CANNES

A FESTIVAL VIRGIN'S GUIDE

Attending the Cannes Film Festival for filmmakers
and film industry professionals

6th Edition

Benjamin Craig

CINEMAGINE

Cinemagine Media Publishing

London

Published By

Cinemagine Media Limited
Kemp House, 152 City Road, London EC1V 2NX, United Kingdom.
www.cinemagine.com

1997- 1998 (Online Editions), 1999 (1st Edition), 2000 (2nd Edition),
2001 (3rd Edition) 2002 (4th Edition), 2006 (5th Edition), 2013 (6th Edition)

ISBN-10 0-9541737-5-9 / ISBN-13 978-0-9541737-5-3

Enquires for sales and distribution, textbook adoption, advertising, foreign language translation, editorial, and rights permissions concerning this book should be addressed to the publisher.

CannesGuide Online

www.cannesguide.com and follow us on Twitter **@CannesGuide**

Preface and Acknowledgements

Welcome to the sixth edition of "Cannes - A Festival Virgin's Guide". This book was born of a first-time visit to Cannes many years ago. As a young Australian filmmaker, it seemed like a good idea at the time to drop in on the world's most famous festival during my travels in Europe. But as it turned out, not only was I completely confused by the festival's structure and operation, Cannes itself was not the most hospitable place for someone new to the industry and travelling on a shoestring budget. Fortunately, that particular trip was designated "reconnaissance only" and out of my discoveries, experiences, and mistakes, the seeds of the Festival Virgin's Guide were sown.

Since then I have been to Cannes many times and had lengthy conversations with others who are true Cannes veterans. The fruits of this work originally existed in the "Cannes - A Festival Virgin's Guide" website, but are now presented for you in this book. As with all good travel guides, the tips, tricks, and recommendations change over time so I urge you to visit the site (www.cannesguide.com) now and then to see what's new. Likewise, great travel resources are born of collaborative effort so feel free to share your experiences with others through the community and feedback areas of the site. You can also follow us on Twitter: @CannesGuide

As always, an endeavour such as this book cannot be undertaken alone. Deserved of my sincerest thanks are the group of Cannes veterans who very kindly made available a slice of their valuable time to provide their own insights into all that is the Cannes Film Festival: Lise Corriveau, Julie Archet, Ben Roberts, Dennis Davidson, Simon Franks, Patrick Frater, Harry Hicks, Stephen Kelliher, Jonathan Olsberg, Bill Stephens, and Jane Wright.

I hope you find the information in this book useful and more importantly, I wish you all the best with your professional and personal exploits at the world's most famous film festival.

Benjamin Craig
London, UK
December 2012

Table of Contents

CANNES - A FESTIVAL VIRGIN'S GUIDE

6TH EDITION

Introduction

It's May. Armed with a wad of business cards, copies of your cinematic masterpiece, a French phrase book, and generous dose of optimism, you've decided to take the plunge and hit the Riviera for a taste of the world's most famous film festival.

Attending Cannes will be one of the most rewarding things you do for your film industry career. But at the same time it can be a somewhat daunting experience. Not only do you have to stay on top of 12 days of hardcore film business, you must also cope with the fact that the event takes place in a country where they don't speak English, and in a city that isn't the largest nor the cheapest place to stay on the Riviera. So where do you start? How do you get to the festival? And where do you find that essential information that will make your visit fun, successful, and most importantly, stress free?

"Cannes - A Festival Virgin's Guide" is for filmmakers and film industry professionals who are interested in learning more about the Festival, how it operates, and how to make the most of their time in on the Riviera. We demystify the city and the festival, and help make your visit both successful and enjoyable. There are four main sections in the book:

The City - covering amongst other things, getting to Cannes, getting around, places to stay, places to eat, and general information;

The Festival - its structure, how to attend, parties and hanging out, and all about the screenings;

The Biz - an overview of how the business side of the festival operates and some advice for filmmakers who are planning to head to Cannes with a project in tow;

The Lowdown - a series of interviews with a selection of Cannes veterans from across the film industry.

In addition to these sections there's a group of appendices containing a wealth of further information.

But a couple of notes before we begin...

How to Pronounce "Cannes"

Hopefully you know this already, but if not, remember: *cans* are what you find in a six pack, **Khan** is the bad guy in the second Star Trek movie (fellow Australians, take note!), and *can* is a city in the south of France, famous for its film festival. Cannes is pronounced can as in "can of beer."

And while we're at it, remember that every Cannes pun you could ever possibly think of has already been done to death. Resist the temptation and your fellow festivalgoers will love you forever.

Prices

All prices in this guide are shown local currency, in this case, Euro. Exchange rates can vary quite dramatically over time, but prices themselves tend to change more slowly so it's simpler for you to make the conversion at the time of your trip. More information on the Euro and obtaining or converting money in Cannes can be found in the section on Money in part one of this book. Where we do show a price in dollars ($), it's always US dollars.

Phone Numbers

Most phone numbers in this guide are shown in the format you would use if you were to call them from within France. To call these numbers from abroad, you need to add your phone company's international access code, the country code for France (33), and then drop the leading zero on any number shown. For example, the Cannes phone number 04 23 82 92 82 would be dialed:

From USA	001 33 4 23 82 92 82
From UK	00 33 4 23 82 92 82
From Australia	0011 33 4 23 82 92 82

You should check with your own phone company for the correct international access code for your service.

And finally...

It's worth remembering that while this book contains a large amount of information about Cannes and the festival, it's by no means 100% comprehensive. As time passes, recommendations change, old places close while new places open, and some suggestions may not suit all tastes. Even the festival itself changes over time. Part of the fun of attending an event like Cannes is building your own library of experiences and anecdotes, and scouting out new places that you can recommend to future Cannes virgins.

*

CannesGuide
ONLINE

Visit Cannes Guide online for the latest on the festival, access to up-to-the-minute information, and a suite of tools to help make your trip a success:

Hotel Booking — online bookings with real-time availability and reservations.

Accommodation Exchange — find and share lodging with other festivalgoers

Restaurant Guide — the lowdown on the best places to eat in Cannes

Travel Desk — cost-effective travel services from CannesGuide partners

Message Boards — share advice and meet new Cannes contacts

www.cannesguide.com
 @CannesGuide

The City

For nearly 200 years Cannes has been a favourite playground for the rich and famous. From humble beginnings as a fishing village in the middle of nowhere, the city has grown to be renowned for its expensive lifestyle, its agreeable Mediterranean climate, and of course its film festival. Tight old streets bustle with a plethora of boutiques displaying the latest from the world's leading designers, with classy restaurants filling the void between. In Cannes even a Big Mac meal can set you back $10 (and yes, you can down a beer while enjoying your Royale with Cheese).

But there is more to Cannes than preconceptions of wealth and opulent Riviera lifestyles. Despite the presence of the well-heeled jet set, the city has managed to maintain a large degree of old world Southern European charm. It's easy to get lost in the fascinating street markets which are hidden away in quiet alleys, and a little local knowledge can help uncover wonderful food that is often great value for money. And if you want to dodge the festival crowds for a day or two, the surrounding region harbours a wide array of medieval villages, abbeys, and museums, as well as wealth of other cultural and historical attractions.

Cannes Facts

Population 70,000

Average May Temperature High 20°C (68°F) Low 13.3°C (56°F)

Measurement System Metric

Time Zone Western Europe (GMT +1, +2 from late-March to late-October)

Electricity 220 volts AC, 50Hz (standard Western Europe round two-pin plugs)

Phone Country Code 33, City Code 04

History

Like most cities on the Mediterranean rim, Cannes has a long and colourful history - a history which dates back far beyond its reputation as a film industry hotspot or playground for the rich and famous.

Archaeological evidence suggests that the area now dominated by the city of Cannes was first settled around 600BC by a group of people known as the Oxybians. By around 200BC, the Roman Empire expanded to include control of the region and many settlements were established. Although by this point the Oxybians had largely been defeated, the villages of *Nikaia* (Nice) and *Antipolis* (Antibes) still suffered regular attacks from the remaining rebels. A call was put out to Rome for support in dealing with the uprising and soldiers arrived soon after to make short work of the remaining Oxybians. To discourage their return the Romans set up a garrisoned trading post in the area which ultimately allowed Cannes to transform from a small fishing village into a *castrum* (fortified town).

Despite the presence of the Romans, the local area still suffered attacks from a handful of left-over rebels. To counter the threat, the nearby city of Marseilles paid for a fort to be constructed on the hill of *Le Suquet* in the heart of what is now modern Cannes. And it is this fort which appears to have indirectly given the city its name. On completion the fort was officially dubbed *Castrum Marseillinum* ("The Fort of Mareilles"), but the name never really stuck with the locals, who simply referred to it as *Castrum Canoïs* due to the abundant *canna* (reeds) which grew at the foot of the hill. Translated from Latin into the local Occitan language this became *Canes*, which first appears on record in 1619. Although this is the generally accepted origin of the town's name, some scholars have also pointed to the fact that the word *canue* exists in the local Ligurian language, meaning "height" or "peak".

Even without an agreed name, documented history of the area began around 410 A.D. with the arrival of a congregation of monks from Italy. Under the leadership of Saint Honoratus, the monks founded a monastery on a small island in what is now the *Baie de Cannes* (Bay of Cannes) with the intention of going about their worship in solitude. The island later became known as *Ile Saint Honorat* (Saint Honorat Island).

For several hundred years the monks lived in relative isolation, conducting a small amount of trade with the Romans and local fisherman, but otherwise keeping to themselves. However, towards the end of the first millennium, Ile Sainte Honorat began to suffer an increasing number of attacks from marauding Saracen pirates. Around 1000 A.D. the monks took steps to counter this menace by commencing a programme of fortification works which would continue for several centuries. Although the Saracen threat eventually dissipated of its own accord and the monks remained fairly secure on their fortified island, the local area continued to remain unstable for several centuries, experiencing reasonably frequent turmoil caused by armies in transit between the various wars in France, Italy, and Spain.

By the 14th Century, the region around Cannes had found its way into the hands of the Counts of Provence, the local aristocracy who ruled a large chunk of what is now the south of France. In 1480 the reigning monarch, "Good King René", died without leaving a clear succession plan. The king's nephew, Charles du Maine, laid claim to the throne even though many believed the title was rightfully that of René's grandson, the Duke of Lorraine. Not wanting to see a civil war break out in his southern neighbour's backyard, the French king, Louis XI, stepped in and brokered a somewhat self-beneficial deal. The Duke of Lorraine was paid to renounce his inheritance and Du Maine was forced to bequeath Provence to the French Crown "for its own protection". Charles and his supporters would have probably been fairly quick to realise that they'd been duped, but for the fact that the very next day, Du Maine 'mysteriously' dropped dead after dining during a visit to Marseilles.

Under French rule, life for the *Cannois* over the next couple of centuries remained harsh, but relatively peaceful. However, things were shaken up in 1615 when France declared war on Spain. France's chief minister (and regent while a 14-year-old Louis XIII sat on the throne), Cardinal Richelieu, became increasingly worried about the possibility of a large-scale naval attack on France's eastern seaboard and ordered fortifications to be built on the *Ile Sainte Marguerite* (Saint Honorat's larger sister in the Lérins island group). Although the forethought proved to be correct, the fortifications failed to keep the armada at bay and the area fell under control of the Spanish crown in 1635. But Spanish rule was short-lived as French troops were able to liberate the area in 1637.

The temporary loss of territory set wheels in motion for more substantial fortifications in the region. Marshal Sébastien Le Prestre de Vauban, the king's leading military engineer, was given the task of constructing a more formidable fort on Sainte Marguerite. Vauban also realised that the island's remote location would make the fort a perfect place to house political prisoners, far away from the courts where they could cause trouble for the king. The *Fort Royale*, as it became known, operated continuously as a prison up until the early 20th century and housed a large number of inmates, the most famous of whom was the Man in the Iron Mask.

The plight of the infamous masked prisoner, incarcerated between 1687 and 1689, was immortalised in the Alexandre Dumas novel, "Le Vicomte de Bragelonne" ("The Viscount of Bragelonne"), but his true identity remains a mystery to this day. Some historians believe he was the elder brother of Louis XIV; others say he was actually Louis' twin brother. Tales of illegitimacy also abound: that he was the fruit of some hanky-panky between Anne of Austria (wife of Louis XIII) and the Duke of Buckingham; or the same Anne and one Cardinal Mazarin (regent of France while Louis XIV was a child). A few even believe that masked man was the illegitimate son of Charles II of England or of Louis XIV himself. Other evidence suggests that he may have been the Italian courtesan, Count Matteoli, imprisoned for espionage during the Franco-Spanish war. But the common thread that runs through all of the various rumours is that virtually everyone believed the man was of noble blood, since he received preferential treatment during his time in prison.

Perhaps the most enchanting rumour of them all is one which would have The Man in the Iron Mask as the grandfather of Napoleon Bonaparte. As the story goes, one night a local Cannes woman visited the masked man in his cell and the horizontal folk-dancing that ensued resulted in the woman bearing a son. For reasons unknown, the child was subsequently fostered out to a family in Corsica. Although the new parents knew nothing of the child's origins, they were assured that he was *de buoné-parte* (of good breeding) and thus named him Bonaparte.

The most recent conclusions suggest that the Man in the Iron Mask may simply have been a royal servant who was incarcerated for knowing a little too much about a series of scandalous financial dealings at the palace. At any rate, the secret died with him in the Bastille in Paris in 1703. Interestingly, one piece of trivia that does survive to this day is the fact that his famed mask was actually made of velvet rather than iron.

In the century following the Man in the Iron Mask's death, Cannes and its surrounds returned to a relatively peaceful state. By the early 19th century, Cannes had grown off the back of a strong local fishing industry and the construction of a better port to facilitate trade with the nearby inland town of Grasse. Not long after, Napoleon I, returning from exile on the Italian island of Elba, used the area as a *bivouac* (camp) for his new army before carving a route through the Alps to Paris. However, Cannes as we know it today was actually born in 1834 with the arrival of an Englishman by the name of Henry Brougham.

Brougham was Lord Chancellor of Great Britain at the time, but more importantly for the future of Cannes, he was also a fan of fleeing the miserable British winter in favour of warmer climes. In 1834 Brougham set off with his daughter, Eleonore-Louise, to visit Italy. Back in those days, if you were an English aristocrat travelling to Italy you did so by sea. Brougham and his daughter arrived in the port of Nice only to find that the King of Piemonte had closed the Italian border to contain a cholera outbreak. Brougham decided to head for the alpine town of Grasse instead, but as it was late in the day he felt it would be best to spend the night at an inn in the port of Cannes before heading inland at daybreak.

The Broughams originally intended only a brief stop in Cannes, but charmed by the beauty of the area and the hospitality of their local hosts, the pair ended up staying for many days. And by the time they left, Brougham had decided to build a home in the idyllic village. Two years later the toast of the British aristocracy flocked to Cannes for the inauguration of Brougham's sumptuous retreat, Villa Eléonore-Louise (named for his daughter). Such was Brougham's influence within London's high society that, before you could say, "By George, I need a winter retreat," a cluster of English villas had sprung up in and around the town.

For the next 10 years Cannes grew steady as a British winter colony. But such was the influence of the British Empire at the time, it also attracted the attention of other well-to-do types in Europe. During a brief visit in 1848, Alexandra Feodorovna Skrypitzine, the wife of the French consul to Moscow, fell in love with the town and returned not long after with a host of Russian aristocracy in tow. The increasing number of high-class visitors prompted construction of Cannes' first luxury hotel in 1858, the Gonnet et de la Reine, which also helped further cement the town's reputation as a resort for the wealthy.

Until 1863, the French aristocracy had taken little notice of the antics on the Riviera so Cannes largely remained a destination for rich foreigners. But that year marked the completion of the *Paris-Lyon-Méditerranée* railway, and with it the town suddenly became easily accessible to wealthy Parisian socialites. French interest in Cannes received a major boost in 1865 with the arrival of Prosper Mérimée, a friend of Brougham's and well-placed member of French high society through his job as France's Inspector of Historical Monuments. After a brief visit to the area on a mission to catalogue the historical value of the Lérins Islands, he became instrumental in promoting Cannes to his Parisian chums. It wasn't long before Mérimée took up full-time residency in the town to take advantage of the area's "therapeutic climate" to help control his asthma.

Indeed, Cannes' reputation as a 'health resort' had been steadily growing for several years, with many prominent British and French doctors singing praises of the restorative powers of the region's winter climate. By 1883 the town had no less than five hydrotherapy centres, where patients came to benefit from range of water treatments targeting a host of ailments. Local doctors published sizable amounts of literature aimed at attracting the widest possible clientele and to cash in on the success of a best-selling book, *L'Hiver à Cannes* ("Winter in Cannes") by Dr Charles-Antonin Buttura.

The appearance of villas, luxury hotels, and health spas was not the only change experienced by Cannes during the second half of the 19th century. At time of Lord Brougham's arrival the diversity of the local flora was fairly limited due to the area's mainly arid climate. For the wealthy new residents this was a problem. It was unimaginable for an Englishman to live without flowers, let alone without a lawn. But the biggest problem was that the region suffered from a lack of a reliable water supply. Most of the watercourses were seasonal mountain streams which were dry for a good part of the year. Not to let this kind of problem stand in his way, Brougham and a few colleagues formed the *General Irrigation and Water Supply Company of France Limited* to address the challenge of supplying water to their homes and gardens (and by extension, to the residents of Cannes). The company's crowning achievement was the construction of the *Canal de la Siagne* which was completed in 1868 and continues to provide water for Cannes to this day.

The introduction of irrigation to the land between the Mediterranean and the mountains had a dramatic effect, transforming the area into a botanical paradise capable of sustaining a huge array of plant life. And the wealthy residents of Cannes spared no expense scouring the globe for the most exotic specimens available. Soon the city was teaming with flora, including citrus trees from the Middle East, eucalyptuses from Australia, and the *Phoenix Canariensis* from Africa. Better known as the classic palm tree, these plants can now be found throughout the region and have become an icon of the city and its famous film festival.

The turn of the 20th Century saw Cannes in persistent growth. More luxury hotels and villas had been built and the area continued to flourish as a winter health resort for Europe's elite. One piece of interesting Cannes trivia from the time suggests that the cupolas of the famous Carlton Hotel (built in 1910) were inspired by architect Marcellin Mayère's fascination with the reputedly ample bosom of a well-known local courtesan named La Belle Otéro.

The carefree lifestyle of Cannes was briefly interrupted during World War I, when the winter health fanatics were replaced by northern refugees and wounded soldiers and many of the luxury hotels were used as makeshift hospitals. But by the late 1920s, a festive spirit had returned to Cannes and the town began to attract summer visitors for the first time. In answer to this new demand, the local hotel managers took the unprecedented step of opening for the summer season in 1931 (previously all the hotels remained closed during the summer) and Cannes adopted its current guise as a year-round resort.

Today, Cannes is a thriving metropolis of around 70,000 people, sitting in the middle of one of France's most prosperous regions. After Paris, Cannes is France's second-most important city for business tourism and hosts international events throughout the year for a wide variety of industries ranging from advertising and music through to tax-free goods and pharmaceuticals. The city is also a major hub for a busy regional tourism industry, hosts the world's most famous film festival, and of course is still one of the top places to be seen on the Riviera if you want to flash some cash.

Getting There

The city of Cannes is located in south-eastern France on the Mediterranean coast known as the *Côte d'Azur* (Azure Coast), or more famously to English-speakers, as the "French Riviera". Cannes is one of France's premier tourist and business travel destinations, so it's well-serviced by a variety of modes of transport. For most people, getting there should pose few problems.

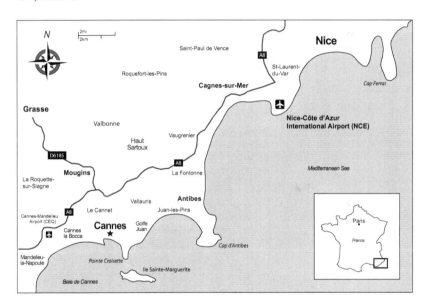

By Air

The main entry point for people flying to Cannes is Nice-Côte d'Azur International Airport (airport code NCE, www.nice.aeroport.fr). As France's second busiest airport, a large number of local and international airlines fly to Nice-Côte d'Azur, either directly or via major European hubs such as Paris, London, Amsterdam, or Frankfurt. A second airport, Cannes-Mandelieu (airport code CEQ, www.cannes-mandelieu.aeroport.fr), is closer to the city, however this is mainly used by private jets and European charter flights. Most flights carrying festivalgoers will arrive at Nice.

For the long-haul crowd, international airlines such as Delta, Air Canada, and QANTAS operate daily services to Nice from key local airports in their respective countries. Within Europe, festivalgoers tend to prefer budget airlines like Easyjet (www.easyjet.com), Air Berlin (www.airberlin.com), or FlyBe (www.flybe.com), which typically offer the cheapest fares. That said, major European carriers like British Airways (www.ba.com), Air France (www.airfrance.com), and Lufthansa (www.lufthansa.com) now find themselves squeezed by their low-cost competitors so sometimes offer pretty good deals of their own. A website called Skyscanner (www.skyscanner.net) is a great starting point to search a range of airlines in one go.

Even though options for flying to Nice are plentiful, it's important to remember that the arrival of May sees much of Europe poised for a leap into peak season. So you will not only be in competition with other festivalgoers for seats, but also against people who've booked early holidays. To get the best fare it's important to book early. For budget airlines, booking in January is recommended; for long-haul, probably before Christmas. Today's airlines run complex booking systems which continually adapt prices to ensure maximum revenues are achieved from each flight. In practical terms, this means the closer you book to your flying date, the more you will pay. Seats on flights are also put under pressure by people travelling to the Monaco Grand Prix, which often coincides with the last weekend of the festival and uses Nice as its main entry point.

Airport Transfers

Once you've arrived in Nice, getting to Cannes is fairly straight-forward. Most people opt to make use of the express shuttle service run by Bus Rapides Côte d'Azur (www.rca.tm.fr). Route number 210 departs from both terminals at Nice and the 25km (16 mile) journey takes about 50 minutes. The service operates seven days a week with the first bus from Nice at 8am. Shuttles run every half hour (except for first thing and last thing when they are hourly), with the last bus at 8pm. A one-way ticket is around 16.50€ and a return, 26.50€.

Tickets cannot be purchased on the bus - you need to buy them from the ticket office at the airport or at the Cannes bus station. When you enter the arrivals hall at Nice, follow the signs out of the airport to the bus station. The ticket office is a small shack on your right after you exit the terminal. Route 210 drops you off in Cannes at the central bus station *Gare Routière*, located at Place Cornut Gentille opposite the port. For your return to Nice, you simply pick up the bus at the same place in *Gare Routière* where you were dropped off. The first bus leaves at 7am and then it's roughly every half-hour until the last bus at 7pm.

The express bus is by far the easiest way to get to Cannes from the airport, but it can be a bit of a bun-fight if you arrive in Nice during the first few days of the festival. Several planeloads of festivalgoers arriving at once results in a lot of people waiting at the bus stop, and it can be a bit pushy to get on. Luggage needs to be stowed in the lower compartments of the bus and the driver will normally load your bags for you. Once your luggage is on, you may need to be a little aggressive to ensure you then get yourself on the bus. If your bags are on, but you're not, make sure you tell the driver. You don't want your bags heading to Cannes without you. Things tend to be a bit easier on the return journey, but be careful if you're planning to catch the last bus of the day as they normally fill up quickly.

Local Bus

If you're watching the pennies it's possible to take a local bus, Lignes d'Azur 200, from Nice airport to Cannes. With fares around 1€ it's considerably cheaper, but journey times are about twice as long as on the express. That said, local buses may be more useful than the express service if you are staying outside of Cannes in areas such as Juan-les-Pins, Golfe Juan, or Antibes. These are all located between Nice and Cannes so taking the express bus will result in you having to travel into Cannes then back out again in the direction you've just come from. Regardless, whatever you do, don't catch a bus into Nice itself unless you are planning to visit the city. From the airport, Nice is in the opposite direction to Cannes.

Taxi

If your flight arrives outside of the express bus times then catching a taxi to Cannes is your only real option. However it may also be more cost effective to take a cab if you're travelling in a group of three to four people. A taxi from the airport will cost around 80€, depending on the time of day and how much luggage you have. At the airport simply follow the signs to the taxi waiting area. On your return, you can grab a cab from one of the official taxi ranks which are dotted around Cannes. Alternatively, you can book a taxi with Allo Taxi (Tel. 08 90 71 22 27) although be aware that the operator may not speak English.

Helicopter

If you're living the movie mogul lifestyle or simply believe that money is here to provide access to the better things in life, you might want to consider a helicopter transfer to Cannes. For around 400€ you and up to four 'assistants' can enjoy spectacular mountain and coastal views as you're whisked off to Cannes, high above the rabble in a rather civilised 20 minutes. The helicopter service is operated by Helistation de Cannes (Tel. 04 93 43 42 42; www.nicehelicopteres.com).

By Car

If you live in Europe or simply fancy a road trip, it's entirely possible to drive to Cannes. And if you're travelling in a group and aren't too pushed for time, it can also be more cost-effective than a last minute flight. French roads are generally in excellent condition, comparatively uncongested, and fuel is slightly cheaper in France than the UK. The only thing you do need to be wary of if you're planning to travel on *autoroutes* (motorways) is the wallet-crunching tolls.

Autoroutes crisscross France in almost every direction. They are easily identified by their route number which always begins with the letter "A" and the signs are always blue. Most autoroutes are tollways and prices vary depending on the road and the distance travelled. The tolls may be expensive, but you do get a higher speed limit, less congestion, and a pristine road surface for your money. It's also entirely possible to traverse the length and breadth of France without using the autoroute system. It will obviously take longer, but the journey can be more scenic, and of course there are no tolls.

Major roads which aren't part of the autoroute network have a route number prefixed by the letter "N", for *Route National* and the direction signs are always green. Where N-roads meet autoroutes, you will often see two sets of signs to a town or city: one blue sign showing the autoroute and one green sign with the town name and the words *"par Route National"* (sometimes abbreviated to simply "par R.N."). Minor roads in France are classed as "D" roads and can be anything from a rural dual carriageway to a single lane track.

If you're driving from the UK it's more than likely that the French part of your trip will start in Calais. The journey from Calais to Cannes is about 1,120km (696 miles) and takes around 11-12 hours on the road. Tolls will set you back at least 45€ (or up to 80€ if you opt for autoroutes all the way). The shortest (and cheapest) route starts in Calais on the A26. Simply follow the signs towards Lyon, via Reims and Dijon, then take the A43/A48 to Grenoble. From there, pick up the N75 towards Sisteron (via Digne-les-Bains) and change for the N85 to Cannes just outside Sisteron itself. The drive along the N75/N85 takes you through some spectacular mountain scenery and the latter route is steeped in history. Known as the *Route Napoléon*, the road was literally carved out of the mountains by the emperor's army to allow it to march on Paris after Napoléon's return from exile in Italy.

If you're bringing a car from the UK or elsewhere in the Europe, you should check that your insurance meets the minimum requirements in France. Thanks to omnipotent presence of the EU, most policies must now provide minimum cover in all member states (plus countries like Norway, Switzerland, and Iceland). However, minimum cover tends to only mean third-party coverage. Some visitors are surprised to find that cover for theft and damage may not be automatically extended while in France. Likewise, check that you have the correct safety gear. It's now a legal requirement for all vehicles to carry a breathalyser and a high-viz jacket.

Speed limits in France are higher than in many other countries. On autoroutes the limit is normally 130kph, dropping to 110kph in wet weather. For dual-carriageway "N" roads, it's 100kph, and for other roads outside built-up areas it's 90kph. Within town limits it's 50kph unless otherwise signposted. Emergency breakdown assistance is available on most major routes from Inter-Mutuelles (Tel. +33 800 75 75 75) although not on autoroutes as these have their own breakdown services (use the orange emergency telephones). It's unusual for breakdown operators or mechanics to speak English.

By Train

Cannes is serviced by local, international, and TGV (fast) trains from a variety of destinations across Europe. Unless you're travelling from another area in the south of France it's more than likely you will need to change trains in Paris (typically for either Gare de Lyon or Gare de l'Est). Paris to Cannes is approximately five hours by TGV or eight hours by sleeper train. If you're coming from London, the Eurostar/TGV combination is a viable option and can sometimes work out cheaper than a flight. The journey takes about seven hours from the point you leave St. Pancras to your arrival in Cannes, including the change in Paris.

The train station in Cannes (Gare du Cannes, Tel. 08 92 35 35 35) is located right in the centre of town at Place de la Gare. For more information, fares, and timetables, contact France's national railway operator SNCF (www.sncf.fr), visit Rail Europe (www.raileurope. co.uk), or Eurostar (www.eurostar.com). If you're under 26 you should always enquire about the possibility of discounts as many European rail services have special 'youth fares' available.

By Bus

It's entirely possible to travel to Cannes by coach from other cities within Europe, but with the prevalence of budget airlines and the train service, there probably isn't much point. If you're hell-bent on travelling this way, contact your local travel agent or visit Go by Coach (www. gobycoach.com) for timetables, fares, and bookings. There are two bus stations in Cannes: one by the train station; the other outside Hôtel de Ville near the port. Most intercity bus services use the latter.

Travel Made Simple

Make sure your take a few moments to visit the Travel Desk at CannesGuide.com for good deals on hotels and flights from many cities around the world. www.cannesguide.com

Finding Your Way

Cannes is home to a sizable population and forms part of an urban sprawl that covers the coast from the Italian border to Saint Tropez, but mercifully most of the festival action is concentrated into a small area in the centre of town. So once you learn the lay of the land, finding your way around is a breeze.

Districts of Cannes
The City of Cannes is divided into nine official districts - well, 10 to be precise, because Cannes La Bocca is technically two districts, *Nord* (North) and *Sud* (South). But that split isn't relevant for festival purposes. The key districts of Cannes are:

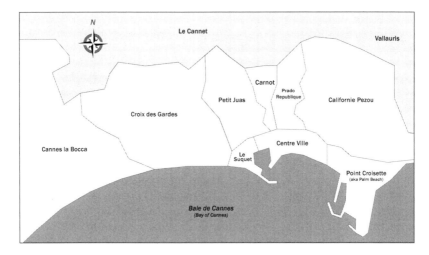

Centre Ville
Sometimes referred to by Cannes regulars as "The Ring", the roughly semi-circular area formed between the N7 main road and the waterfront is home to 95% of the festival action. Centre Ville abounds in restaurants and hotels, and staying in this area affords a great deal of convenience. But convenience does of course come at a price.

Le Suquet
Also known as the "old town", Le Suquet is the area situated on the hill above the port. It's a veritable maze of pedestrian alleys, mainly occupied by small apartments, and is crowned by the *Musée de la Castre* (the largest museum in town which inhabits the former Saracen fort.) You will also find the city's most popular and rustic restaurant strip in this area, running up an alley called Rue Sainte Antoine.

Pointe Croisette

Located at the far-eastern end of the *Baie de Cannes* (Bay of Cannes) is a large peninsular, also known as "Palm Beach". The area is built up predominantly with residential apartments although there are also a few smaller hotels present.

Californie Pezou

Here you'll find an area full of expensive villas owned by some of the Riviera's richest residents. Many of the properties are let for the festival to those with the means, and as a result, the area sees some of the poshest parties. Geographically, Californie Pezou is a little removed from the festival action so taxis to and from are the norm.

Prado République

Backing up against the train station, this district stretches in a thin corridor northwards until it hits the A8 autoroute (and boundary between Cannes and the town of Mougins). The south end of 'République' offers a good range of hotels which are still within walking distance of Centre Ville.

Carnot

Similar to neighbouring République, Carnot also backs up to the train station and stretches northwards. The main arterial road, Boulevard Carnot, cuts a dead-straight line through the middle of this area and is home to a range of slightly cheaper hotels and restaurants which are priced for locals. The south end of Carnot is within easy walking distance of the festival action.

Petit Juas

The area behind Le Suquet stretches back northwest to the A8. It's mainly occupied by flats and houses for the locals, but there are also a few large villas, including Lord Brougham's original Villa Eléonore-Louise (privately owned). Most festivalgoers have little reason to visit Petit Juas, although if you're lucky enough you might find yourself at a party in this area.

Croix des Gardes

This sprawling mainly residential district also stretches northwest behind Le Suquet. The area is dominated by a large municipal park and a range of expensive villas, but as you move further north you can almost watch the wealth evaporate. The far north of the district is occupied by locals who may be living close to the Riviera, but are very far from the dream.

Cannes la Bocca

The most separate of Cannes' districts, La Bocca is predominantly residential with a mix of regular apartments and some fancy villas. A few festivalgoers opt to stay in La Bocca to save some pennies, but as we'll discuss in the section on Accommodation, this is a false economy and therefore not recommended.

Outside of Cannes

Outside of the city limits, there are a few areas which you may come across reference to from time to time, particularly in relation to being cheaper places to stay. Le Cannet, Antibes Juan-les-Pins, Golfe Juan, Mandelieu la Napoule, and Mougins are all viable alternatives for accommodation if you can't get something closer to town. We'll talk more about these areas in the chapter on Accommodation, but it's worth noting that none are within walking distance of Cannes (for festival purposes anyway).

Navigating Centre Ville

A basic map of the Centre Ville area can be found at the back of this book. The area is also fully-covered by online mapping services such as Google Maps (including Street View) and Bing Maps. If you prefer the reassurance of an old-school physical map, these can be obtained for free from either of the two tourist offices (*Office du Tourisme*) in town:

Palais des Festivals
Esplanade Georges Pompidou
Tel. 04 92 99 84 22
Open seven days, 9am to 8pm

Gare du Cannes (train station)
Place de la Gare
Tel. 04 92 99 19 77
Open Monday to Friday, 9am to 7pm.

The entrance to the tourist office at the Palais is clearly sign-posted and can be found to the left of the Théâtre Debussy steps. The tourist office at the train station is on the ground floor at the eastern end of the building (on the right if you are facing the station from Rue Jean Jaurès). The train station branch is generally quieter, so the staff members tend to be friendlier due to not being constantly harassed, but it is closed on weekends.

With map in hand and a basic understanding of the main districts of the city, you should take a bit of time after you arrive to familiarise yourself with the location (and pronunciation) of the following places. Some of these are used for various functions of the festival itself, others you will simply find it useful to know their locations. All are shown on the maps at the back of this book.

City Streets & Buildings

Boulevard de la Croisette
"The Croisette" is the palm-lined beach-front drag. It's dotted with classy hotels, expensive restaurants, designer stores, and crowds several miles deep. Most of the festival action takes place here so people-watching can be a great pass-time. *Croisette* is pronounced "KWA-SET".

Rue d'Antibes
A couple of blocks inland from the Croisette is Rue d'Antibes, the retail backbone of Cannes. All manner of shops line this tight street and for some reason, almost all of the banks (and therefore ATMs). *Antibes* is pronounced "ON-TEEB".

Gare du Cannes
Also known as *Gare SNCF*, this is the central train station in Cannes. Besides the obvious, there are several reasons for being familiar with its location. Firstly, it's used as a reference point for many places described elsewhere in this book, but also because it generally separates the business area of Cannes (for festival purposes anyway) from the rest of the city. Gare du Cannes is located on Rue Jean Jaurès and *gare* is pronounced "GAR".

Gare Routière
The main bus station in Cannes. Located at Place Bernard Cornut Gentille, opposite the port, this is where the airport shuttles arrive and depart, and where most of the local buses connect. There's also a taxi rank which is less busy late at night than those closer to the Palais des Festivals.

Major Hotels
The big six hotels in Cannes are important locations for festival purposes. Even if you're not staying in one it's highly likely you'll need to visit them during the festival for a meeting or to do some networking in one of the numerous bars (assuming your credit card is prepared for the assault). Almost all of these hotels are located on the Croisette: Majestic Barrière (normally referred to as just, "The Majestic") is at the corner with Rue des Serbes; the JW Marriott (formerly the Noga Hilton) at the corner with Rue Frédéric Amouretti; the Grand Hotel (or just "The Grand") a little further down the road at 45 Boulevard de la Croisette; the Carlton Intercontinental on the corner with Rue François Einesy; and the Martinez a slightly longer stagger at the junction with Rue Latour-Maubourg. The odd one out is the Grey d'Albion, which can be found one block back from the Croisette, straddling Rue des Etats-Unis and Rue des Serbes.

Festival Buildings & Locations

Palais des Festivals

Officially known as the *Palais des Festivals et Congrès*, but more commonly referred to as simply "The Palais", this massive conference centre is located on the waterfront smack in the middle of town. The Palais is home to the main festival action including the official screenings, festival administration, the press centre, and a good deal of the Market action. Access to the Palais is strictly controlled by the festival's beige-blazered, no-nonsense security men. An accreditation badge or official invitation is required for entry and in today's heightened security climate, expect some delays while bags are searched and you and your fellow festivalgoers are scanned (and occasionally frisked) for metal objects. The Palais has five levels which you'll often see referred to as Level 0, Level 1 etc. Note that where you see Level 01 this means the basement. The Palais is open from 9am to 6pm daily during the festival. *Palais* is pronounced, "PAL-AY".

Riviera

Built to take up the overflow from the Palais this 7,000sqm space now houses a good chunk of the Market and has eight state-of-the-art screening theatres. You will find the Riviera directly behind the Palais, accessible either through the bowels of its older brother or via its own entrance on the east side of the building. You will need your accreditation badge to enter.

Cinemas

In addition to the various theatres and screening rooms in the Palais and Riviera, there a range of other venues where films are screened during the festival. These are dealt with in the "Screenings" chapter, later in this book.

Village International

At festival time a veritable Bedouin village springs up on the waterfront as many national film commissions and other organisations pitch their tents on the beach outside the Palais. Officiallly this space is known as the Village International, but most festivalgoers just refer to it as the "Pavilions". Although the pavilions tend to offer a range of services for their nationals (such as informal meeting space, seminars, light refreshments, and free internet access), many are also normally accessible to other accredited festivalgoers during the day. In the evening, most are closed for private functions from about 6pm onwards. More details about the pavilions can be found in the chapter on Parties and Hanging Out.

Village International Pantiero

The number of pavilions now vastly exceeds the space available outside the Palais so a second Village International springs up each year in Espace Pantiero, a public space opposite the port. Most of the pavilions at Pantiero are run by festival sponsors or French media outlets, but some national ones are now located there too. Festival accreditation is also required to enter the Village International Pantiero area.

Gare Maritime

The old ferry port no longer sees departures servicing the Lerins islands of Sainte Marguerite and Saint Honorat (these now leave from Quai Max Laubeuf on Rue Jean Hibert), but the space is used during the festival to manage accreditation for day passes and also houses the left luggage service.

Festival Boutiques

You can pick up all of your festival merch at either of the two official boutiques. There's one located at the far eastern end of the Village International, the other can be found outside the Village International Pantiero, about half-way between the Palais and Gare Routière. The festival boutiques are open to both accredited festivalgoers and the general public.

For additional information on festival locations, visit out one of the various information booths (called *Points d'Informations*, marked with a yellow "i") which are dotted around the Palais and Riviera buildings. Multi-lingual hostesses are available to answer your questions.

Getting Around

Fortunately for most festivalgoers, getting around Cannes is a breeze as almost all of the action takes place in the Centre Ville district... and the good news is that this is walkable. Indeed, with the road closures, traffic, and thick crowds, walking is about the only effective way of getting around this part of town.

The longest walk is from the port to the Martinez Hotel, which could talk you half an hour (or more if you walk slowly), but it's still likely to be quicker than any other method. That said, even when walking you should always avoid the area around the Palais near screening times as there are additional road closures plus extra thick crowds vying for a position to see the red carpet. Unless you are specifically going to the Palais, it's best to stay one block back until you've moved past Rue des Serbes (to the east) or Rue Jean de Riouffe (to the west). And if you're heading to the Village International, a neat trick is to walk behind the Palais on the western side. There's an access road next to the casino which swings around behind the building and delivers you on the crowdless-side of the barrier right in front of the pavilions. You will need your accreditation badge to walk through this area.

If you are staying outside of Cannes, there are several transport options available to get you in and out of town.

Buses

The most cost-effective way to travel in and out of town is by local bus. The service is operated by Bus Azur (www.busazur.com) and there are routes all over Cannes as well as to neighbouring towns. Fares are a standard 1€ for a single journey and you can save a few extra euros by buying a book of 10 tickets or a travel card. In terms of schedules, on weekdays most routes have busses every 15-20 minutes between 6am and 9pm. After hours things can be patchy, although a 'night bus' service is available on some routes. Likewise, expect a significantly less-frequent service on Sundays and public holidays. Online route information and timetables are available on the Bus Azur web site. It's only available in French, but if you select *Horaires de ligne* from the home page the functionality is fairly self-explanatory. And if you're stuck, you can always run the site through Google Translate (www.google.com/translate).

Trains

The train service operated by SNCF can be extremely useful if you're staying outside of Cannes near one of the stations. Unlike the buses, the trains run until midnight on weekdays, don't get stuck in traffic, and aren't subject to the driver's own personal philosophy on time-keeping. The one thing they do have in common with the buses however, is the vastly reduced service on Sundays and public holidays. Train fares are also a little more, but at 2€ - 3€ for an *aller simple, deuxieme class* (single ticket, second class) it's hardly going to break the bank.

Taxis

After 9pm, taxis become the main mode of transport between festival central and a cosy bed. Rates are pretty much on par with what you'd expect to pay in most modern cities. It's 3€ at flag-fall then between 1.80€ - 2.40€ per kilometre, depending on the day and time. There are additional charges for luggage, airport trips, tolls, and putting a fourth passenger in the cab. Tipping isn't necessary with French taxies and the taxi charter prevents drives from demanding a tip. However, like everyone else drivers will be appreciative of a little extra if you feel the service was good. It's also common to round up to at least the nearest euro.

One key difference between taxis in France those in other countries is that you cannot hail a French taxi from the roadside. By law they are not allowed to pick you up, although inevitably some will. To get a taxi you need to find one of the official taxi ranks which are located all over the city. The rank next to the main bus station is a good option late at night, particularly when every taxi within a mile of a Palais is fair game for the post-screening hoards. Alternatively, you can book at taxi from Allô Taxi Cannes (Tel. 04 92 99 27 27, www. taxicannes.com).

Driving (and Parking)

Forget about driving in Cannes. Tight streets, thick crowds, and road closures near the Palais make driving a nightmare best avoided. And this is before you face the problem of finding somewhere to park. So the advice is, if you're staying in Cannes itself you don't need a car because virtually everywhere you need to go will be within reasonable walking distance. If you're staying away from the centre of town, or in one of the neighbouring areas, your best bet is to use your car to come into town in the morning then join the foot-crowd for the rest of the day.

When it comes to parking, there around 5,500 spaces in the various lots around town. This might sound like a large number, but given that around 1,400 go to official vehicles in the Palais and Pantiero car parks, and there are over 200,000 people in Cannes during the festival, it doesn't leave many to go around. If you must drive into town the moral of the story is get there early. Parking rates vary a little between car parks, but are generally in region of 2€ - 3€ per hour. A full day's parking, multiplied by the number of days you are in Cannes can add up to a small fortune, another reason why it's best to avoid using a car if at all possible. The following car parks are all within walking distance of festival-central:

Parking Croisette (280 places)
Enter off Port Canto, La Croisette

Parking Ferrage (400 places)
Enter off Boulevard Victor Tuby

Parking Forville (700 places)
Enter off Rue Pastour, Avenue Sainte Louis, or Rue de la Miséricorde

Parking Lamy (400 places)
Enter off Rue d'Antibes or Boulevard de Lorraine

Parking Laubeuf (350 places)
Enter off Boulevard Jean Hilbert

Parking République (126 places)
Enter off Rue Docteur Calmette

Parking Vauban (280 places)
Enter off Rue Raphaël, Avenue de Grasse

Gray d'Albion (475 places)
Enter off Rue des Serbes

Gare SNCF (660 places)
Enter off Rue Jean Jaurès

Parking du Noga Hilton (458 places)
Enter off La Croisette or Rond-Point Duboys d'Angers

In addition to the car parks, metered street parking is available in the areas surrounding Centre Ville. In most cases the maximum stay is limited to a few hours and traffic wardens are active across the city during the festival. There are a few unmetered spaces here and there, but as you can imagine, they fill up very quickly. As with most cities the parking restrictions tend to be relaxed in the evenings and on Sundays or public holidays, but be careful not to accidentally park in a tow-away zone (marked by a small sign showing a tow-truck and car) as these are often in operation 24/7.

If you do return to find your car has been visited by one of the city's meter-maids (yes, for some reason they are all women) then you can pay the fine at most tabacs around town. To settle your ticket you purchase stamps from the tabac, attach these to the ticket, and simply pop it in a post box. If you return and your car has disappeared completely, your first port of call should be the local impound depot, Fourrière Municipal (Tel. 04 93 94 53 46).

Car Rental
You shouldn't need to rent a car to get around town, but if you have some spare time it may be cool to grab some wheels for the day and check out the areas surrounding Cannes. A few suggestions for day-trip destinations can be found in the "Getting Away" chapter of this book. As always, it's generally cheaper to book your rental car before you leave your home country and you will need to be at least 25 years old (although some companies will rent to people between 21-25 for an additional premium).

Ada Location
91 Boulevard Carnot.
Tel. 04 93 38 38 93

Avis
Place de la Gare
Tel. 04 93 39 26 38

Hertz France
147 Rue d'Antibes
Tel. 04 93 99 04 20

Europcar
3 Rue du Commandant Vidal
Tel. 04 93 06 26 30

If you're looking to head to an evening screening in style, limousines (with driver) can be hired from the following locations:

Chabé Riviera
11 Rue Latour Maubourg
Tel. 04 93 43 90 91

Limousines Agence Côte d'Azur
1 Rue Philibert Delorme
Tel. 04 93 38 11 91

Scooters

Most of the locals seem to be single-handedly keeping the scooter industry alive as this is the main form of independent motorised transport. Easy to park, cheap to run, and simple to manoeuvre through the gridlock, scooters are probably the best way to get around if you find the old two-leg method objectionable. Rates are 28€ - 30€ per day or 175€per week and scooters can be hired from the following places:

Mistral Location
4 Rue Georges Clémenceau
Tel. 04 93 99 25 25
www.mistral-location.com

Finazzo Alain
Palais Miramar, 65 La Croisette
Tel. 04 93 94 61 94

Multi Location Service
5 Rue de Latour Maubourg
Tel. 04 93 43 60 00

Bicycles

A trusty tredley is another good way to make short work of getting around town and there are plenty of places that rent them out. Expect to pay 10€ - 14€ per day or 63€ per week.

Cycles Daniel
2 Rue du Pont Romain
Tel. 04 93 99 90 30

Mistral Location
4 Rue Georges Clémenceau
Tel. 04 93 99 25 25
www.mistral-location.com

HB Cannes-Holiday Bikes
32, Avenue Maréchal Juin
Tel. 04 93 94 30 34

Accommodation

Of all the things you need to sort out as part of a trip to Cannes, accommodation is by far the most trying. Finding a well-located, affordable, and spacious place to stay in town during the festival is a mission unto itself. It doesn't matter whether you're an indie producer or a famous actor... as Uma Thurman found out some years ago when she gratefully accepted a $30 a night room in a hostel run by local hippies. When there's no room in the inn, there's no room in the inn. Even Robert Redford is reportedly fond of recounting how he slept on the beach in Cannes, many moons ago.

Finding decent accommodation in Cannes during the festival is difficult for several reasons. Firstly, a good deal of apartments and hotel rooms never become available on the open market. They are protected by a myriad of opaque deals - everything from sub-letting to backhanders - which ensure wealthy and/or influential people are able to keep their regular digs for the festival. And many other rooms and properties are block-booked well in advance by companies for use as offices during the event.

The second reason is basic economics. Extreme demand for lodging creates a seller's market and this results in high prices. The problem is compounded by the fact that most hotels will only take bookings for the entire festival period. In other words, even if you only want to stay for a week, you'll be charged for the entire 12 days regardless. Likewise, most apartments are also rented at a single price for the entire festival, irrespective of how long you intend stay. So the upshot is, it's pretty much essential for you to book your accommodation as far in advance as humanly possible, and to make use of every contact, option, scheme, opportunity, and excuse at your disposal.

Apartments
Generally, renting an apartment for the festival is the best value option, particularly if you have a group of three or more. As France's second-busiest destination for business travel, Cannes has one of the highest densities of short-term rental apartments of any city in the world. Prices in Centre Ville start at around 1,500€ for a studio which sleeps 2-3 and max out around 14,000€ for something über luxurious. Realistically, the cheapest you can probably do a Cannes apartment for is around 500€ per person for the festival period. You should also expect to pay extra for linen and maid services, often in cash.

While apartments are definitely the best value accommodation in Cannes, if you're shopping at the lower end of the price range, expect the property to be small. In most cases, the number of people any given apartment "sleeps" includes having at least one person on a fold-out bed in the lounge. Likewise, you should always check with the owner or agent to find out whether they're counting double beds as one or two people. Either way, most affordable accommodation will undoubtedly be cramped so festivalgoers tend to use their apartments simply as a place to sleep and get changed. A list of booking services can be found in Appendix V.

Villas
Although the hills around Cannes are dotted with eye-wateringly expensive villas, there are plenty in the middle of the road, pricewise, which can offer reasonable value for money if you have a decent size group or planning to do some serious entertaining during the festival. There aren't any villas in the Centre Ville area, but well-situated properties can be found in Croix des Gardes, Petit Juas, and Californie Pezou. Unless you're looking to spend

silly money, prices range from 300€ - 750€ per night, depending on the size, number of bedrooms, location, and facilities available.

Hotels

Even without a particularly scientific count, it's obvious that the number of hotels in Cannes and the surrounding area is easily pushing 1,000, if not more. Hotels can be found in most of the districts of Cannes, but the heaviest concentrations are in Centre Ville, Carnot, and Prado République. As you'd expect, quality varies from basic to super lux, but for reasons outlined earlier, prices at the bottom end are probably higher than you'd ideally want to pay for what you actually get. A hotel's star rating can give you some idea of what to expect, but it's important to understand what this system covers (and what it doesn't).

The hotel star system in France is a national, government-mandated rating which gives hotels three, two, one, or no stars. The stars are intended to help visitors understand the facilities available at a hotel, based on a defined set of objective criteria such as the number of rooms, average room size, bathroom facilities, heating/air-conditioning, elevators, etc. They *do not* measure subjective criteria of the hotel, such as décor, quality of service, or cleanliness. As such, a 2-star establishment can be subjectively 'better' than a 3-star establishment and therefore may also be more expensive! Yay, France.

Prices for hotel rooms are mainly dictated by location, with those in the centre being costlier than those further out. In Centre Ville, prices start at around 75€ per night for a zero/one-star establishment; 150€ for a two-star; and normally over 200€ for a three-star. Prices in neighbouring districts are pretty much on par, but taper off a bit the further from Centre Ville you go. Expect prices for rooms in the big hotels along the Croisette to be orders of magnitude higher (and entry-level rooms at the Hotel du Cap-Eden-Roc, the region's most luxurious hotel, will set you back in excess of 1,000€ per night).

If you book early (i.e. prior to Christmas), it's sometimes possible to get a reasonably-priced hotel room (by Cannes standards anyway) via one of the major online booking services. A good place to start is the official website for this book: www.cannesguide.com/hotels. You can also check sites like Booking.com, Hotels.com, and Laterooms.com for deals.

Another option for booking hotels in Cannes is the service operated by the official Cannes tourist office. The advantages are: they speak English, can usually find you a place to stay, often within your budget, and will help you make the necessary arrangements. Although they won't be finding you a room in the Carlton for 25€ per night, the service is free and very thorough. Start at the web site, www.cannes-destination.com, or call them on +33 4 92 99

84 22. When contacting them, you'll need your visit dates, number of people, number of beds, and your realistic price range.

If you experience any problems during your stay with a hotel you've booked in Cannes, the festival runs a free hotel mediation service. The service can't help you with bookings, only problems you experience with the hotel after you have arrived. The service is available throughout the festival and can be found inside the Palais near the main entrance on Level 0. It can also be contacted during the festival (and for a couple of weeks afterwards) via email to hotelsmediator@festival-cannes.fr.

Budget Options
Unfortunately, cheap accommodation in Cannes is a little thin on the ground at festival time. With the recent closure of Le Chalit, and Hostel les Iris giving up the accommodation game to focus on its core business as a Mexican restaurant, there are now no hostels in Cannes which are available for festivalgoers (note that the you may hear about a hostel called Logis des Jeunes de Provence, but this only offers long-term accommodation for locals).

If you're travelling on a tight budget and can't manage an apartment-share, your best option is probably one of the two caravan parks/campsites near Cannes. And if you do decide to rough it a little, you definitely won't be alone. When the clock strikes 6pm you are virtually guaranteed to see a tuxedo or evening dress emerge from a small tent as other festival-goers make their way into town for a screening. Neither site is within walking distance of Centre Ville, but both are easily accessible via a short bus journey.

Distancewise, there isn't much in it. The cheaper and closer of the two (by about 1km) is three-star rated Le Ranch (www.leranchcamping.fr), located in Le Cannet just northwest of Cannes. Set amongst two acres of pine trees, the facilities are excellent, including free showers, a swimming pool, laundry, and a small grocery store. There are around 130 sites for tents/caravans, and also a number of basic cabins which are great value for money. Prices start at around 15€ per night for a campsite, but the real value is in the cabins, which range from 260€ per week for 1/2 people, through to 500€ per week to sleep six. To get to Le Ranch, pick up bus number 10 from Gare Routière heading *vers* (towards) Les Pins Parasols. After about 15 minutes, get off at the stop *Le Ranch* and you've arrived.

The other caravan park near Cannes is Parc Bellevue (www.parcbellevue.com), located in Cannes la Bocca. With 200 spaces it is slightly larger than Le Ranch and also includes an on-site bar/restaurant. Prices are around 17€ for a campsite. To get there, take bus number 2 from Gare Routière in the direction of Les Bastides and get off at the stop *Les Aubepines*, on Avenue Maurice Chevalier. Parc Bellevue is also on this road, a short walk away.

Staying Outside of Cannes

You may hear people who've been to the festival before suggest you stay outside of Cannes to save a bit of money. While it's true that accommodation will be cheaper and slightly more plentiful, ultimately, staying outside of Cannes is a false economy and not recommended for the following reasons:

1) **Travel**. What little money you save on lodging, you are bound to blow in one go on a taxi home after a late night out. Not to mention the lost time.

2) **Hassle**. Staying outside of town means you need to carry everything with you for the entire day to avoid the hassle of having to go back to your accommodation. Things like heading back to get changed for your evening thus become a major headache.

3) **Isolation**. You will feel detached from the festival and so much of the Cannes experience is serendipity. The last thing you want is to have the "how I am I going to get home" niggle in the back of your mind or feel the need to head home early to avoid an expensive taxi fare.

If you're hell-bent on staying outside of Cannes then it's best not to stay too far away. Your first choice should be areas which are on the train line, such as Golfe Juan, Antibes-Juan Les Pins, or Cannes la Bocca. You can use Google Maps to see how close your potential accommodation is to a station before you book. If you have your own transport, or are happy to do buses by day and taxis by night, you can also stay in Le Cannet, Cap d'Antibes, Mandelieu-la-Napoule, or Mougins. Do not stay in Nice, Saint Raphaël, or Grasse unless you really want to feel separated from the action.

Accommodation Scams

With the number of international festivals and conventions taking place in Cannes each year, there are sadly some opportunistic crooks who attempt to make a quick buck by taking advantage of unwary visitors. Scams come in various forms, but the central theme seems to be as follows. You see website or receive an email offering apartments for rent in Cannes at what seems like a decent price. You then go through a booking process which involves paying a deposit (or in full) and you receive confirmation via email. Safe in the knowledge that you're all set, you show up in Cannes… only to find the accommodation you've booked doesn't actually exist or it was never booked for you in the first place and is occupied by someone else. And the helpful 'agent' you dealt with during the booking process suddenly stops responding to emails and phone calls.

Fortunately, scams are still fairly rare, but you should remain vigilant none-the-less. To protect yourself, book through trusted agents such as Immosol, Everything Cannes, Destination Cannes, Dovetail Foks, or Central Cannes. There are of course also many other honest booking services and property owners out there, so with some caution and a little common sense you should be fine. When booking accommodation in Cannes, keep in mind the following questions:

1) Suspiciously Cheap? During the film festival accommodation in Cannes is in massive demand. Prices reflect this. Any apartment or hotel within 15 minutes' walk of the Palais should *always* feel expensive for what it is. If you find yourself thinking the price sounds reasonable, approach with a healthy scepticism.

2) Short Stays? As already mentioned, high demand means most hotels and properties within the Ring are offered on a block-booking basis only. Be wary of a well-located property which offers bookings on a daily basis. It may still be legit, but this is so rare that it's worth approaching with caution.

3) Photos? You should insist on seeing photos of the actual property before booking. These should look like they've been taken by a normal person, not a professional photographer. Raise your guard where the photos feel like they've come straight out of a furniture catalogue or lifestyle magazine, as stock photos can easily be used to hoodwink potential victims. And always insist on seeing at least one photo of the exterior of the property. Cannes has pretty good Street View coverage in Google Maps, so in many cases it's easy to verify the building is where they say it is.

4) What's Nearby? If your suspicions have been stirred, a good trick is to ask the owner or agent to recommend local shops and restaurants which are near the property. You can then use Google Maps to verify, although bear in mind that Google Maps isn't updated super frequently.

Accommodation Exchange

If you are looking for somewhere to stay in Cannes, make sure you visit the Accommodation Exchange at CannesGuide.com. This free service lists offered/wanted accommodation, villas, and last minute deals, and is a great place to form groups and meet new Cannes contacts.

www.cannesguide.com/ax

5) Payments? It's common for property owners or hotels to ask for payment in full up-front. Again, this is driven by it being a seller's market. Where possible, pay by credit card or PayPal, as these are traceable and you normally have some recourse if things go wrong. Wires/bank transfers are the other most common method of payment, but take note of the country to where payment is being sent. Obviously France is fine, as are many other countries in Western Europe, since many European nationals own rental property in Cannes. But it's not advisable to send money to banks located in Eastern Europe, and certainly not anywhere outside of Europe.

6) Western Union? As a rule you should never pay for anything online via cash transfer services like Western Union. They are favoured by scammers because of the low ID requirements and lack of traceability at the receiving end. Use Western Union to send money to your friends and family overseas. Never use it to pay someone you don't know for anything whatsoever.

7) Official Partner? Don't rely on 'official partner' logos which may appear on a third-party website as these are easily copied. Companies can only be verified as official partners if they are listed on the festival (www.festival-cannes.org) or Market (www.marchedufilm.com) websites.

8) Unsolicited Email? Avoid lodging providers who send you unsolicited emails offering accommodation in Cannes. While not necessarily scammers, they are certainly spammers. You can do your bit to discourage the practice by not responding. If response rates become low enough, they might just give it up.

The official website for the Marché du Film outs the following companies as known to have been involved in scams in the past: Premier Destinations, Euro-Events (with hyphen), Global Living Group, The Ultimate Living Group, Riviera Network, Business Travel International, and Expo Travel Group. This list is not exhaustive and new scammers appear from time to time. The old mantra, *if it's too good to be true, it probably is,* remains the best protection.

Eating

Eating is a national pass-time in France so French food should be a major highlight for any visitor. And Cannes is no exception. The city is teaming with eateries of all types, from small family-run cafes through to multi Michelin-starred world-beaters. You certainly won't be pushed for choice, regardless of the type of cuisine you desire, or to a large extent, on price.

Restaurants and cafes are dotted all over the city, but the highest density can be found in Centre Ville and Le Suquet. The two main strips are Rue Félix Fauré and the block formed by Rue Fères Pradignac and Rue de Bateguier. Both team with restaurants and are also good options for late night eats. For a more traditional experience there is also a multitude of restaurants on the pretty Rue Saint Antoine in Le Suquet (although most are not open super late). Further back into town, you'll find a range of slightly cheaper restaurants by the train station on Rue Jean Jaurès, but the quality can be variable. Outside of Centre Ville, restaurants are predominantly the domain of locals and as such, are often cheaper than those in the Ring. But it depends on whether you want the walk.

Dining in Cannes is a fairly informal affair. With a few exceptions most places do not require reservations, although there may be a wait at some of the better establishments around peak times (8pm – 10pm). That said, if you have a large group it's always advisable to visit or call ahead to make a reservation; particularly as many of the better restaurants in town are quite small.

A large number of restaurants in Cannes will have menus available in English (although perhaps as a matter of principle, some of the better ones won't). Either way, you may need to ask. In most cases at least one person on the wait staff will speak English to some degree and will normally be happy to explain anything on the menu in more detail. Having a pocket phrasebook can also be a good idea as menu translations (and waiter's English) may not be as comprehensive as you'd like. It also helps to ensure there are no surprises when your meal comes - important because the names of some French dishes or ingredients can look similar to English words, but are in fact quite different.

For example, a traditional French dish is *Steak Américain avec frites*, served *tartare*. An American-style steak with fries, right? Wrong. *Steak tartare* is raw beef mince mixed with onions and herbs, served with a raw egg on top. While the dish itself is quite good, it may not be to all tastes. A couple of less extreme examples include the different meanings of the words *menu* and *entrée*. In French, a *menu* is a set menu of two or more courses, normally at a fixed price. Whereas, to ask to see the menu you actually need to request *la carte*. Likewise, Americans may be used to an *entrée* being the main dish, but in the rest of the world, including France, an entrée is a starter (aka first course).

Another area of common confusion for foreigners in France is coffee. It's likely that you'll need a caffeine hit at some point while you're in Cannes, so it's helpful to know what you're ordering. If you want an espresso or "short black", ask for *un café*. For a standard white coffee, it's best to ask for a *café au lait* (CAFÉ-OH-LAY). You can also ask for a *café crème* (CAFE-CREM), however some people may interpret this as an espresso with a dash of milk, so if in doubt, ask for *un grande café crème*. Decaf coffee is *un déca,* and fortunately for the sweet-tooths, cappuccino is the same in every language.

Unusually for a modern city, Cannes is completely devoid of Starbucks or any similar caffeine dealers. Indeed, the takeaway coffee culture familiar to those from English-speaking countries just doesn't exist in France. In most cases, if you want coffee you will need to order it in a café and sit in to drink it. A few places may do you a cup to take away, but you need to look hard to find them. Gap in the market, anyone?

Fast Food

Like most cities, Cannes is brimming with fast-food options to ensure you're fed in a cheap and speedy manner. Staples such as burgers, kebabs, and paninis are ever-present and complimented by more traditional French fare like the veritable *croc monsieur* (toasted ham and cheese sandwich), *croc madame* (toasted ham, cheese, and egg), and a baguettes with a range of *chaud* (hot) or *froid* (cold) fillings. In recent years, sushi has also become increasingly popular in Cannes and there are now a range of restaurants which also do takeaway.

Corporate fast-food is noticeably absent in Cannes, with McDonalds being the sole offering. You should give Maccers a miss in favour of the smaller local joints. Our favourite fast-food takeaway in Cannes is Chick 'n' Chips, located on the eastern end of Rue Jean Jaurès near the corner with Rue Hélène Vagliano. Originally a 'hole in the wall' takeaway, the owner has recently expanded into the small bar next door. The menu includes burgers, paninis, and rotisserie chicken, but the *Sandwich Américain* (basically a burger and fries in a baguette) is highly recommended. Other good options include the excellent Lebanese traiteur Al Charq on Rue Rouaze, Snack Le Croq'in on Rue Félix Fauré near Hôtel de Ville, Kiosque Gambetta Americane on Rue Chabaud, Sushi Time on Rue Notre-Dame, and the sandwich/patisserie chain Paul, which has an outlet on Rue Meynadier near the corner with Rue Rouguière. You can also pick up cheap eats from the various kiosks along beach-side of the Croisette, although prices tend to be inversely proportionate to the distance you are from the Palais (i.e. the further you are away, the cheaper it gets). If you can't resist, you'll find McDonalds at Square Lord Brougham (off Allées de la Liberté), where a slightly un-amused statue of the city's founding father looks on as the local kids breakdance and eat their Big Macs.

Cheap and Cheerful

When it comes to eating in Cannes, if you're watching the pennies the best advice is to stay off the Croisette. You may not be seen in the right places, but at least you'll come out with your wallet intact. Cheaper eats can be found in most areas of the city – it's simply about checking menus and avoiding places which appear to be more about posing than eating. In restaurants, the best value normally comes in the form of the fixed-price menu. Referred to as *prix fixe* or simply, *le menu,* these typically include a starter, a main, and a desert. A palatable price range for a menu is 12€ - 15€, but you can pay anything up to 30€ or more. It's also worth checking out the *plat de jour* (daily special), as these are often put on at a decent price.

Cheap eat-in restaurants in Centre Ville do exist, but aren't as common as they are in other areas of the city. A good place to start is the restaurant area attached to Al Charq, mentioned earlier. Located across the road from the traiteur on Rue Rouaze, the restaurant is cheap, casual, and fast. On Rue Emile Négrin you'll find Délices Yang, which serves up a range of cheap and tasty Chinese, Thai, and Vietnamese dishes. La Pizza, at Quai Sainte Pierre is a Cannes institution and has great pizza and pasta at reasonable prices. Not to be confused with La Piazza, just across the road which also does similar fare and is reasonably priced (and if you're meeting people at either, make sure everyone is clear on exactly which restaurant you're going to). In the same area, there's also one of our favourite haunts in Cannes, affectionately known as the 'Cristal'. It's actually two branches of the same bar (Le Cristal and Cristal Café) which are almost next to each other on Rue Félix Fauré (near the corner with Rue Gazagnaire). In addition to offering a wide selection of pizza, pasta, salads, and grills at reasonable prices, the Cristal is also open and serving food pretty much all night during the festival.

Another Cannes Guide favourite in the 'cheap and cheerful' bracket is Aux Rich-Lieu, which serves up a range of regional dishes. The 10€ *moules et frites* (mussels with fries) shouldn't be missed and their prix fixe menus are also great value. You can find Aux Rich-Lieu on Rue Meynadier near the corner with Rue Loius Blanc. If it's full, La Socca next door also isn't bad. Le Ksar, a small Moroccan restaurant just up from the bus station on Rue Georges Clemenceau is also amazingly cheap and tasty. More centrally, you can try Bistro Casanova for nice alfresco dining (Rue Casanova), Restaurant Esméralda for lunch (Rue Tony Allard, behind the Grand Hotel), or the excellent crêperie, La Galette de Marie, on Rue Bivouac Napoléon.

Middle of the Road

The vast majority of the eating options in Cannes fit into this category, so it tends to be more about personal preference than anything else. For starters, try the wonderful home-cooked Provençale cuisine on offer at the cosy Petit Lardon (Rue Batéguier) or Cannes' oldest restaurant, Auberge Provençal on Rue Saint Antoine. For seafood with a champagne chaser, try La Marée on Boulevard Jean Hibert. It's a short walk around the port, but La Marée has great views over the Baie de Cannes. On the way, you will also pass Gaston Gastounette (Quai Saint Pierre) which Cannes regulars almost unanimously vote as offering the best seafood in town. You will need to book Gaston Gastounette at peak times.

For a French twist on the seafood/steakhouse theme, La Cave, on Boulevard de la République has been consistently great for years (bookings required at peak times). Or if a lively evening of food and music is more your style, Au Bureau ("The Office") is a great pub on Rue Félix Fauré. Fans of Greek food can get a fix at Restaurant Tovel Beth-Din on Rue Gérard Monod and for contemporary Chinese cuisine, the stylish Le Jardin de Bamboo (16 Rue Macé) is a popular choice. If you're interested in a truly unique dining experience, try La Brochette de Grand-Mère ("Grandmother's Wheelbarrow") on Rue d'Oran, where you sit down at Granny's table and she keeps bringing you food until you say stop (closed Sundays).

Other tried and tested middle of the road options include, Aux Bon Enfants on Rue Meynadier, the Caribbean-themed bar/restaurant Coco Loco on Rue Frères Pradignac, and sushi bar Carré des Sens on Rue Saint Dizer at the top of Rue du Suquet/Rue Saint Antoine.

Expense Account Time

For those with the means, the French Riviera has no shortage of restaurants that will challenge your wallet as well as your palette. If you're a fan of ultra-fresh shellfish and other *fruits de la mer,* then you shouldn't leave Cannes without at least one visit to Astoux et Brun. Opened in 1953 and still going strong Astoux et Brun is pricey, but you won't be disappointed. Find it on the corner of Rue Félix Faure and Rue Louis Blanc. For a more refined dining experience, you can't go past the glamorous and elegant Le Merchant Loup on Rue Saint Antoine. Neighbouring restaurants, Le Mesclun and Le Maschou are also fantastic. The latter is extremely popular with the Hollywood executive crowd and is often booked up days in advance so it's advisable to reserve early.

Restaurant Guide

Visit **CannesGuide.com** for access to a large database of eateries in Cannes across the full spectrum of prices and styles. The database also includes maps, reviews, contact details, and you can also add your own review in due course.

For ultra-fine dining, there are two restaurants in Cannes with Michelin stars. Le Park 45 at the Grand Hotel holds a one star, serving diners during the festival in the beach annex, Plage 45. The other, La Palme d'Or at the Martinez, has held two stars since 1991 and offers sumptuous art deco décor with great views over the Croisette and Baie de Cannes. Just on the outskirts of Cannes, you will also find La Villa Archange (Rue de l'Ouest, Le Cannet). With two Michelin stars, this beautiful but relaxed restaurant is set in an 18th century Provençal house with exquisite food and service.

Top Riviera dining is also available at many famous regional restaurants outside of Cannes. A-listers and studio bosses can always be found dining on the terrace at the Hotel du Cap-Eden-Roc (Boulevard John F. Kennedy, Antibes), but the most famous fine restaurant in the area is probably Le Moulin de Mougins (1432 Ave Notre-Dame de Vie, Mougins). Originally the stomping ground of Roger Vergé, one of the greatest French chefs of the 20th century, the restaurant opened in 1969 and over the 30-odd years of Vergé's leadership developed a legion of fans, from presidents to movie stars, amassing three Michelin stars in the process (the most a restaurant can be awarded). It's no surprise then that Le Moulin de Mougins has for decades played host to the annual AmFAR (www.amfar.org) charity dinner, which takes place during the festival's second week and is attended by virtually all of the biggest stars in town. Vergé retired in 2003 and took his three stars with him so these days Le Moulin de Mougins has only one Michelin star. But the food is still amazing and the surroundings of the 16th century former mill are beautiful.

Self-Catering
If you're staying in an apartment or villa, or are simply looking to save a bit of money, you can buy provisions at one of the many *supermarchés* (supermarkets) in town. Most are fairly small and will stock the sort of items you would find in your local corner shop at home. National supermarket chains are also represented in town, albeit by small-medium size branches: Carrefour Market on Rue Meynadier (near the corner with Rue Rouguière), Monoprix on Rue Jean Jaurès (the food section is upstairs), Casino on Boulevard Alsace (corner with Rue Volta), Intermarché Express on Boulevard de la République (just outside the Ring), and Monop' on Place Gambetta.

Alternatively, if you take a wander along the pedestrianized Rue Meynadier you'll find a wide selection of specialty shops offering gourmet delights to temp all of your senses. If you're out in the morning, this walk will also land you at the Forville Marché (market) where all of your fresh produce needs (meat, seafood, fruit, and vegetables) can be met. The market is open 7am - 1pm every day, except Mondays.

It's worth noting that most shops, including grocery stores, close for lunch each day for up to two hours, although the bigger supermarkets such will stay open. Pretty much everything is closed on Sundays and public holidays so make sure you're well-stocked by close of business on Saturday.

Late Night Eats

Most restaurants in Cannes will serve meals much later into the evening that those in some other cities around the world, but if you're looking to sit down for a full meal much beyond 11pm your options will start to become more limited. Late service is available at Caffe Roma (opposite the Palais), Au Bureau (Rue Félix Fauré), Caffe 50 (Rue Frères Pradignac), and Cristal Café (Rue Félix Fauré near the corner with Rue Gazagnaire). Check out other restaurants along Rue Félix Fauré and also the fast-food options mentioned earlier, as some, such as Snack Le Croq'in, are open well into the wee hours.

Money

Although the euro has taken a bit of a battering of late, it's here to stay - certainly in France. As one of the main architects of the single currency the French are proud of their achievement and very few people mourn the passing of the franc. Indeed, after more than a decade of euro-power few signs remain of the old currency bar the occasional till receipt which includes a franc conversion for the seniors.

The euro is a modern, simple currency to use. Gone are the excessively high-denominations that plagued many European currencies prior to 2002. The euro was designed, structurally at least, to operate much like the US dollar and comes in a range of coins and notes. Coins are available in one and two euro values, and like the dollar, one euro is made up of 100 cents, with coins in 50c, 20c, 10c, 5c, 2c, and 1c denominations. It's best to try and avoid the copper coins (5c, 2c, 1c) as they are largely useless and in the case of the 1c coin, irritatingly small. All coins minted in the Eurozone have the 12-star symbol of the European Union on one side and an image chosen by the coin's country of origin on the other. However, all coins are legal tender in all Eurozone countries.

Euro notes are available in seven denominations: 500, 200, 100, 50, 20, 10, and 5. For anti-counterfeiting reasons, unlike the coins euro notes are uniform in their design across the zone regardless of where they were printed. Euro notes can be withdrawn from ATMs and also from a *Bureau de Change* (money changer), although the latter are nowhere near as common in town as they used to be so it's best to use these services at the airport. It's also a good idea not to get your cash in 200€ or 500€ notes. Many places will not accept them due to a recent spate of counterfeit notes found circulating in Europe (but also because it's tough to make change).

Credit/Debit Cards

In France, credit cards are known as *cartes bancaires*, but you will often see signs abbreviating this to simply, "CB", indicating that payment via card is accepted. With major credit cards, such as Visa, MasterCard, American Express, and Diners Club, you'll have no problems in Cannes (although as always, you will find some establishments don't accept the latter two). Likewise, where cartes bancaires are welcome you will also be able to use an international debit card (e.g. one bearing the Cirrus or Maestro logo). But it's worth checking with your card issuer to find out what charges are levied on payments in foreign currency, as sometimes these can be excessive. Domestic credit and debit cards are probably best left at home unless you are 100% sure they will work in France. When travelling internationally, it's also always good to bring multiple credit cards in case one is lost, stolen, or simply won't work for unknown reasons.

Banks and ATMs

All major French banks have branches in Cannes and oddly, most of them can be found within a couple of blocks on the western end of Rue d'Antibes. This also means that most of the ATMs in town can also be found here. In France, an ATM (aka cash machine) is known as a *distributeur de billets* (abbreviated to "DAB" after the old-school name *distributeur automatique de billets*). Most accept major credit and debit cards, although some don't so it's always a good idea to check the logos on the outside of the machine first.

Here is a list of banks with ATMs, broken down by the area of the city:

Near the Port
Crédit Mutuel, corner Rue Maréchal Joffre and Rue Félix Fauré
Crédit Agricole, corner of Rue Félix Fauré and Rue Marius Isaia dit Tony

Near the Palais
HSBC, corner of Rue Buttura and Rue Bivouac Napoléon
Banque Populaire, 25 Rue Bivouac Napoléon
Société Générale, corner of Rue Bivouac Napoléon and Rue Jean de Riouffe

Near The Grand Hotel
Barclays, Rue Frédéric Amouretti
EuropeArab Bank, 45-47 Boulevard de la Croisette

Rue d'Antibes
CIC, corner of Rue d'Antibes and Rue Buttura
LCL, corner of Rue d'Antibes and Rue Jean de Riouffe
Crédit Agricole, 85 Rue d'Antibes
BNP Paribas, corner of Rue d'Antibes and Rue Buttura
Caisse d'Epargne, 16 Rue d'Antibes

It's worth remember that, although ultimately part of the same group, Cannes branches of familiar banks (e.g. HSBC and Barclays) are not directly connected to your bank back home.

Lastly, a word of caution about ATM fraud. Skimmers - small electronic devices which are attached to ATMs to steel your details - are rife in Europe. Some also use pinhole cameras to capture your PIN. Always cover the keypad while you are entering your PIN and avoid any ATM where you spot anything unusual about the card slot. When withdrawing money, also be wary of people around you as another common tactic is for one person to distract you at the penultimate moment (e.g. by talking to or 'accidentally' bumping you), while an accomplice makes off with your cash.

Travellers Cheques
In the days of easy plastic and ubiquitous ATMs, traveller's cheques are a throwback to a bygone age. Usage has fallen dramatically over the last decade and as a result, so has the number of places which accept them. If you insist on bringing traveller's cheques, the only place you will likely be able to exchange them is in a bank.

Sales Tax
All countries within the European Union levy sales tax in the form of VAT ("Value Added Tax"). In French, this is known as *TVA* and the standard rate is currently 19.6%. By law, all taxes

---

Online Currency Conversion

The Internet contains a wealth of real-time currency information. A great place to visit is **Olsen & Associates** (www.oanda.com), where you can not only get the latest exchange rates, but you can print out a mini 'cheat sheet' to take with you to Cannes for help with quick on-the-spot conversions. Alternatively, download the free O&A app for from iTunes or the Android Market.

must be included in the price, so as in most civilised countries, the price you see if the price you pay.

Festivalgoers from outside of the European Union can claim a refund of most of the TVA paid on purchases in France when leaving the country. Refunds are only available where the receipt total is over 175€. A small administration fee is charged, so realistically the maximum refund of TVA you'll see is around 17%, but that can still represent a decent amount of cash. To claim the refunds, make sure you obtain a TVA receipt from the shop and present it to the VAT Refund desk at Nice Airport on your return home. For more information, visit the French Customs website: www.douane.gouv.fr.

Tipping

Restaurants and cafes in France are required by law to include service in the final bill (*service compris*), so there is generally no need to tip. However, most people do leave a few coins on the table unless the service has been particularly bad. There is also no need to tip for drinks in bars, although greasing a barman's palm in a busy establishment can often ensure speedy service for the rest of the evening. Likewise, tipping generally isn't required for taxi drivers or maids, but everyone will be appreciative of something extra if the service they have provided is good.

Budgeting

The question of how much you should budget per day for your time in Cannes can best be described as one of the many 'string length' questions we face. A lot will depend on the type of experience you want, how far away you're staying, whether you can self-cater, and also how successful you are at getting party invites (you can save a lot of money via free drinks and by living off hors d'oeuvres). As a basic rule, after you have paid for your accommodation, the bare minimum you can probably get by on and still enjoy your stay is probably 25€ per day. A more realistic figure probably averages somewhere between 35€ - 50€ per day, which assumes you're not self-catering, but also that you're not buying rounds at the big hotels either.

Mobile Devices in Cannes

Back in the day, the communications worries of most international travellers were limited to finding the nearest payphone and hoping you had enough coins in the local currency to keep it fed for the duration of your call. But in today's hyper-connected age most of us now fly around the globe packing a range of portable electronic devices which are thirsty for connectivity.

Like most European countries, France is well-serviced in the mobile communications department. Indeed, you will often find coverage in France is better than many other countries and with more choice when it comes to providers. This is particularly true if you hail from the United States, where coverage is often dictated by your choice of technology and a local monopoly provider. In France, and certainly in Cannes, 3G coverage is ubiquitous and there is a selection of carriers. When it comes to 4G, as of this writing service has yet to reach Cannes, but it will only be a matter of time. Marseilles was the first French city to get the 4G treatment in March 2012. And by the end of 2013, coverage is expected to reach the vast majority of the French population. But for now, the main question is of course: will your device work in Cannes? To answer that we'll need to take a brief digression into the history of the technologies which drive mobile communications.

As tends to happen in a competitive landscape, two different technology standards for mobile communications have emerged and been adopted around the world. The first is *Code Division Multiple Access*, commonly known as "CDMA2000" after the year the standard was ratified by the International Telecommunications Union. The second is the *Global System for Mobile Communications*, or "GSM" from the acronym of the original French name for standards group, *Groupe Spécial Mobile*. GSM is by far the most widely adopted standard internationally, used exclusively in Europe and also in Asia, Africa, South America, and Australaisa. GSM is available in North America, but CDMA2000 is the dominant standard there. And of course the two technologies are completely incompatible with each other.

So it would appear that international mobile communications exist in a situation akin to the age-old 'PAL vs NTSC' discord, familiar to filmmakers everywhere. If only it were that simple. In addition to the fundamental differences in the underlying technology, these services have been deployed on different frequencies in various countries. So even if your device supports the necessary standard, it still may not work unless it's capable of operating on the frequencies used by local carriers. For GSM coverage in Europe, 3G is provided on 900MHz, 1800MHz, and 2100MHz, so in order to make calls and access data services your device must support at least one of these frequencies. 4G services in Europe are being rolled out predominantly on 850MHz, 1800MHz, and 2.6GHz.

Returning to the original question, "Will your device work in Cannes?", the answer depends on the country where your device has its home network. For festivalgoers from France or other parts of Europe there should be no technical issues preventing use of your device in

Cannes. Likewise, if you're arriving from the southern hemisphere and your device supports the GSM standard, you should also be fine. Unfortunately it's North Americans who are most likely to face compatibility issues in Cannes. Those on CDMA2000 networks (e.g. Verizon, Sprint, Bell Mobility etc) will have the most trouble because the standard is not supported at all in France. In most cases GSM users should be fine if you have a recent device, however to be sure you should check that it supports at least one of the frequencies used in Europe. If you have a 4G device, it's worth remembering that even if it doesn't support the European 4G frequencies it may still be able to connect via 3G, which isn't the end of the world.

Of course, the other thing you should check is that your device's price plan supports international roaming (for both voice and data). Some cheaper 'Pay as You Go' (aka 'Pre-Pay') plans exclude data usage overseas, and sometimes roaming altogether. Likewise, before you leave you should also check that there are no bars in place from your carrier or employer which prevent international calls or data connections.

Network Coverage

France has three mobile network operators who provide national coverage. These are:

Bouygues
(Pronounced "BWEEG")
www.bouyguestelecom.fr

Orange
(Pronounced "ORR-ON-SHJ" in French)
www.orange.fr

SFR
(Pronounced "ESS-EFF-AIRH" in French)
www.sfr.com

Making Calls

The process of making a call when roaming is a little different to that when you're at home. Regardless of whether the number is local or not, you need dial using the full international access code and country code. You must also drop any leading zero from the phone number. For example, say the number you want to call in Cannes is 08 36 68 02 06. To call on your phone while roaming, you must dial the French international access code (00), followed by the country code for France (33), then the local number without the leading zero (8 36 68 02 06). Fortunately, most mobile phone handsets allow you to substitute the plus sign (+) for the international access code, so in this example you could simply dial +33 8 36 68 02 06.

Outgoing calls made while roaming are normally charged at your phone company's international rates, regardless of whether the call is to a local number in France or not. This is because the host carrier you are using while roaming charges your phone company for the call and your company passes that charge, plus some of their own, on to you. Needless to say, if you're watching the pennies it's probably worth keeping your calls as short as possible.

Receiving Calls

If you receive a call when roaming there's also a bit of a sting in the tail. If someone in your home country calls you, or you receive a call from another person in Cannes, the caller pays for the leg of the call between their location and your phone company's exchange, then you pay the remaining leg between the exchange and your location. This of course is also charged at your phone company's international rates.

To contact your phone while you're in Cannes, people in your home country can simply dial the same number they would use to reach you when you're in town (and they pay their normal rates for calling a mobile phone). However, if someone in Cannes wants to call you, they must dial your number as if it were international, using either the international access code (00) or the plus sign, *your* country code (e.g. 1 for USA/Canada, 44 for the UK, 61 for Australia etc), followed by your number minus any leading zero. The caller pays international rates on the call between their location and your phone company's exchange; you pay the rest per when someone calls you.

Data

So long as you have a compatible device and data roaming isn't blocked by your carrier, no additional configuration should be required to get data connectivity in Cannes. Connectivity will most likely be at 3G speeds, but may fall back to the slower EDGE standard in areas where the signal is weaker. At the time of writing 4G coverage was unavailable in Cannes, but expected to be in place by the end of 2013. Regardless of the connection method, you should be aware that accessing data services while roaming can be eye-wateringly expensive, particularly if your home network is outside of the European Union.

Keeping Your Bill Small(ish)

For most festivalgoers, using your device in at some point in Cannes is an inevitability so having a larger than normal bill when you get home is something to make your peace with from the outset. It's just part of the Cannes experience. That said, there are plenty of ways to reduce the 'bill shock' on your return.

Divert All Calls to Voicemail.
Using this strategy allows you to avoid paying the cost of incoming calls. You only pay when you check your messages, which is likely to be far cheaper than receiving the original call. And for those who use a data-driven voicemail service (e.g. Visual Voicemail or HulloMail), you can always check your messages for free via the nearest wifi connection. Either way, it's also worth noting that the method by which you access your voicemail in France may be different to that at home. Check with your phone company before you leave.

Use VOIP Services.
These days, wifi connections are ubiquitous in Cannes so it's entirely possible to make your outgoing calls via a Voice Over IP (VOIP) service such as Skype, Viber, or Fring. These apps offer substantially cheaper (if not free) calls to both local and international numbers, and can be installed on laptops, tablets, and most smartphones.

Text Text Text.
Nearly all mobile phones support text (SMS) services, charged at a fixed price per message. Although rates for sending texts are always higher when roaming it can be more cost-effective than calling, particularly when you take into account that the receiver is also potentially paying for a call. Text will never be a great medium for an in-depth conversation about the film you saw last night, but it is extremely useful for making plans and the inevitable, "where are you right now?" question.

Disable Data Roaming.
Most mobile devices include a setting allowing data connectivity to be disabled while roaming. If you're looking to keep your bills under control it's a good idea to do this. Many apps installed on smartphones and tablets include functions which automatically and silently download information from the Internet at regular intervals. So without even realising, you can be churning through roaming data at a wallet-crunching rate. Although some apps can be controlled individually, it's often easier to just completely disable data roaming when you're not actively using an app that requires it. Alternatively, iPhone users can download a free app from iTunes called Onavo Count which will keep track of how much data each app is using.

Special Roaming Tariffs.
With a little prodding from their regulators, mobile phone companies have begun to wise up to the fact that their customers are sick of being shafted for international roaming. As a result some companies now offer special tariffs or add-ons which deliver better value for international travellers. For example, both Vodafone and O2 in the UK offer a 'world

traveller' service which, for a small monthly or daily fee, allows significantly cheaper calls and data. Before you leave, contact your own mobile provider to see if there are any options available for your phone and plan.

Ditch the Pre-Pay Phone.
Pre-pay mobile phones may seem cheap out of the box, but calling and data is often more expensive than on contract phones. Further, many do not support international roaming at all and even when they do, there's also the added hassle of having to top-up while you're away. If you analyse your monthly spend, you may find it's actually cheaper to go contract and that will almost certainly make life easier when roaming too.

Get Local Pre-Pay SIM Card.
One of the most common strategies used by travellers to save money when roaming is to replace your home SIM card with a local one. The key advantage is this allows you to pay local prices for data and calls (and no charges for receiving calls). On the downside, your number will be a local number instead, which is more of hassle for incoming calls, but you can always set the voicemail on your normal number to inform callers of your temporary Cannes number.

The other consideration when opting for a local SIM is to ensure that your device is not locked to your home carrier. Locked devices will not accept SIM cards from other carriers. Your carrier will be able to tell you whether your device is locked (and whether it can be official unlocked by them). Alternatively, if you're technically minded and understand the risks,' jailbreaking' is also an option to unlock many devices running iOS or Android. Either way, make sure you sort out your device's locked/unlocked status before you leave home.

In terms of getting your hands on a local SIM in Cannes, your best bet is to head to one of the local mobile phone shops in town. In most cases someone on the staff will speak decent English and they are normally extremely helpful. The flagship stores for each of the main carriers are:

SFR
23 Rue d'Antibes

Orange
28 Rue d'Antibes

Bouygues
19 Rue des Serbes

SFR have been extremely helpful in the past and are recommended as a first port of call. Orange is literally across the road and has been an official festival partner for many years. They also maintain a stand in the accreditation area of the Palais, but if you're considering Orange, it's best to visit the shop. Some festivalgoers have reported that the staff on the stand have been less helpful and provided conflicting advice on available price plans and device compatibility. You can also avoid the crowds.

Rent a Phone.
As a last resort (or if you have a CDMA2000 device), there are several companies in Cannes who offer rental phones for the festival. Different options are available, depending on whether you need calls and data or calls only. Prices start around 8€ per day for the device and you will need to pay for calls/data on top.

A company called Cellhire has been the official festival partner for many years and operates desk in accreditation area of the Palais:

Cellhire
Tel. +33 (0)6 75 37 15 55
www.cellhire.com/cannes/

It is also worth checking with competitor, Com and Call, as you may be able to get a better deal:

Com and Call
5 Avenue du Maréchal Juin
Tel. +33 (0)4 93 94 56 56
www.comandcall.com

Language

Although at times it's easy to forget, Cannes is of course in France and that means everyone speaks French. This can certainly add to the confusion felt by first-time visitors to the festival, but it's definitely not something to worry too much about. Those who are lucky enough to be versed in the language of love will obviously encounter no problems. For the rest of us, it isn't really as daunting as it may seem as there are several factors that work in favour of Anglophones visiting the festival.

First off, you'll remember from the history of Cannes that the modern city was effectively founded by a Brit, so speaking English here is nothing new. Secondly, English is the undisputed international language of business. For example, when a Brazilian needs to do business with a German, they will most likely speak in English. As much as this may annoy the traditionalists who stare wistfully into a past when French was the *lingua franca*, both the festival organisers and the city itself are largely happy to support English as a second language.

That said, when it comes to dealing with people who aren't connected to the festival (e.g. staff in shops or restaurants) it's always polite to at least attempt to start the conversation in French. This way, you will experience the pleasant and helpful side of any Francophone you encounter. Even if you stumble on the vowels, massacre the pronunciation, or cross-dress an object, your efforts will be appreciated. And in many cases, if a French person detects that you're an Anglophone they will often speak to you in English even if you speak to them in French.

Regardless of how much or how little French you're comfortable attempting during your visit, you should definitely master the phrase, *Parlez vous anglais?* (PAR-LAY VOOS ONG-GLAY) – "Do you speak English?" After your exchange of pleasantries, you can politely pop this question. The usual response is "a little" and you're in business. But remember, when someone says "at little", they mean a *little*. Make sure you speak slowly and clearly (but not loudly) so that you're easily understood.

In general, the written word is a little easier to grasp than the spoken one. Because English is closely related to French the two languages share a large number of words. Many other French words are similar enough to their English counterparts to allow you to guess their meaning. French grammar and punctuation, on the other hand, are a little different; not to mention a slew of irregular verbs and the inexplicable practice of assigning gender to inanimate objects. However, you can often get the general idea of what signs, labels, menus, and other written words mean pretty easily.

You should at least try your hand at French while you are in Cannes. You never know, you might find that the little bit you perhaps learnt at school comes flooding back. The main challenges you'll face with spoken French are the speed at which natives speak and the colloquial terms found in common speech. If you get a stream of incompressible babble, you can always ask the person to repeat themselves, *répétez s'il vous plait* (REP-ET-AY SI-VOO-PLAY), or to speak a little more slowly, *Est-ce que vous pourriez parler plus lentement?* (ES-KE-VOO POO-REE-AY PARLAY PLOO LONT-MON). Finally, you could always resort to, *Pardon. Je ne comprends pas* (PAR-DON. ZJUH-NEY COM-PRON PAR) – "Sorry. I don't understand." An introduction to French, including a collection of useful words and phrases can be found in Appendix III.

You will generally find that most people in Cannes, particularly those there for the festival, will speak at least some English. Cannes has more of an international flavour than many other French cities and with the huge influx of Americans, Canadians, Brits, Aussies, Kiwis and others, you're bound to hear plenty of understandable chatter. If you find yourself craving some English-speaking company take a visit to either the American or Irish Pavilions, or the UK Film Centre. English-language books and magazines can also be found at the Cannes English Bookshop (11 Rue Bivouac Napoléon), which is run by a friendly expat Aussie.

General Info

Different countries and cities always come with their own quirks, especially for visitors. Here's a collection of handy hints and tips about Cannes, and France in general, to help make your stay as smooth as possible.

Weather
Cannes has a typical Mediterranean climate, with warm dry summers and cool wet winters. The average daytime temperature in May is a pleasant 20°C (68°F), but it's not uncommon for temperatures to occasionally nudge 30°C (86°F) during the festival. Night-time temperatures in May rarely fall into single figures, but it can feel a bit chilly without a jacket latter in the evening. When it's out, the sun can be quite strong, particularly for denizens of the northern hemisphere who have just come out of winter, so decent sunscreen is a must. However, because May is technically still spring you're also guaranteed to see at least one or two days of fairly heavy rain during the festival. Make sure you bring a brollie. Check weather reports for Cannes online at Yahoo! Weather (weather.yahoo.com) or France's national weather service, Météo (www.meteo.fr).

What to Wear
The basis of your Cannes wardrobe should be comfortable, neat summer wear. During the

day, the dress code is fairly laid-back with most people opting for a business casual look. But remember to pack a couple of warmish items in case it gets nippy later in the evening.

If you're planning to take in a red carpet screening or a swanky party, you'll also need your formal gear as the evening dress code is strictly enforced. For the blokes this means a tux with a bow-tie; the latter being essential lest you find yourself being forced to purchase one at an exorbitant price while you wait in line for the screening. For the ladies the rules are as always, at little looser. Classy, elegant evening wear is a given, but you should also give some thought to practicality of needing to traverse stairs, stand in line, and potentially walk a reasonable distance to and from a screening. Which leads us to the most important item... shoes.

You should pack at least two pairs of shoes for Cannes. The first should be the most comfortable pair you own, to provide some consolation to your feet for the amount of walking you'll be doing. The other pair should be your knock 'em dead evening shoes to match your formal attire; although ladies, it's advisable to keep your glam shoes at least a little sensible. The red carpet can be treacherous and later on there may be a need for some fancy footwork to pull of entry to an exclusive party.

Internet Access
These days, getting online while you're in Cannes is fairly straight-forward. Most accommodation includes some form of internet connectivity and during the festival free internet terminals are available in the Palais and many of the pavilions. Most locations also offer wifi access, although in the Palais this is only available to those with Market or Press accreditation. Wifi in the pavilions tends to be free, but not always super speedy. You may also need to get the password from the pavilion staff. If you're really stuck, a growing number of cafes and restaurants, including McDonalds, also offer free wifi for their patrons. Look for signs indicating *Wifi Ici* (Wifi here). Note that, in French, *wifi* is pronounced WIFF-EE.

Tabacs
Part newsagent, part grocery store (and occasionally part bar), tabacs are France's corner shops. Across the country they can easily be spotted by the universal tabac symbol of an elongated orange diamond shape, called *la carotte* (the carrot) by the French. Tabacs are your source of newspapers, tobacco, phone cards, gum, and other staples.

Payphones
Thanks to the ubiquity of mobiles, payphones are fast becoming a relic of the past. If for some reason you do need to use a payphone, they are reasonably well-located around town. But your best bet is to use the phones inside the Palais or Riviera complexes as the

environment is much quieter than out on the street. Virtually no French payphone accepts coins these days, so you must either pay using a credit/debit card, a calling card from home, or pick up a *télécarte* (local phone card). Télécartes are available from tabacs, post offices, and anywhere you see the sign, *Télécarte en Vente Ici*. When making international calls, dial 00 followed by the country code and number. Remember to drop any leading zero when dialling foreign numbers.

Print/Photocopy/Fax

If you need access to printing, photocopying, or fax services, there is a business centre located on Level 01 (basement) of the Palais. Market badge holders can also make use of the Purple Lounge, also inside the Palais on Level 01. Outside of the Palais, you'll find Buro Copy at 6 Rue Notre Dame and Telecourses Bureautique at 16 Rue Louis Blanc. Some of the pavilions, such as the UK Film Centre, also offer basic printing and photocopying services, and these are sometimes free for nationals of the respective country.

Post Office

A mini post office (La Poste) is located in the Palais (Level 01) and open during the standard hours, but also on Sundays and public holidays. Inside the Ring, full-size post office branches can be found at 22 Rue Bivouac Napoléon (near the Palais), 13 Rue Saint-Dizier (Le Suquet), and 19 Rue Hoche (near the train station). Post-office branches are open 9:30am – 6:30pm Monday to Friday, and 9:30am – 1:00pm on Saturdays. Branches are closed on Sundays and public holidays.

Times

All times in France are shown in 24 hour notation, sometimes referred to in English-speaking countries as "military time". The hours in the morning commence with 00:00 (midnight, which can also be shown as 24:00) and continue 01:00 (1am) through to 11:00 (11am). Midday (12:00) is followed by 13:00 (1pm), 14:00 (2pm), and so on up until 23:00 (11pm). Unlike in English-speaking countries, hours and minutes are not separated with a colon or full stop. Instead the French use the letter "h", for *heure* (hour). For example, 6:30pm in French is *18h30*.

Prices/Numbers

You should be aware that, when it comes to numbers, most Europeans use commas and decimal points in completely the opposite way to English-speaking countries. Commas are decimal points and decimal points are used as thousand separators. For example, the price 5.99€ will be displayed as 5,99€ and the number 1,000 would be shown as 1.000. With prices, you will also occasionally see the euro symbol used as a separator, as in 5€99.

Business Hours

France is the home of the 35-hour working week, which is great if you work in an office, but a total pain if you want to get anything done in the middle of the day because most business close at lunchtime for about 2 hours. Exact closing times will vary depending on the type of business. Banks and offices are normally closed between 12pm and 2pm, while for shops it can be 12:30pm – 2:30pm, and sometimes 1pm – 3pm. Restaurants in the Ring are normally open all day (*service non stop*), as are larger supermarkets, although it's important to remember the latter will be closed on Sundays and public holidays.

Public Holidays

Depending on the dates for a given year, there are several public holidays which can sometimes fall during the festival. If the festival runs early watch out for *Victoire 1945* (celebrating the Allied victory in World War 2) which is 8 May. And for years where Easter is very late, *Lundi de Pentecôte* (Pentecost/Whit Monday) may also take place during the festival.

First-Aid

A first-aid post with a doctor on duty is operated by the *sapeurs-pompiers* (fire brigade) in the Palais during the festival. It can be found on Level 0, near the Artists Entrance at the rear of the building. For out of hours or serious medical assistance, contact details for local hospitals and emergency services can be found in Appendix II.

Beaches

Non-Europeans will find the situation with beaches in Cannes a bit of an oddity. In most countries, ample beaches are usually available at no cost. In Cannes, most of the beaches are owned by the big hotels and consequently reserved for the sole use of their guests. For the rest of us, there is a small slice of municipal beach in front of the Palais between the Village International and the water (an accreditation badge is necessary to enter this area), and a fully-public beach available at the Cinéma de la Plage during the day. You can also venture west of the old port where you'll find Plage du Midi and Plage de Cannes la Bocca, both of which are free and far less crowded.

Driving

As with all Continental Europeans, the French drive on the right-hand side of the road. Not a problem if you hail from North America, but filmmakers from 'lefty' countries like the UK, Ireland, Australia, and New Zealand, should take extra care when driving and crossing the road. Speed and distance are also measured in the metric system, so all road signs are in kilometres or metres.

Electricity

In Europe the electricity supply operates on 220 volts at 50Hz. This is compatible with that found in the UK, Australia, and much of Asia, but not with the system used in North America (which is 115 volts at 60Hz). For visitors from the USA or another country where the supply is less than 220 volts there is a real danger of blowing up your device unless it's multi-region or you use a transformer. Either way, you will also need an adaptor plug to convert your local cable to the double round pin plug used in Europe. If you need to purchase an adaptor once you're in Cannes, visit Monoprix on Rue Jean Jaurès or FNAC on Rue d'Antibes.

Time Difference

France observes the standard Western European Time (WET), which is one hour ahead of Greenwich Mean Time (GMT). This translates to be one hour ahead of the UK and Ireland, six hours ahead of US Eastern Time, eight hours ahead of US Mountain Time, and nine hours ahead of US Western Time. Australia and New Zealand are 7-12 hours ahead, depending on whereabouts in these countries you are. Alternatively, if you prefer to let someone else worry about all this 'four hours forward, six hours back' stuff, you can use the World Time Server (www.worldtimeserver.com) to make the calculation for you.

Left Luggage

An official left luggage service is accessible to accredited festivalgoers for the duration of the festival. It's open 9am – 7pm every day, although it closes at 5pm on the last Sunday. The service is day-only (i.e. bags cannot be stored overnight) and it's located in Gare Maritime. If you're an exhibitor in the Market or friendly with someone who is, there's also a special left luggage service (including overnight) available in Hall Méditerranée in the Palais, Level 0.

Lost Property

The festival's official lost property desk can be found in Gare Maritime. Any items which are handed in at one of the festival venues are taken here (assuming they haven't been blown up by the anti-terrorist police). The lost property office is open from 9am – 1pm, and 2pm – 6.30pm every day during the festival. If you have lost an item elsewhere in town you can try the City of Cannes lost property service, located at 1 Avenue Saint Louis.

Vigipirate

Vigipirate is the French national anti-terrorist programme and is in force in Cannes during the festival. It's manifested mainly in visible anti-terrorist policing - look for the guys with dark sunnies, big guns, and mean-looking dogs - but also in the entry controls for the Palais and Riviera. Expect to be subjected to bag searches and metal-detectors when you enter these buildings. If you notice a suspect package or someone behaving suspiciously you should contact a member of staff in the Palais immediately. And it goes without saying that you shouldn't leave your own luggage unattended as, assuming it isn't stolen first, it may be removed and destroyed.

Personal Security

Overall, Cannes is a very safe city. So long as you exercise the usual common sense you should get through the festival without incident. The main risk you face in Cannes is petty theft. Be very careful of pickpockets in crowded places and take extra care when withdrawing money from ATMs to ensure no-one is too close. A common trick used is to wait for the point where the cash is released, then distract you by asking a question or bumping into you while the cash is grabbed. You should also be ultra-careful with your bag in public places. Ensure it is securely closed at all times when you're walking or standing in line (ideally locked) and never take your eyes off it for a second when you sit down.

Incidents of violent crime are extremely rare in Cannes, but you should take the usual precautions when travelling alone at night. Likewise, always keep an eye on your drink when you are in a public bar or club. There have been rare instances of people having drinks spiked with 'date rape' drugs like Rohypnol.

Getting Away

Attending any major film festival is an amazing experience, but it can also be very draining. Late nights (often involving more than a little alcohol), early starts, and far too many screenings have the power to take it out of even the most seasoned campaigner. And this effect can be magnified exponentially if you're attending a festival with a business agenda. Fortunately, many festivals take place in locations where there are a variety of interesting ways to take time out and recharge... and Cannes is no exception. So if after a few days you're finding the madness of festival-gripped Cannes a little too intense, then there are plenty of places nearby where you can escape the hordes and take some time to enjoy a bit of what the South of France has to offer.

Shopping

If the shopping experience is part of your nature, Cannes won't disappoint. The city is brimming over with all manner of retail establishments waiting to help you part with your money. The obvious starting point is a walk along Rue d'Antibes where you'll find a range of boutiques, shoe, and gift shops. If your credit card is feeling brave, along the Croisette in between the hotels and restaurants you'll find most of the big name designer stores. For more eclectic items, a wander along the pedestrianized Rue Meynadier can be rewarding. There are also bargains to be had at the clothes market in Place Gambetta (open daily from 7am – 1pm).

Musée de la Castre

At the top of Le Suquet (also known as Mont Chevalier) is La Castre, the last incarnation of the city's fortifications. Built in the 11th Century, the fort complex is now a museum housing a range of collections including paintings from local artists, artefacts from the Mediterranean and Middle East, and over 200 antique musical instruments. The pretty 12th Century Chappelle Sainte-Anne also sits below the fort's clock tower. The Musée de la Castre is open daily (except Mondays) from 10am – 6pm, but closed for lunch from 12pm – 2pm. Tours are available in English on request. Excellent museum aside, La Castre also commands magnificent views of Cannes and the waterfront.

Where? On the hill above Gare Routière. Get there by wandering up Rue Saint Antoine from Place Cornut Gentille. A little way up the hill, take the stairs on the left.
How Much? Views, free. Museum, 5€ for adults, free for students and children.
Time Requirement? 1-3 hours.

Iles de Lérins

Situated 3km off the coast of Cannes, the islands of Sainte Marguerite and Saint Honorat form a group known as the Iles de Lérins. At 3.2km by 0.9km, Sainte Marguerite is the larger of the two and home to Aleppo pines, eucalyptus trees, tranquil walks, and Le Fort Royale. The fort is the former prison of The Man in the Iron Mask, but now houses the Musée de la Mer, an excellent museum which provides information on the famous prisoner and displays a range of relics recovered from several ancient shipwrecks. A small number of rooms are also available in the fort for overnight stays (although the ferry schedule makes these unsuitable for general festival accommodation). The museum is open daily (except Mondays) from 10.30am – 4.45pm, but closed for lunch between 1.15pm – 2.15pm.

Ile Saint Honorat (1.5km by 0.4km) sits directly behind its big sister and is named in honour of the monk St Honoratus who, along with seven disciples, settled on the island in 410 A.D. Today the island is still in monk hands, being the property of the Cistercian Congregation of Senanque. The inhabitants grow grapes and herbs, and like all good monks, produce a few varieties of speciality booze. The island is open to visitors daily and regular services are conducted in the 11th Century fortified monastery, Abbaye de Lérins (www.abbayedelerins.com).

Where? 3km off the coast of Cannes. Get there by ferry from Quai Laubeuf.

How much? Allez retour (return ticket) from Cannes to Sainte Marguerite, 12€ and Cannes to Saint Honorat, 14€. Musée de la Mer (Ile Sainte-Marguerite), 5€ for adults, free for children and students.

Time requirement? Half or full-day trip.

Château de la Napoule

Now a museum, this stunning 14th century seafront castle is a fantastic example of Saracen architecture and houses a range of interesting art collections. The building was acquired in 1918 by Henry Cluse, an American sculptor, and accommodates a number of his major works as well as an extensive collection from other artists and sculptors. There are also extensive gardens, a lovely tea room, and the area around the castle is a popular swimming beach. Visit the official web site (www.chateau-lanapoule.com) for more information.

Where? 7km west of Cannes. Get there by train or Bus 16 from Place de la Gare.

How much? Museum entry circa 5€, plus bus/train fare.

Time requirement? Half day.

Mougins

300 metres above Cannes in the Alpes-Maritimes is the old fortified village of Mougins (pronounced MOO-GAN). The village is full of fantastic restaurants (including the famous Michelin-starred Le Moulin de Mougins) and has great walks in the La Valmasque Forest Park. There are also a range of historical and cultural sites to visit including the Museum of Photography, Musée de l'Automobile (Motor Museum), and the beautiful churches of Saint Jacques le Majeur and Chapelle Notre-Dame de Vie.

Where? 7km north of Cannes. Get there by taking bus 3VB towards Valbonne from outside the train station.

How much? Your bus fare only, although some museums have entry fees.

Time requirement? Half to full day.

Valbonne

This well preserved 16th century Provençal village is a great place to offload some time and enjoy the flavour of the South of France. There's a 12th Century abbey and the Roman Aqueduct of Claussonnes to visit, and the walk along the River Brague path from Valbonne village to Biot is magic.

Where? 14km northeast of Cannes. Get there by taking the train or bus (3VB from Place de la Gare).

How much? Your bus fare only.

Time requirement? Full day.

Grasse

High above Cannes is the world capital of the perfume industry, Grasse (pronounced GRAS). Many of the famous perfume factories conduct tours and of course are happy to sell you their product at source. If the perfume trail gets a bit overpowering, you can get some fresh air visiting the town's 12th Century Notre Dame Cathedral (home to three original Rubens), excellent maritime museum, and Princess Pauline Gardens.

Where? 17km north of Cannes. Get there on bus 610 from outside the train station or take the N85 in a car.

How much? Your bus fare only, although some museums have entry fees.

Time requirement? Full day.

Saint Paul de Vence

This scenic village (pronounced SAN-PAUL DE VONCE) is set against the mountains within fortified walls and has been a source of inspiration for some of the world's greatest painters, including Picasso and Monet. Today the artistic influence is still alive in the town through a local centre for artists, painters, and writers, and two fascinating museums.

Where? 27km northeast of Cannes. Get there by taking the train from Cannes to Cagnes-sur-Mer and then take the bus 233 from the station vers (towards) Vence. Get off at the village of Saint-Paul de Vence (before Vence itself).

How much? Bus/Train fare.

Time requirement? Full day

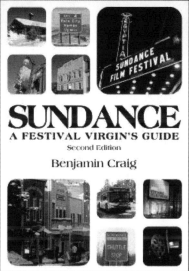

The Festival

For 12 days each May, the city of Cannes is transformed from a quiet seaside resort into the densest concentration of film industry activity on the planet. Over 200,000 people – filmmakers, film fans, studio executives, and star-gazers alike – decend on the Croisette to take part in the the Festival de Cannes, more commonly known to English-speakers as the Cannes Film Festival. During these two weeks, thousands of films are screened, deals worth millions are inked, careers are made (or ruined), and stars from all over the world gather to bask in the limelight.

Ever since the early 1950s, when a bikini-clad Brigitte Bardot frolicked on the beach for the cameras, Cannes has grown to embody two of the world's favourite pastimes: sex and cinema. Now easily the most famous film festival of them all, the mere mention of Cannes conjures up images of red carpets, palm trees, scantily-clad starlets, the blinding flashes of a million paparazzi cameras, and of course, celebrity parties.

History

On the surface, it seems strange that a city such as Cannes plays host to what has become the world's most famous film festivál. It's not a capital city, or even near one. Yes, cinema as we know it was invented in France, but that was in Paris, not Cannes. And sure, the weather in Cannes may be nice, but that certainly isn't a unique selling point. So just how did a small resort town end up hosting the most prestigious film festival there is?

Like much of the world as we know it today, the Cannes Film Festival exists as an indirect result of the rise of the fascist regimes in Europe during the 1930s. Its roots date back to 1932 when the first competitive international film festival was held in Venice, Italy. In those days, the *Mostra di Venezia* – and chiefly its awards – was as much about the national prestige of the participating countries as it was about the films. As time marched on, both the official selection and the prize-winners began to noticeably favour the countries of the fascist alliance, particularly Germany and Italy.

Matters came to a head in 1938 when Jean Renoir's "La Grande Illusion" was overlooked for the festival's top prize, known back then as the *Coppa Mussolini* ("Mussolini Cup"), despite being the clear favourite among both festivalgoers and jury members. Instead, the Coppa was jointly-awarded to a two-part German film called "Olympia", commissioned by Joseph Goebbels to document Nazi successes at the 1938 Berlin Olympics, and Italian film "Luciano Serra, Pilota", made under the supervision of Mussolini's son. When the results were announced, the French were of course outranged and withdrew from the festival. Both the British and American jury members also resigned in protest at the idea that politics and ideology were able to stamp all over artistic expression. "La Grande Illusion" – ostensibly an anti-war film – was subsequently banned in Germany and Italy, with Goebbels himself publicly labelling it as enemy propaganda.

In a classic case of ironic karma, it was Venice's folly would ultimately turn out to be Cannes' triumph. Later that same year, a group of critics and filmmakers got together to petition the French government to underwrite the cost of running an alternative international film festival in France, one where films could be compete without bias or political censorship. The government was initially lukewarm to the idea, worried about potentially upsetting Mussolini, but the powerful lobby group wasn't easily dissuaded. Spearheaded by Philippe Erlanger (leader of *Action Artistique Française*), Robert Favre Le Bret (who would become the festival's longest serving president), and Louis Lumière (the co-inventor of cinema), the group ratcheted up the pressure until the government eventually caved and gave the green light.

Several locations were initially considered for the festival, but the final choice came down to either Biarritz on the Atlantic coast or Cannes on the Mediterranean. Officially, it was the city's "sunny and enchanting location" which clinched it for Cannes, however most people acknowledge that the real reason for selection was the fact that, unlike in Biarritz, the municipal authorities in Cannes agreed to cough up the dough to build a dedicated venue for the event.

With a home secured, the inaugural *Festival International du Film* was slated to kick-off in September 1939 - the month chosen by shrew city officials who quickly realised that the festival could be used to extend the summer tourist season by a couple of weeks. But the fledgling festival only managed to get through its opening night before being closed down the next day because of the outbreak of World War II.

Things remained in hiatus during the war, but the festival remerged for a second attempt on 20 September 1946 under the aegis of the French ministries of foreign affairs and education. The city had yet to make good on its promise of a dedicated venue so the first festival-proper took place in the old winter casino, with Louis Lumière taking on the duties of inaugural jury presidency. Films presented in 1946 included Billy Wilder's "Lost Weekend, David Lean's "Brief Encounter", Roberto Rossellini's "Rome Open City", George Cukor's "Gaslight", Walt Disney's "Make Mine Music", Alfred Hitchcock's "Notorious", and Jean Cocteau's "Beauty and the Beast". Films from Charles Laughton, Howard Hawks, and Cecil B. De Mille were also screened out of competition.

With the first festival regarded as a success by all and sundry, the 1947 edition was moved under the wing of the newly-formed *Centre National de la Cinématographie* (CNC), a government body charged with supporting and promoting the cinematic arts and preserving France's screen history. Amongst its other general responsibilities, the CNC also took over the co-ordination of the submissions and selection process for the event. Indeed, in the early days, films were actually nominated by the governments of their respective countries, rather than the festival itself, and the number of berths available to a given country was proportionate to the volume of its cinematic output. This meant that back then, Cannes was more of a 'film forum' than the competitive event we know today, with the CNC trying very hard to ensure every film screened went home with some kind of award.

Although the 1947 festival had been successful by most measures, things faltered in 1948 with budget problems seeing the event dark for a second time. Financial woes also prevented the 1950 festival from going ahead, but in between, the 1949 festival managed to secure an impressive line-up of international cinema, including Fred Zinnemann's "Act of Violence", Michelangelo Antonioni's "L'Amorosa Menzogna", Joseoph L. Mankiewicz's "House of Strangers", David Lean's "The Passionate Friends", and Carol Reed's "The Third Man" (the top prize-winner for that year). 1949 also saw the City of Cannes finally make good on its promise of a dedicated venue with the opening of the Palais Croisette on the site of what is now the JW Marriott hotel.

By the early 1950s, the festival had experienced significant grown in both scope and renown. Many observers begun to note that Cannes was losing out on world premieres to festivals such as Venice and Berlin, which took place earlier in the year. So it was agreed that Cannes should be bought forward from September to April, a move which also garnered wide support from the local tourist industry, who had begun questioning the wisdom of holding such a large event at the end of the season when things were naturally winding down.

After the wobble in 1950, the festival found its footing, going from strength to strength as the decade progressed. Between 1951 and 1953 over 105 feature films were presented in competition, including George Stevens' "A Place in the Sun", Alfred Hitchcock's "I Confess", Orson Welles' screen adaptation of "Othello", John Ford's "The Sun Shines Bright", Raj Kapoor's "Awara", and a back-to-back triple play from Luis Buñel ("Subida al Cielo", "Los Olividados", and "El"). And in 1954, two things happened which would change the image of Cannes forever.

The first change involved an idea, initially floated by Parisian jeweller Suzanne Lazon, that the festival award trophies should incorporate a palm motif, since the trees had long become an icon of the city. The idea was picked up by Lazon's friend, legendary French director Jean Cocteau, who sketched out an initial concept. The design went down so well with the festival brass that for the 1955 festival the top prize, hitherto known as the *Grand Prix*, was renamed the *Palme d'Or*.

The other change experienced by the festival in 1954 was the introduction of 'sex' to the festival's image. During a photo call for Robert Mitchum, French starlet Simone Sylva inaugurated what would become an infamous tradition of 'getting one's boobs out' on the beach for the cameras. A slightly bemused Mitchum stood by as Ms Sylva's assets hit the international news wires, and with them, a lasting image of Cannes was cast in the world's mind. This was only strengthened by images of a bikini-clad Bridgette Bardot, who by the end of the 1950s had become an almost permanent fixture on the beach during the festival.

Despite the headline-grabbing off-screen antics of its attendees, the festival continued to present a range of films from top international directors. Indeed, the 1950s selection saw a list of films from what started to look like a bunch of usual suspects, as many Cannes alumni were invited back with their next films. Highlights included Fred Zinnemann's "From Here to Eternity", Walt Disney's "The Living Desert", Satyajit Ray's "Pather Pantchali" and "Parash Pathar", Federico Fellini's "Nights of Cabiria", Louis Malle's "Le Monde du Silence", Stanley Donen's "Funny Face", and a trio from Ingmar Bergman, " Smiles of a Summer Night", " The Seventh Seal", and "So Close to Life".

In the early days, Cannes was largely an event for tourists and socialites, who were often more interested in attending the parties than watching the films. However, as the festival's popularity increased it also started to become a place for the international film industry to gather, do business, and discuss future projects. The first "Marché du Film" was kicked off by 10 participants who, in 1959, set up a canvas screen on the roof of the Palais Croisette to show their films to potential buyers. The idea of using Cannes as a forum for film sales then gathered momentum so quickly that by 1961, it had become an official part of the festival.

The arrival of the 1960s brought with it large-scale social and economic changes in many western countries, but the festival was able to capitalise on the success of the previous decade and continue growing apace and pushing boundaries. 1965 saw the appointment of the first female jury president, when Olivia de Havilland took the reins, followed the next year by Sophia Loren. Films shown during the 60s festivals included Fellini's "La Dolce Vita", Buñuel's "Viridiana", John Fankenheimer's "All Fall Down", Sidney Lumet's "Long Day's Journey into Night", Robert Mulligan's "To Kill a Mockingbird", François Truffaut's "Le Peau Douce", Masaki Kobayashi's "Kwaidan", David Lean's "Doctor Zhivago", Orson Welles' "Chimes at Midnight", Michelangelo Antonioni's "Blow Up", Costa-Gavras' "Z", and Dennis Hopper's "Easy Rider".

Although during the 1960s the festival was able to screen seminal films from some of the world's greatest directors, a feeling had been growing in some quarters that it was becoming increasingly difficult for newer filmmakers to get their work shown in Cannes. In 1962 this sentiment lead to the creation of the world's first festival 'side-bar', the Semaine Internationale de la Critique (International Critics' Week), a parallel section focussed on presenting work from first and second time directors.

By the end of the 1960s, the festival was able to move beyond its shaky financial past and remained active for almost the entire decade. But there was to be one more hiccup in 1968. Amidst an undercurrent of general discontent in France, the head of the CNC, Henri Langois, was forced to resign by the French Minister of Culture, André Malraux, over a long-running budget dispute. Langois was an extremely popular and respected figure, particularly with powerful 'New Wave' directors like Jean-Luc Godard and François Truffaut, who immediately smelled a political motive. When news of the sacking, coincidentally timed with the 1968 festival, hit the Riviera, all hell broke loose. Directors Louis Malle and Roman Polanski immediately resigned from the jury, supporting calls from Godard, Truffaut, and a host of other French filmmakers for the festival to be shut down in protest. Tempers ran so hot that on 19 May, a group of directors, including Godard and Truffaut, burst into a noon screening and literally hung from the curtains to prevent the festival from continuing.

Shortly after, festival organisers conceded defeat and the event was canned as a wave of unrelated nationwide strikes brought France to a standstill.

The French government eventually brokered a deal to end the strikes and the filmmakers successfully forced Malraux to reinstate Langois to the CNC, although it was too late to resume the festival. But the events of 1968 did leave an deep impression on another group of French filmmakers, amongst them Robert Enrico and Jacques Doniol-Valcroze. Both were appalled at the thought that the festival had been used as a political tool by Godard and Truffaut in clear defiance of its founding principle. Together with a group of colleagues, they formed the *Société des Réalisateurs de Films* (Film Director's Guild) and gave birth to the festival's second side-bar, the *Quinzaine des Réalisateurs* (Directors' Fortnight). The intention of the Quinzaine was to pick up the mantel of the festival's original principle by creating a forum where films could be presented free from "... all forms of censorship and diplomatic considerations." The spirit of this idea was immortalised by a mildly-Orwellian quote from French director and fellow-founder, Pierre Kast: "All films are born free and equal. We must help them to remain so."

The arrival of the 1970s brought with it profound change, both in the world of filmmaking and within the festival itself. In 1972, the festival's board of directors decided to end the practice of allowing participating countries to select their own films and announced that from then on, it would take over the process of choosing participating films itself. This set the blueprint for the selection process used by most modern film festivals today. As for the films, the 1970s was largely dominated by the new 'golden boys' of American cinema.

With Hollywood in a transitional phase - the studio system was long dead, but the corporations had yet to become interested in movies - directors such as Martin Scorcese, Francis Ford Coppola, and Robert Altman, were given unusually free rein and had moved to the forefront of cinema in the 1970s. In effect, these directors and their peers were America's answer to the French New Wave, and Cannes certainly approved. Over the course of the decade American 'new wave' films screened at the festival included Robert Altman's "M.A.S.H" and "3 Women", Francis Ford Coppola's "The Conversation" and an unfinished "Apocalypse Now" (which still managed to clinch the Palme d'Or), Martin Scorsese's "Alice Doesn't Live Here Anymore" and "Taxi Driver", and Steven Spielberg's "The Sugarland Express".

But the 1970s in Cannes weren't only about American movies. Filmmakers from Europe and further afield were also well represented by films including, John Boorman's "Leo the Last", Louis Malle's "Murmur of the Heart", Milos Forman's "Taking Off", Andreï Tarkovski's "Solaris", Ken Russell's "Mahler", Rainer Werner Fassbinder's "Fear Eats the Soul" and "Despair", Wim Wenders' "Kings of the Road" and "The American Friend", Roman Polanski's

"The Tenant", Ridley Scott's "The Duellists", Alan Parker's "Midnight Express", and Werner Herzog's "Woyzeck".

By the mid-70s, the official competition was bulging at the seams so festival boss, Maurice Bessey, decided to expand the scope of the event by introducing three new 'out of competition' side-bars: *Les Yeux Fertiles* ("Rich Vision"), *l'Air du Temps* ("Spirit of the Time"), and *Le Passé Compose* ("From the Past"). While seemingly a good idea at the time, it quickly became apparent that the new side-bars simply over-complicated the official selection. So in 1978, the festival's new *Delegate Générale*, Gilles Jacob (now festival president), rationalised the three side-bars into a single selection which has been retained to this day, *Un Certain Regard*. That same year, Jacob also introduced the *Camera d'Or* (Golden Camera), an award for the best feature film by a first-time director in any section or side-bar of the festival.

By 1980, the festival had begun to face the reasonably serious problem of having outgrown its home in the Palais Croisette. Unwilling to lose the prestigious and lucrative event to another city, the local authorities in Cannes commissioned a new conference centre on the site of the derelict old winter casino. Completed in December 1982, the dual-purpose *Palais des Festivals et Congrès* hosted its first festival in 1983. To celebrate, the City of Cannes invited many stars of the time to leave their hand prints in clay outside the building on Esplande Georges Pompidou.

On the movie front, the 1980s were heralded by the comeback film from Akira Kurosawa. The legendary Japanese director had been languishing in bankruptcy, but with financial help from George Lucas and Francis Ford Coppola, Kurosawa was able to make "Kagemusha", which not only signalled a return to form, but also managed to pick up the Palme d'Or for 1980, an honour shared that year with Bob Fosse's "All That Jazz". Other key films screening at Cannes during the 80s included Bruce Beresford's "Breaker Morant", Bernardo Bertolucci's "Tragedy of a Ridiculous Man", Michael Mann's "Violent Streets", Costa-Gavras' "Missing", Jean-Luc Godard's "Passion", Terry Jones' "Monty Python – The Meaning of Life", Peter Weir's "The Year of Living Dangerously", Win Wenders' "Paris, Texas" and "Wings of Desire", Alan Parker's "Birdy", Peter Bogdanovich's "Mask", Roland Joffe's "The Mission", Peter Greenaway's "Drowning By Numbers", Krzysztof Kieslowski's "A Short Film About Killing", Jane Campion's "Sweetie", and Steven Soderbergh's "Sex, Lies, and Videotape" (a surprise Palme d'Or winner in 1989).

The 1990s kicked off with a continuation of the independent theme set by Soderbergh the year before. Early in the decade, the festival featured films such as David Lynch's "Wild at Heart", Ken Loach's "Hidden Agenda", the Coen Brothers' "Barton Fink", Lars von Trier's

"Europa", and Spike Lee's "Jungle Fever". Other notable films included James Ivory's "Howard's End", Robert Altman's "The Player", Joel Schumacher's "Falling Down", Mike Leigh's "Naked", and of course Quentin Tarantino's "Pulp Fiction". In 1993, New Zealander Jane Campion also made festival history, becoming the first female director to win the Palme d'Or, for "The Piano".

Although most of the action during the 90s took place on-screen, the festival did pause in 1997 to celebrate its 50th anniversary. To mark the occasion, a host of previous Palme d'Or winners were invited back for a photo call and to pay tribute to half a century of film in Cannes. The festival also presented legendary Swedish director, Ingmar Bergman, with a special award – the *Palme des Palmes* (Palm of Palms) – in recognition of his true mastery of the cinematic medium. The following year, the festival also acknowledge the role played by film schools in developing new talent with the creation of *Cinéfondation*, a side-bar dedicated to showcasing the best work from film students around the world.

For the remainder of the decade, the festival maintained a focus on presenting an eclectic mix of films from across the globe. Highlights included Emir Kusturica's "Underground", Larry Clark's "Kids", Lars von Trier's "Breaking the Waves", the Coen Brothers' "Fargo", Ang Lee's "Ice Storm", Curtis Hanson's "LA Confidential", Thomas Vinterberg's Dogme 95 offering, "Festen", Terry Gilliam's "Fear and Loathing in Las Vegas", Pedro Almodovar's "All About My Mother", and Takeshi Kitano's "Kikukiro".

As the world finished partying like it's 1999 and the clocks ticked over on the year 2000, the festival was busy putting together an official selection which highlighted the importance of digital technology to the future of filmmaking. The first Palme d'Or of the new millennium went to Lars von Trier's digitally-shot "Dancer in the Dark", opening the doors for a whole host of films not shot on celluloid to appear in the official selection. In addition to the shift in the way films were being made, the 'naughties' also saw several other key changes at the festival. In 2002, the brand got a makeover and the event's somewhat lengthy title, the *Festival International du Film de Cannes*, was given a haircut, becoming simply, the *Festival de Cannes*. Organisers also experimented with new additions to the official selection. Some, such as the world cinema programme, *Tous les Cinémas du Monde*, were short-lived. But others such as *Cannes Classics,* a side-bar which presents a selection of old films of archival importance, have thrived and remain permanent fixtures.

On the film front, the last decade has seen its share of triumphs and controversies. Films which have received accolades include Wong Kar-Wai's "In the Mood for Love", the Coen Brothers' "The Man Who Wasn't There", Baz Luhrmann's "Moulin Rouge", Michael

Winterbottom's "24 Hour Party People", Roman Polanski's "The Pianist", Michael Moore's "Bowling for Columbine" (the first documentary film ever accepted in competition), Lars von Trier's "Dogville", Gus van Sant's "Elephant", Walter Salles "The Motorcycle Diaries", Robert Rodriguez and Frank Miller's "Sin City", and Atom Egoyan's "Where the Truth Lies". Other films, such as Vincent Gallo's "The Brown Bunny" and Lars von Trier's "Antichrist" have caused stirs for different reasons (unwatchable, self-indulgent rubbish in the case of the first, and genital mutilation for the latter). Indeed, as the first decade of the new millennium gave way to the second, former golden boy Von Trier found himself declared a *persona non grata* (an unwelcome person) by festival organisers in 2011, after comments he made at the press conference for his film, "Melancholia".

Today, as Cannes continues the march towards its 75th anniversary, it remains both the most famous of all film festivals and one of the largest media events on the planet. The festival has an annual budget in excess of 25m euro, half of which comes from the French government via the Ministry of Culture and Communications (through the CNC), with the rest from the City of Cannes, various regional authorities, and a whole host of corporate sponsors. Each year more than 1,500 films from over 100 countries are submitted to be considered for a very limited number of berths in the official selection. And although the sexy image of the festival has somewhat waned, the stars still show up to bask in the limelight, the crowds still gather to watch, and Cannes' reputation as the king of film festivals just gets stronger each year.

Structure

"In Competition", "Out of Competition", "Official Selection", "Critics' Week", "Directors' Fortnight", "the Market"... having been the first film festival to develop side-bar events, a casual observer could be forgiven for thinking Cannes now appears to be a bit of a confusing mess. In reality, there are actually five organisations overseeing eleven major sections that comprise what is commonly referred to as the "Cannes Film Festival".

Festival de Cannes
Originally known as the *Association Française du Festival International du Film*, the Festival de Cannes is the 'official' organisation which runs the event. Headquartered in Paris, the Festival de Cannes manages the six core film programmes (participation in any of which affords a film permission to be promoted as having gained "Official Selection" at Cannes). The six programmes are:

Compétition (Competition)

The competition is the festival's main event and where you'll find all the glamour, glory, and occasionally, controversy. Films screening in this section are referred to as being "in competition" and vie for an assortment of awards. The Holy Grail is of course the *Palme d'Or* (Golden Palm) for best picture, one of the most prestigious film awards on the planet. Although it doesn't always translate into box-office gold like bagging a Best Picture Oscar, a win can still give a film a massive lift. For art-house films it can help secure a wider release and increased revenue; for foreign-language films it means worldwide distribution. Historically, the competition has only been open to narrative films, but documentaries have occasionally slipped in (such as Michael Moore's "Fahrenheit 9/11", which won the top prize in 2004).

Courts Métrages (Short Films)

The short film competition runs in parallel to its bigger brother, presenting a selection of films from around the world which vie for the *Palme d'Or du Court Métrage* (Golden Palm for Short Films) and a range of special jury prizes. The programme normally includes around 7-10 films.

Hors Compétition (Out of Competition)

Very early on in the festival's development, organisers realised there was value in inviting high-profile films to premiere at the event, even if they didn't necessarily qualify for the competition. More red carpets, mean more celebrities to pose for photo calls. In turn, this works to enhance the festival's image in the press and by extension, its reputation in the minds of the cinema-going public. And all without compromising the artistic value of the competition. Each year, the festival invites around 5 - 10 films to screen out of competition, ranging from highly-anticipated Hollywood blockbusters to the latest work from a respected European auteur. Recently this programme has also been expanded to include several 'midnight screening' slots, reserved for films which lean towards the cult end of the spectrum.

Un Certain Regard

Created in 1978 to roll-up several ambiguous programmes, Un Certain Regard (which loosely translates as "at a glance") is the main showcase section of the festival. Intended to be a "survey of current world cinema" it typically focuses on films from newer directors, films which use innovative storytelling techniques, and also work from countries which have a low cinematic output. Historically, Un Certain Regard was purely showcase, but these days the festival appoints a jury which bestows an award for the best film in the selection. They jury can also award Special Jury Prizes to other films as it sees fit.

Cinéfondation

Added in 1998, Cinéfondation is the festival's competition for short films made by students in educational institutions around the world. The Short Film Competition jury also casts its critical eye over Cinéfondation, making awards to the best films in the programme. Cinéfondation awards also come with a cash prize for the filmmakers.

Cannes Classics

In recognition of the importance of film heritage, the festival added a new section in 2004 which has become known as Cannes Classics. The programme is used to showcase new or restored prints of classic films and also rediscovered footage from days gone by. The festival works closely with major international archive collections and leading restoration companies to present around five films in the programme each year.

Séances Spéciales (Special Screenings)

Not strictly an official section per se, in recent years the festival has also screened a handful of films outside the official programmes (and rather confusingly, these have not been considered part of the Out of Completion selection).

Semaine Internationale de la Critique (SIC)

Founded in 1962 by the *Syndicat Français de la Critique de Cinéma* (French Film Critics Association), the *Semaine Internationale de la Critique* (International Critics' Week) was the world's first film festival sidebar, Although the event takes place in Cannes during the film festival it is run independently from the Festival de Cannes. Comprising competitive programmes for features and shorts, plus a host of special screenings, the main aim of the Critics' Week is to bring work from first and second time directors to a wider audience.

Films screened in the sidebar are selected by an international panel of critics and sponsors, with prizes awarded for the best film in each category. The Critics' Week has a long history of launching talented filmmakers on to the international stage. Alumni includes, Bernardo Bertolucci, Barbet Schroeder, Ken Loach, Neil Jordan, John Sayles, and Kevin Smith, amongst others. In Cannes, the Critics Week runs all screenings and other activities from its base at the Miramar.

Quinzaine des Réalisateurs

The *Quinzaine des Réalisateurs* (Directors Fortnight) is the second major sidebar which sprung up alongside the Festival de Cannes. Started in 1968 by a group of French filmmakers, its founding principle was to create a forum in which films could be presented free from politics, censorship, or elitism. Since then the sidebar has unofficially expanded its mission to include presentation of films which have an interesting directorial voice. The

Quinzaine enjoys a slightly higher profile in Cannes than the Critics Week due to its larger programme (20+ features and normally around 15 shorts) and is the only section of the 'Cannes Film Festival' which goes on tour to a selection of other European cities after the event. Like its older brother SIC, the Quinzaine is run completely independently of the Festival de Cannes. During the festival, the Quinzaine sets up camp in a townhouse known as *La Malmaison*, which can be found on the Croisette next to the JW Marriott hotel.

L'ACID

The *Association du Cinéma Indépendant pour sa Diffusion* (Independent Film Distributors' Association) has long played a part in the festival, mainly through its support of programmes and awards in the Critics' Week. However, since 1993 it has also managed a showcase programme of its own, presenting nine feature films from around the world that embody the independent spirit and are yet to find distribution. More recently, this programme has been given enhanced status by the Festival de Cannes (even though it is run independently) and is now considered by many to sit comfortably alongside the older sidebars. After Cannes, L'ACID also presents its programme in Paris and Normandy.

Marché du Film

Literally, the "film market" but simply referred to as "The Market" by most, the Marché du Film is the largest event of its type in the world. As the name suggests, it's the commercial end of the festival where the movie industry gets together to do business, primarily the buying and selling of films. Although it takes place at the same time as the Festival de Cannes (and is run by a dedicated division of that organisation), the Market is not prestigious. It's simply a tradeshow open to anyone who is looking to buy or has something to sell. The Market has been an official part of the Cannes Film Festival since the 1960s.

In addition to traditional participation as either a buyer or seller, the Market now offers several specialist registration streams:

Producers' Network
A special programme of events and workshops which run throughout the festival, intended to help newer producers make international contacts and get business done in Cannes and beyond.

Producers Workshop
A new initiative (launched in 2012) which provides a series of workshops at the outset of the Market to help neophyte participants understand the international marketplace and make the most of their Market experience.

Short Film Corner
A dedicated market for short films which also includes a series of events and workshops for short filmmakers.

More details on how to register for the Market can be found in the section on Attending.

Other Festival Events

The films are of course the feature presentation at Cannes, but to bolster the festival spirit there are always a range of other official events taking place in town at the same time. Some are permanent fixtures on the Cannes calendar while others pop up for a single year only. Full details for the special events at each festival are always available at the official web site, www.festival-cannes.org. Regular events each year include:

Master Classes
Since 1991, the festival has run a series of 'master classes' (in reality, lectures) where an established and respected film practitioner is invited to speak. There are now three different master classes held during Cannes: *La Leçon de Cinéma* (directors), *La Leçon d'Acteur* (actors), and *La Leçon de Musique* (film composers). Previous speakers in the various categories have included Oliver Stone, Stephen Frears, Kar-Wai Wong, Catherine Deneuve, Max von Sydow, and Patrick Doyle.

Exhibitions
From the early 90s, the festival has included a programme of exhibitions with themes that are strongly linked to cinema, such as tributes to the work of a particular filmmaker, or a collection of items relating to a single cinematic theme. Exhibitions are normally free and take place in various locations around the city.

Tributes
Each year at an evening gala, the festival pays tribute to one or more internationally-renowned artists from the film industry. Recipients are presented with a special festival trophy and a selection of their work is screened for the audience. Recent tributees include, Luis Buñel, Melanie Griffith, Raj Kapoor, and Billy Wilder, Morgan Freeman, and Liza Minnelli.

L'Atelier du Festival
Launched at the 2005 festival as part of the Cinéfondation sidebar, L'Atelier du Festival is a special programme to help young filmmakers bring their projects to the screen. Project

submissions are accepted in the period leading up to the festival, of which around 18 are selected for participation in the programme. Successful filmmakers are brought to Cannes for a series of meetings with industry professionals who may be able to help them get their projects off the ground.

La Résidence du Festival

Outside of the festival itself, the Festival de Cannes runs two six-month film development programmes for young and new filmmakers. The residences take place in Paris and there are two sessions each year, one running October – February, and the other, February – July. During the residences, filmmakers are provided with a range of financial and professional support functions to help support the development of their projects, while also offering cultural opportunities to broaden their horizons.

Submissions and Selection

Outwardly, most major international film festivals, including Cannes, present their submissions process as an entirely neutral affair where films are selected purely on their artistic merit. But the reality is often quite different. It's not uncommon for a lot of horse-trading to go on behind the scenes, with spaces reserved for favoured filmmakers, publicists twisting arms to secure berths, and even national film commissions exerting their own special kind of pressure. So when it comes to submitting to the world's most famous film festival, to a degree, anything goes.

This may go some way to explain why, counter-intuitively, Cannes actually receives fewer submissions than many other A-list events (notably Sundance). Not that competition for a place isn't still fierce. In 2012 over 1,800 feature films were put before the selection committee for a total of 53 berths (a success rate of just under 3%). However, the number of films selected for official programmes during the festival does increase once you add the Critics' Week, Directors' Fortnight, and L'ACID sidebars, but the chances of selection remain very slim.

Submissions Overview

Submissions for the various sections of Cannes are managed by the respective organisations outlined earlier. But despite the fact that the processes are separate, these organisations do quietly co-operate behind the scenes to ensure a film of worth finds its way into the most suitable section. It's still necessary, however, to make a separate submission to each organisation and the eligibility rules do vary slightly between programmes. All organisations now require submissions to be made online via their respective websites.

Festival de Cannes

In order for a film to be considered for the Festival de Cannes' programmes it must meet certain eligibility criteria:

Completion Date

Films must have been completed in the 12 months prior to the festival.

Prior Screenings

Being the world's most prestigious film festival means you can insist on world premieres. To be eligible for consideration, a film must not have been exhibited on any other festival or event, been made available on the Internet, or had a theatrical release outside of its country of origin.

Running Time

Apart from the short film competition, all films submitted must have a running time of at least 60 minutes. The running time for shorts must not exceed 15 minutes (including credits), however this requirement is relaxed for the Cinéfondation programme, where a running time of up to 60 minutes is acceptable.

Submission Format

For feature films, the festival accepts a wide variety of submission formats, but the most common are DVD, HDCAM, and 35mm prints. For shorts, only DVD screeners are accepted (note that Blu-ray discs are not).

Screening Format

There are no requirements relating to shooting formats, however for a film to be accepted into the official programme, either a DCP or two 35mm prints must be available. The cost of preparing screening prints or a DCP is at the producer's expense. If you are going down the digital route, you should also check that your DCP meets the festival's required specification.

Subtitles

Films which are submitted for consideration with dialogue in a language other than French or English must also include subtitles in one of those languages. If a film is accepted into the official selection, it must be subtitled according to the festival's rules, depending on the original language. For French-language films, subtitles in English must be provided. For all other languages, subtitles must be provided in both French and English. With the exception of films selected for the Cinéfondation section, all subtitling must be done at the producer's expense.

Article 1
All films submitted for consideration must also respect Article 1 of the festival's rules and regulations, which states: "The spirit of the Festival de Cannes is one of friendship and universal cooperation. Its aim is to reveal and focus attention on works of quality in order to contribute to the evolution of motion picture arts and to encourage development of the film industry throughout the world."

Historically, the official selection has mainly focussed on narrative films, although the definition of what exactly constituted 'fiction' has always been very loose. In recent years, several feature-length documentaries have made it into the festival line-up, most notably, Michael Moore's "Fahrenheit 9/11" which won the Palme d'Or in 2004. There is no separate section or entry procedure for documentaries - the same process and eligibility criteria applies.

Submissions normally open in December each year. For the exact dates, complete rules and regulations, and the submission form, visit www.festival-cannes.org.

International Critics' Week
The submission rules for the International Critics' Week are the same as those for the Festival de Cannes in the following areas: Completion Dates, Prior Screenings, Running Times, Screening Formats, and Subtitles. There are however, some areas where the rules differ:

First or Second Film
For features, the film must be the director's first or second film, however only previous films which have had theatrical distribution count towards the tally. This rule does not apply to shorts.

Submission Formats
The International Critics' Week will only accept screeners in the following formats: 35mm, Digibeta, DVD, Blu-Ray, or DVCAM. In the case of video formats, you must also explicitly request for the screener to be returned if you want it back.

Submissions for the International Critics' Week normally open in December around the same time as those for the Festival de Cannes. For the full rules and regulations, plus the submission form, visit www.semainedelacritique.com.

Directors' Fortnight

Submission rules for the Directors' Fortnight also largely mirror those of the Festival de Cannes. Unlike the Critics' Week, there is no requirement for films to be first or second features, however the acceptable submission formats are the same.

The Directors' Fortnight normally opens submissions in mid-January, and the full rules and regulations, along with the submission form, are available at www.quinzaine-realisateurs. com.

L'ACID

As the most separate of the various organisations which form the 'Cannes Film Festival', L'ACID has managed to keep its submissions rules fairly simple.

Running Time

Films must be feature-length, measured as a running time of 60 minutes or more. Short films are not accepted by L'ACID.

Prior Release

Films must not have had a theatrical release or been broadcast on television in France prior to the festival.

Completion Date

Films must have been completed within the 18 months preceding the festival.

L'ACID normally opens submissions in January each year. The full rules and regulations, along with the submission form, can be found at www.lacid.org. The site is in French, but an English version of the regulations and forms is normally available via a link in the main navigation.

Market / Short Film Corner

As the Market is not part of the official programme there is no submissions process per se (although the Short Film Corner does have some entry criteria). If you wish to screen a feature film in the market, you simply register for market accreditation then make use of the screening facilities provided to market attendees (at a cost) to screen your film. The Market is discussed in more detail later in this book in the section, The Biz.

The Short Film Corner is also part of the Market and there is no prestige associated with presenting a film here. So for anyone who may feel the urge, it's best not to go around telling all and sundry that your film "got into Cannes" when you have it in the Short Film Corner. Basically, pretty much any narrative or documentary short film is eligible for submission, subject to some minimum criteria to prevent people from registering music videos or their kid's birthday party tape. The criteria are:

Completion Date
The film must have been completed it the 18 months prior to the festival.

Running Time
Films must be no more than 35 minutes, including credits.

Subtitles
Films must be subtitled in either French or English, where the dialogue is not already one of those languages.

One Film Per Director
A new regulation added in 2012, the Short Film Corner will now only accept one film per director per year.

All submissions are reviewed by the Market to ensure that the film has "cinema artistic values". This is not a measure of quality, rather simply that the film is not a music video, training piece, or a home movie.

Submissions for the Short Film Corner are managed via the official website www.cannescourtmetrage.com and normally open in February.

Dates and Deadlines
You should check the respective websites at the beginning of the year for the exact deadline, but typically deadlines tend to be as follows:

Cinéfondation:	Mid-February
Festival de Cannes:	Mid-March
Critics' Week:	Early April
L'ACID	Early April

Directors' Fortnight:	Mid-April
Short Film Corner:	Mid-April

Once submissions have closed, the various festival organisations spend a few weeks compiling the final list of films before announcing their selections. By tradition, the Festival de Cannes always announces first at a press conference in Mid-April. The Critics' Week follows a few days later and the Directors' Fortnight normally the next week. L'ACID typically announces its line-up in late April via a press release on its website. There is no formal announcement for films submitted to the Short Film Corner - notification of acceptance or rejection is normally sent via email within 48 hours of submission.

Avoiding Scam Events

The sheer scale of an event like the Cannes Film Festival inevitably attracts interlopers with a variety of intentions. Some, such as the pop-up event Cannes in a Van (www.cannesinavan. com) are run with the same love and dedication as the official events. Others, such as the Cannes Independent Film Festival (www.cannesfest.org), are of a more dubious nature. Before submitting to any event that suggests it's connected to the Cannes Film Festival (either explicitly or implicitly), do your research to make sure it's both genuine and can offer real value to your film. This is particularly important if a submission fee is involved.

With regards to the Cannes Independent Film Festival specifically, we recommend filmmakers avoid this event. Despite a professional-looking website and some lofty claims about pedigree, in previous years the 'festival' has had zero presence in Cannes itself and has appeared to try and leverage its standard market accreditation to somehow suggest an official link to the Festival de Cannes. It's more likely that this event is one of a growing number of awards and screenplay competitions which attach themselves to prestigious locations in an attempt to bolster legitimacy, but appear to be primarily about generating revenue for their operators via submission fees. In other words, they are scams. More on this in Appendix IV, but specifically in relation to Cannes, don't waste your time or money with the Cannes Independent Film Festival.

Juries and Awards

A whole host of awards are up for grabs across the Cannes Film Festival and its sidebars. The task of selecting the prize winners falls on the members of a group of juries appointed by the various festival organisers. Jurors are chosen from all walks of the film industry, based on their body of work and general regard amongst their peers. And the presidencies of these juries are typically bestowed on a kind of 'lifetime achievement' award basis.

Festival de Cannes

The Festival de Cannes appoints four separate juries to take responsibility for the various awards on offer:

Feature Film Jury

Normally comprised of nine members including a president, the Feature Film jury has the unenviable task of selecting the award-winners from the films screened in Compétition. Over the course of the festival the jurors view all of the films in the programme, discuss them at length with the other jurors, before finally casting a vote for the film they feel is most deserved of each award. Voting is conducted by secret ballot and the winners are determined on an absolute majority basis. The festival's president and artistic director are also present during the deliberations, but do not take part in the voting process. The festival's charter obliges the Feature Film jury to bestow the following awards:

> Palme d'Or (Golden Palm) – for the best feature film of the festival.
> Grand Prix (Grand Prize) – for the film which shows "the most originality"
> Prix d'Interprétation Féminine (Best Actress)
> Prix d'Interprétation Masculine (Best Actor)
> Prix de la Mise en Scène (Best Director)
> Prix du Scénario (Best Screenplay)

In addition to the obligatory gongs, the jury also has the power to confer one or more Prix du Jury (Special Jury Prize) awards to films they feel deserve particular recognition.

Where there is a tied ballot for the Palme d'Or or Grand Prix, the jury president has the power to split the award equally between two recipients, although the festival rules only allow one shared award per year. In practice such shared awards are rare, having only happened three times in the festival's history: 1979 between Völker Schlondorff's "Die Blechtrommel" ("The Tin Drum") and Francis Ford Coppola's "Apocalypse Now"; in 1980 between Bob Fosse's "All That Jazz" and Akira Kurosawa's "Kagemusha"; and in 1997 between Shohei Imamura's "Unagi" ("The Eel") and Abbas Kiarostami's "Ta'm e Guilass" ("The Taste of Cherry").

Short Film Jury

A five-member jury is appointed to take responsibility for handing out the awards in the short film competition and Cinéfondation programmes. As with the Feature Film jury, voting is conducted by secret ballot and winners are determined by absolute majority.

The Short Film Jury bestows the following awards:

Palme d'Or du Court Métage (Golden Palm, Short Film) - for best short in competition.

Mention Spéciale, Court Métage (Special Mention, Short Film) – up to two special jury prizes

Premier Prix de la Cinéfondation (Cinéfondation First Prize)

Deuxième Prix de la Cinéfondation (Cinéfondation Second Prize)

Troisième Prix de la Cinéfondation (Cinéfondation Third Prize)

The Cinéfondation/Short Film Jury also has the power to confer joint awards, however a special waiver must be granted by the Festival President for a tied Palme d'Or du Court Métage or Premier Prix de la Cinéfondation.

All of the Cinéfondation awards come with cash prizes attached: 15,000€ (for first place), 11,250€ (for second place), and 7,500€ (for third place). The winner of the Premier Prix de la Cinéfondation is also guaranteed that their first feature film will be presented at a future Festival de Cannes.

Un Certain Regard Jury

A president heads up a five-member jury which makes a small number of awards to films being showcased in the Un Certain Regard programme. The main award is the *Prix Un Certain Regard*, for the best film in the section, but the jury also has the power to bestow one or more special jury prizes on other films they feel are worthy.

Camera d'Or Jury

Introduced in 1978, the *Prix de la Caméra d'Or* (Golden Camera) is a prize presented to the best feature film by a first-time director in the Festival de Cannes, International Critics' Week, or Directors' Fortnight. The task of selecting the winner of this prestigious award is handed to a special six-member jury appointed by the Festival de Cannes. For a film to be eligible for the Caméra d'Or, it must not only be the director's first feature, but it must also respect Article 1 of the award's regulations:

"The aim of the Caméra d'Or award is to reveal and to assist a first film shown in the Cannes Film Festival, whose qualities seem to be of a nature to encourage his or her director to undertake a second film."

International Critics' Week

Unlike the Festival de Cannes, the Critics' Week does not appoint an independent jury, rather awards are determined by members of the parent organisation, Syndicat Français de la Critique (SIC), and the various sponsors who provide awards in this programme. Prizes tend to vary each year, depending on the sponsors who are taking part, but SIC always awards the *Grand Prix de la Semaine de la Critique* (Critics' Week Grand Prize) for the best feature film in the programme. Other common awards include the *Prix SACD* for best screenplay, sponsored by the Société des Auteurs et Compositeurs Dramatiques; the *Prix ACID/CCAS* which provides a cash prize and distribution support for the selected film; *Prix Canal+* for the best short film in the programme; the Prix Découverte, for new talent in short or medium length films; and the *Rails d'Or,* selected by a group of railway worker film enthusiasts who attend the festival and select their best feature and short film in the programme.

Feature films in the International Critics' Week from first-time directors also qualify for the Caméra d'Or award.

Directors' Fortnight
The Directors' Fortnight itself does not offer any awards, but the programme's sponsors sometimes below awards on films they feel have merit. As the sponsors tend to vary from year to year, so too do the awards. It's always best to check the official website for the most up-to-date information for the next event.

First features in the Directors' Fortnight are also eligible for Caméra d'Or consideration, and since 2002 the programme's parent organisation, the Société des Réalisateurs de Films, has continued a practice of bestowing a kind of 'life-time achievement' award, known as the *Carrosse d'Or* (Golden Coach), on one of their own.

Attending

Cannes almost unique amongst film festivals in that it's an event predominantly reserved for film industry professionals and the press. Accreditation, entry to screenings, and admission to official venues is strictly controlled, with public access to the vast major of the festival virtually non-existent. Films screening in the Directors' Fortnight programme, or at the Cinéma de la Plage (beach cinema) offer some consolation for non-industry types via a small ticket allocation in the case of the former, and the 'first come, first served' nature of the latter. Film enthusiast groups from France (and occasionally overseas) can also see festival films via the Cinéphiles programme, although these screenings take place in a different part of town. In most cases, everyone else just has to be happy star-gazing and enjoying what the south of France has to offer.

If you're a filmmaker, attending the festival for the first time will probably be one of the most valuable things you can do for your career. Twelve days in Cannes will teach you more about how the international film industry works than a year at film school or a truckload of books. Above all, you will realise pretty quickly that films are simply a commodity to be bought and sold in a market which is governed by the age-old rules of commerce: create something that other people want and sell it to them for more than it cost you to make.

For this reason, the people who tend to get the most value out of attending the festival are producers, those involved in buying and selling films (e.g. sales companies and distributors), financiers, and quasi-industry types such as film lawyers or accountants. Those of a more directly creative nature – writers, directors, actors etc – may find the in-your-face commercialism mildly unpalatable, but this is the nature of the beast. Attending the festival will still be an immensely valuable experience because it provides an opportunity to make loads of new contacts outside of your normal circle, see a wide range of films, attend a host of parties, and write off a visit to the French Riviera as a business trip.

Who Can Attend

Accreditation for the Festival de Cannes is open to a variety of industry professionals as well as those who work for companies which service the film industry, and of course, the press. Although the Festival de Cannes oversees the process, the nitty-gritty of getting people vetted and accredited is split over a raft of different organisations according to the profession of the individual concerned. In the past, it was necessary to deal directly with the organisation which looked after your specific discipline however, thankfully, the festival now manages accreditation requests centrally via their website, automatically routing applications to the relevant body for approval.

So do you actually need accreditation to attend the festival? Technically no, as it's still possible to do business in Cannes without going into the official venues. But this is not recommended. Being in Cannes without accreditation will put you in for a whole world of hassle because you won't be able to get into key business areas such as the Palais, Riviera, or Village International. You will also have a hard time getting into the major hotels (for meetings) because most use the festival badge as a simple way of filtering out the professionals from the star gazers who are simply trying to find out if George Clooney is staying at the hotel.

Types of Accreditation

There are five main types of accreditation available for Cannes and each has a different set of rules, fees, and eligibility criteria:

Festival Accreditation

Occasionally referred to by its old name, "professional accreditation", this is your bog-standard credential for entry to official screenings and venues in Cannes. Festival accreditation is free and available to professionals working in film and associated industries. There is however, a catch. You will be asked to provide proof of your eligibility for accreditation in the discipline you select (e.g. producer, director, writer, actor etc). In previous years, the festival simply asked you to name three feature films you'd worked on, but in the days of heightened security and ever-increasing crowds, the rules have tightened up considerably.

For filmmakers, you will be expected to show evidence of work in your chosen discipline on one or more feature films in the last three years. The rules on what exactly constitutes 'evidence' are fairly opaque, but in the past the festival has made mention of things such as marketing materials (e.g. posters, flyers etc), contracts (employment, distribution etc), or membership of an approved professional body. A large amount of emphasis is also placed on your IMDB credits, particularly for actors, so make sure your listing is fully up-to-date before you submit your accreditation request. Having a professionally-designed website, clearly showing that you operate in the film industry, will also help support your application.

Ironically, those seeking accreditation in disciplines which aren't directly related to filmmaking will perhaps have an easier time, so long as the organisation you work for has a reasonable profile and clearly operates in a space which is related to filmmaking. The type of evidence accepted in this case will vary depending on the individual requirements of the accrediting body and will be outlined during the online application process. But having a website which shows a connection to the film industry will be paramount.

Applications for festival accreditation normally open beginning of February and must be made via the Festival de Cannes website (www.festival-cannes.org). You can find the link to the form under the "Pro/Press" section of the site. If you were accredited for the previous year it's normally possible to retrieve your last set of details to save time. Either way, you must then step through the various form pages and provide or confirm the information required. Although the site has got better over the past few years, the usability of the online accreditation process still has a lot to be desired so patience and a little time are essential.

Once you've completed the online process, you'll need to send any supporting materials requested to the relevant accreditation body (the address details will be provided during the registration process). You should receive an initial confirmation of your request via email, with an update on the status a few days later. If your request is rejected, carefully study the reason(s) given by the accrediting body as some have been prone to mistakes or misunderstandings in the past. It's always worth asking them to reconsider. Be polite, but argue you case and make sure all your supporting materials (and IMDB profile) are fully up-to-date. It's also worth remembering that just because you had accreditation in previous years, doesn't mean you automatically qualify again, particularly if your credits are starting to look a little stale.

The deadline for festival accreditation requests is normally the beginning of April.

Market Accreditation
Officially known as "Accreditation Marché du Film", this is the registration stream for individuals and companies who wish to participate in the Cannes Market. More than 10,000 professionals register each year. Market accreditation is available to employees and directors of:

- Companies whose main activity is production, distribution, exploitation, or international broadcasting of cinematic films;
- Companies which provide related services, including technical, business, financial, or legal services;
- Institutions, associations, and professional organisations whose principal work is in relation to the film industry.

Like festival accreditation, the market flavour provides access to official venues and screenings, however market badge holders get preferential treatment when it comes to tickets for the red carpet. In addition, Market accreditation provides access to various activities and facilities run by the Market (additional fees can apply) and services such as free wifi in the Palais. Market attendees also receive listing of their company, projects, and personnel in the official market guide. Historically this has been a veritable brick of a book which is given to all market participants on arrival, but these days also includes listing in the online market database at Cinando (www.cinando.com). More on that later.

Only companies and other eligible organisations can register for market accreditation, but it is not necessary to be an incorporated business to qualify because the minimum number of personnel a company can 'send' to the festival is one. Unlike the festival flavour, market accreditation isn't free. The fee for registration is around 299€ per participant, however a discounted fee of 250€ is offered for registrations received before the end of February. Despite the fees, market accreditation can be a good option if you're planning on doing a lot of business in Cannes or if your recent feature credits aren't quite up to scratch (because there's money in it for them, the rules are ever so slightly looser for market accreditation).

As with festival accreditation, initial applications must be submitted via the official website (www.festival-cannes.org). The first step is to nominate one person who will be the company's main contact for accreditation purposes. That person can then register themselves and any colleagues who will also be attending. If it's the first time you're registering a company, the festival will conduct similar checks to those used for festival accreditation, so you should ensure your website is up-to-date and clearly shows your film industry credentials. Once validated, the main contact will receive an email confirmation containing details of how to register themselves and additional participants on via the website. For companies which were registered for the previous year there aren't normally any additional checks – you simply go ahead and register previous participants using the stored details and add additional participants as necessary.

The deadline for market accreditation is normally the end of April, however to have your company and participants listed in the market guide, applications must be received by the end of the first week in April.

Producers Network
Created in 2004, *Le Réseau des Producteurs* is a special flavour of market accreditation for independent producers. Its aim is to provide a collection of services and events to help producers develop their projects, meet co-production partners, and ultimately bring their projects to market. Services include a programme of daily networking breakfasts hosted by a moderator with a range of guest speaks from across the industry, listing in a special catalogue which is distributed to a range of key industry players, and a series of online tools to help producers get their projects off the ground. This is in addition to the standard benefits bestowed by market accreditation.

To qualify for Producers Network accreditation, you must have at least one producer credit on a feature film that's been commercially released in the past three years. Note that "Executive Producer", "Line Producer", or "Associate Producer" credits do not qualify towards this requirement. A film is deemed to have had a 'commercial release' if it's been screened for at least one week in a cinema which is open to the public.

In practice, Producers Network accreditation is most useful to producers who are looking to make their second or third feature films. Obviously, the eligibility criteria rules out those without feature credits, but producers who have made more than three or four films probably won't benefit from a good deal of the services offered by this type of accreditation.

The fee for Producers Network accreditation is around 335€, but as with standard market accreditation, there's an earlybird discounted rate of 299€. To register, follow the

Accreditation Marché du Film track on the official festival web site (www.festival-cannes. org).

Producers Workshop
Not to be confused with the Producers Network, the Producers Workshop (new in 2012) isn't a fully-blown flavour in its own right, rather a subset of standard market accreditation. This is primarily aimed at accreditees who are attending the Marché du Film for the first time. For an additional fee of around 50€ on top of standard market accreditation, the Producers Workshop provides access to a series of events aimed at helping you navigate the marketplace, both in Cannes and the world at large. There is also normally at least one networking event.

Producers Workshop is worth the money if it's your first time visiting the market. The events provide a great introduction to the mechanics of Cannes and also to the international business landscape of the day. But if you've been to Cannes before, you probably won't learn anything new for the money.

Short Film Corner
It took until 2004 for the festival to finally introduce a formal market for short films, and alongside, an accreditation track for a large number of filmmakers who were previously excluded from Cannes by the feature film credit requirement. When a short film is accepted into the Short Film Corner market, two of the film's representatives (normally the producer and director) are entitled to Short Film Corner accreditation. This provides access to official venues and screenings (albeit at a lower 'priority' to those with market and festival accreditation), as well as a range of special activities and events for short filmmakers. Probably the most valuable are the breakfast meetings with short film distributors and the daily happy hour, the latter being a good source of free beer and new friends.

For new filmmakers or those without feature credits, Short Film Corner accreditation represents your best option for gaining access to Cannes. The fee for entering a film in the Short Film Corner is 95€ for the first film, and additional films are charged at a rate of 3.50€ per minute. Note that only one film per director is acceptable and only two representatives can attend the festival, regardless of how many films are registered for the Short Film Corner. All films must also be under 35 minutes, including credits.

The deadline for Short Film Corner registration is normally around the first week of April. Register via the official Short Film Corner website (www.cannescourtmetrage.com).

Press Accreditation

Cannes is one of the largest media events in the world and attended by more than 4,000 journalists, representing 1,500 media outlets in over 75 countries. Media access is managed directly by the Festival de Cannes via a dedicated press office. Press credentials come in a range of flavours, based on media type and audience size. In other words, the higher your profile and the more people you reach, the better the access that will be provided.

The Press Accreditation Commission maintains a database of previous accreditees, so if you've held press accreditation for the previous year, and your situation hasn't changed (i.e. a change of company or media type), then it's fairly straightforward to gain entry to the next festival. For new requests, or where there's been a change, the accreditation process simply involves supplying samples of your work.

The various media types eligible for press accreditation are:

- Written Press
- Television
- Radio
- Press Photographers*
- Press Agencies
- Photo Agencies
- Audio-Visual Press Agencies
- Online Press

* Press photographers must be assigned by a media company - it isn't possible for unassigned freelancers to get accreditation.

There are two main steps required for press accreditation. Firstly, you need to prepare the various supporting materials for your application. The nature and volume of material required depends on whether or not you are applying for accreditation for the first time and which of the media types you would like to be accredited for (you can only be registered for one). Once you've collected all of the necessary materials, they must be sent via regular post to the Press Accreditation Commission (note that email submissions and web links are not accepted). Information regarding the various requirements for each media type can be found in the Press section of the official festival web site (www.festival-cannes.org).

On receipt and validation of your materials, the press office will provide you with a unique reference and an address for the pre-registration web site where you'll need to complete the accreditation application forms (step two). Once you've submitted your application you can monitor its progress at the same site.

Applications for press accreditation open in mid-January and the deadline is normally the end of March.

Cinéphiles Accreditation

Organised by the City of Cannes, in association with the Festival, Cinéphiles accreditation enables local residents to see films from the official selection and sidebars in several cinemas around Cannes and some screenings in the Palais. Cinéphiles accreditation is also open to film enthusiast and education groups (both French and foreign).

Requests for Cinéphiles accreditation from groups within the PACA region of France should be sent to:

L'OMACC
La Malmaison
47 la Croisette
06400 Cannes
Tel. 04 97 06 44 90

All other requests for Cinéphiles accreditation should be sent to:

Festival de Cannes
Service des accréditations
3 Rue Amélie
75007 Paris
Tel. +33 (0)1 53 59 61 19
cinephiles@festival-cannes.fr

Requests for Cinéphiles accreditation must be accompanied by documentation certifying membership of a group which is either resident in the PACA region or a recognised film enthusiast or educational group. Cinéphiles accreditation opens in mid-January and closes early March.

Public Access

As mentioned earlier, the general public is largely cut out of the festival. Without accreditation it's not possible to enter any of the official venues, the Village International, or most of the big hotels. Screenings, other than those in the Directors' Fortnight and Cinéma de la

Plage, are also largely off-limits. As such, it's best to make sure everyone in your party has accreditation of some kind, lest they feel extremely left out.

Late Registration

If you've managed to miss the various deadlines it's still possible to obtain Festival or Market accreditation once you arrive in Cannes. But do not use this as an excuse to be lazy. Late registration in Cannes is more expensive, excessively bureaucratic, and in no way guaranteed. Success is largely up to the whim of the person who is processing you.

Presumably because there's money in it for them, the Market tends to be more accommodating to late registration. At around 350€ per participant the fees are inflated and you'll miss out on listing in the market guide, but in the days of Cinando that's no biggy really. It isn't possible to register late for the Producers Network, Producers Workshop, or the Short Film Corner.

To discourage late requests for Festival accreditation it's common to see language like "subject to severe restrictions" and "only in exceptional circumstances" used in official literature and on the website. In practice, if you show up in Cannes with your supporting materials, a healthy IMDB profile, a professional company website showing your film activities, and a good deal of patience, you should be able to get yourself accredited. Unfortunately late Festival accreditation is not free – there's an 85€ 'administration fee' levied, presumably to cover the costs of having you wait around while they check your credentials. The late registration desk is located at the Accreditation Centre in the Palais, which can be accessed via a dedicated entrance next the *Office du Tourisme*.

Day Passes

It's possible to obtain a day pass while you are in Cannes which provides access to the Palais, Riviera, and Village International areas. Passes are valid for 1 - 3 days and cost 20€ per day. It's not possible to renew or extend a day pass and they do not entitle the holder to attend screenings, but can be useful if you are only in town for a couple of days and have meetings in the official venues. You will still need to prove that your work in the film industry or a related area, however an official-looking invitation from a company which is exhibiting in the Palais should also secure you a pass with minimum fuss. The day pass office is located in Gare Maritime, in between the Palais and the Village International Pantiero.

Collecting Your Badge

On arrival in Cannes, after you've dumped your bags at your accommodation the next thing you should do is collect your badge. This is done at the Accreditation Centre which can be found in the basement of the Palais and is accessible via a dedicated entrance next to the

Office du Tourisme. Accreditation is open from 9am on the Tuesday before the festival and throughout. If you're arriving on the first Wednesday, Thursday, or Friday, it can get very busy so it's advisable to get there early if at all possible.

To collect your badge you simply line up as directed, show your passport, and you're all set. If it's your first Cannes, the process can take slightly longer as they will need to photograph you and print your badge. You will also be given a piece of paper with a detachable voucher on the bottom. The page itself contains instructions on how to attend screenings and this is tailored specifically to your flavour of accreditation so take note. The voucher itself allows you to collect your accreditation pack, which can be picked up from another desk in the same area. The pack's contents vary between Festival and Market accreditation, but all contain the official festival guide, a screening schedule (official films only), and normally some sponsor bumph. All this will all come in an official festival satchel or shoulder bag (the quality of which varies from year to year, but is often ok for a freebie).

You may also notice there's a large recycling bin near the exit. Before you leave it's best to spend a few minutes going through the bag and jettisoning anything you obviously don't need. Believe me, your shoulders and back will be eternally grateful, particularly if you're not planning to head back to your accommodation until later in the day. Likewise, if you have Market accreditation, you will be offered a free copy of the Market Guide when you collect your pack. Think long and hard about whether you absolutely, positively need a physical copy of this book. All of the information contained within is available online at Cinando (www.cinando.com) and annual membership of this site is included in the price of your accreditation. Some people still prefer to flip through the pages, but the book weighs the same as about three bricks (literally!) so the previous comments about the relationship with your back and shoulders at the end of the day doubly apply here.

Your badge is your single most important festival position. Carry it *always*, day and night, regardless of what you're wearing or where you're going. And don't lend it to anyone. If you're unfortunate enough to lose your badge, head to the Accreditation Centre immediately so they can cancel it and issue a new one.

Screenings

Despite the presence of the international film industry and the hyperactive Market, Cannes is of course first and foremost, a film festival. Over the 12 day event more than 120 films are screened in the official selection and festival sidebars. And being the world's most prestigious festival means that this crop will definitely include some of the best new cinema available, so you'll probably want to see a couple of films while you're in town.

Venues

Cannes as a festival location has come a long way since the early days when films were shown in the old winter casino. Most of the official selection is screened in the various cinemas within the Palais, however the size of the event and the presence of the various sidebars (not to mention the needs of the Market) mean that the screenings also spill over into most of the cinemas across town. Fortunately, all of the festival screening venues are located within the Centre Ville area.

Palais des Festivals

As well as housing the press corps, market, and accreditation activities, the Palais is also the main screening venue for the festival. Inside, you'll find the following cinemas and screening rooms:

Grand Théâtre Lumière

Unmistakable due to the rather large amount of red shag out the front, this massive state-of-the art cinema seats over 2,200 people and is the festival's flagship screening venue. Films in and out of competition have their premiere screenings here.

Théâtre Claude Debussy

The second-largest cinema in Cannes seats around 1,000 and is home to screenings in Un Certain Regard, the short films competition, and a raft of press screenings during the day. It is one of only three cinemas in the Palais with an exterior entrance, which you'll find on the western end of the building.

Théâtre Buñuel

Home to screenings in the Cannes Classics and Cinéfondation programmes (and also some Critics' Week and press screenings), the Buñuel can be found inside the Palais on Level 5.

Salle Soixantième

Located on the roof of the Palais, this temporary cinema hosts 'Day-After' screenings of feature films from in and out of competition. Entry is via a set of stairs on the east side of the Palais, opposite the Village International.

Théâtre Bazin

This 280-seat cinema shows 'Day-After' screenings of films in the Un Certain Regard programme and also some press screenings. You can find it on Level 3 inside the Palais.

Théâtre Bory

At 147 seats, Bory is the smallest of the cinemas in the Palais (if you don't count screening rooms). It is mainly used for market screenings. Bory is also sometimes referred to by its former name, Auditorium K.

Auditoriums B – J, L, M

These screening rooms are dotted around the upper levels of the Palais and host market screenings throughout the festival. L and M have 80 seats; the remainder 40 seats. These rooms are sometimes referred to simply as "Palais B", "Palais M" etc.

Riviera / Lerins

These temporary screening rooms can be found downstairs and upstairs respectively in the Riviera building. They are used solely for market screenings and normally referred to by name and number, e.g. Riviera 1, Lerins 6 etc.

Cinéma de la Plage

The beach cinema is located at Plage Macé on the seafront at the intersection of Rue Macé and the Croisette. With the huge screen scaffolding, it's hard to miss. During the day the screen is packed away and the beach is the only strip available on the Croisette for sunbathers and swimmers. Once night falls, the screen is rolled out and various films from the official selection are shown over the water. These are normally films from the Cannes Classics or Special Screenings sections (never competition films). Screenings normally kick-off around 8.30pm and access is open to all, on a first come, first served basis.

Other Cinemas in Cannes

Espace Miramar

Located in an old hotel (now an apartment complex), the Miramar is the main screening venue for films in the International Critics' Week. You can find it on the corner of Rue Pasteur and the Croisette (the entrance is on Rue Pasteur).

Théâtre Croisette

Officially, this cinema was recently renamed *Théâtre Jacques Doniol Valcroze* in honour of one of the founders of the Directors' Fortnight, but the name has yet to stick. As such, most of the time you'll see it referred to as Théâtre Croisette, or by one of its older names, Théâtre Palais Croisette or Théâtre Noga Croisette. The cinema is located within the JW Marriott hotel, which itself sits on the site of the original festival venue, the Palais Croisette. Théâtre Croisette is the main screening venue for films in the Directors' Fortnight sidebar and the entrance is hard to miss on Rue Frédéric Amouretti.

Les Arcades

Les Arcades is the home of screenings in the L'ACID sidebar, but is also used for some Directors' Fortnight, market, and press screenings. Les Arcades is located at 77 Rue Félix Fauré, near the corner with Rue Rouguière.

Olympia

This cinema is located on the tiny Rue de la Pompe (off Rue d'Antibes). In the past it has been used for market screenings and special events, but more recently has mainly operated as a normal cinema with current releases. In case you're tempted, note that these films, if not in French already, will be dubbed in French and shown without subtitles.

Star

This small, slightly run-down cinema is used for market screenings during the festival and can be found at 98 Rue d'Antibes.

Gray d'Albion 1-5

To meet the high demand for screens in Cannes during the festival, some of the banqueting space in the Gray d'Albion Hotel is converted into temporary screening rooms, mainly used by the market. You can find the rooms on the first floor of the hotel and the entrance on Rue des Serbes.

Outside of Cannes

Unless you have Cinéphiles accreditation, there should be no reason for you to visit a cinema which isn't in Centre Ville, but you may see them referred to in official literature:

Théâtre de la Licornes

Located in Cannes la Bocca, this is the main venue for Cinéphiles screenings, but also shows some Directors' Fortnight and Critics' Week films. 25 Avenue Francis Tonnor, Cannes la Bocca.

MJC Picaud

Also known as Studio 13, this cinema is attached to the cultural centre of the same name in Cannes la Bocca. It is used mainly Cinéphiles and repeat screenings of films from the International Critics' Week and Directors' Fortnight. 23 Avenue Docteur Raymond Picaud, Cannes la Bocca.

It's worth noting that cinemas in Cannes are sometimes referred to using the French word *salle* (auditorium), as in "Salle Lumière".

Finding Out What's on Where

With so many different organisations managing programmes of films during the festival, there doesn't tend to be any single definitive schedule of everything screening in Cannes on a given day.

In recent years, the Festival de Cannes itself has got much better at sharing its own schedule - you'll find a full list of films in the various official programmes included in your accreditation pack. The festival also publishes a free daily newspaper which is available in the mornings from the Palais and in the lobbies of the major hotels. This contains the up-to-date screening schedule as well as festival news and reviews. If you're heading to Cannes with a smartphone or tablet, you may also wish to download the free official festival app for iPhone and Android. This is available from the App Store or Android Marketplace from the week before the festival starts. But these options only cover films in the various programmes run by the Festival itself. Films screening in the sidebars or market are not listed here – a task that seems to have fallen on the shoulders of others.

The most laudable effort to create a 'master' screening list goes to the major trade magazines, with Screen International taking the prize for the most comprehensive list. Screen, along with its competitors, Variety and The Hollywood Reporter, publishes a free daily edition which, in addition to news and reviews, normally includes a screening schedule for the next 24 hours across all areas of the festival. Pick up copies of the trades from the dedicated racks dotted through the Palais, but also from pavilions in the Village International and lobbies of the big hotels. Make sure you get your magazines in the morning as by mid-afternoon the supply has usually dried up.

The trades normally do a decent job of including sidebar screenings in their listings, but you can also pick up the schedule for the International Critics' Week and Directors' Fortnight screenings from the respective offices or main theatres. For the Critics' Week, that's Espace Miramar on Rue Pasteur; for the Directors' Fortnight, visit the official tent at La Malmaison, 50 Boulevard de la Croisette (in between the Grand Hotel and the JW Marriott). Some years, the Festival de Cannes also includes these schedules in the accreditation pack.

Market Screenings

While the official selection tends to dominate everyone's attention, there are literally thousands of other films screening in Cannes during the festival. Most of these are shown as part of the Market, where sellers (i.e. sales agents and/or producers) are presenting their product in the hope of attracting the attention of a buyer (i.e. a distributor).

Access to market screenings varies according to a range of factors, but it's predominantly the type of accreditation you have and the size of the screening venue which will determine whether you can get in or not. As the primary focus of the Market is to sell films, festivalgoers with the revered 'buyer' Market badges (mauve stripe) are welcomed with all the zeal of a long lost rich relative, but others with regular Market accreditation are sometimes also admitted. As for holders of press accreditation it's normally tough. Sales agent and/or producers aren't normally prepared to risk an early bad review in case it puts off potential buyers.

Market screenings are usually off-limits to those with other types of accreditation, however if there is a film you are particularly intent on seeing it's sometimes possible to blag your way in. The staff working these screenings are often pretty bored and may let you in if you give them a smile and a half-decent excuse. But be prepared to part with a business card on entry. In saying that, you shouldn't blag you way into a busy Market screening at the expense of a legitimate buyer. It's not fair to the filmmakers and you would certainly expect the same courtesy in return.

Most of the Market screenings take place in the myriad of rooms that honeycomb the Palais and Riviera buildings.

Short Film Screenings

The Short Film Corner occupies a large space in the basement of the Palais (Level 01). Here you will find interactive screening booths where you can view shorts from the Short Film Corner, and also the short films in the official competition. Competition shorts are also screened in the Théâtre Claude Debussy at the appointed time.

Ticketing

Cannes is rather unusual in the world of major film festivals in that access to every film in the programme is completely free of charge. Further, besides films screening in and out of competition, tickets are not required so long as you're an accredited festival attendee. In most cases entry operates on a first come, first served basis. You simply line up outside the screening venue with your badge around an hour or so before the scheduled start time (although for highly-anticipated films it's often necessary to get there earlier).

For films screening in or out of competition, *invitations* (tickets) are required for red carpet screenings in the Théâtre Lumière, but not for repeat screenings of these films in other venues. Invitations are free, but gone are the old days when simply lining up early to get your tickets would suffice. These days the festival uses a process which is overly complex, badly organised, full of favouritism, and varies depends on what discipline you used to gain your accreditation.

The first thing to take note of is whether your type of accreditation allows you access to red carpet screenings. There are two ways to determine this. The easiest is to check the ticketing information supplied to you at the time you collected your badge. Alternatively, check your badge itself for a red dot with the letter "R". This signifies that you can obtain invitations for red carpet screenings. In general, all market accreditations will have this, but not all festival accreditations do. Recently, the festival has introduced a practice of sometimes refusing first-time bearers of festival accreditation access to red carpet screenings (presumably to help reduce demand). In some years, short film corner accreditation has also not provided access to red carpet screenings. Either way, if your accreditation does not provide access to the red carpet, you can still attend screenings in the other programmes of the festival, and also see competition/out of competition films in 'day-after' screenings at other venues.

If your accreditation does provide red carpet access you need to obtain an invitation for any film you wish to see in the Théâtre Lumière. For instructions on how to do this, refer to the ticketing information sheet you received when you collected your badge. For most market and festival accreditations, you will obtain tickets by reserving via the ticketing web site and collecting from the Palais. However certain disciplines, notably actors and those who work the camera department, are still required to use the old method of getting there early and lining up at the appropriate desk within the Palais.

To access the online ticket reservation system, point your web browser at ticket.online-festival.com (note that there is no "www" in this address). You can also access this site via dedicated terminals in *Billetterie Centrale* (central ticket office), located in Hall Méditerranée in the Palais. Either way, on the site you will be greeted by a welcome screen which allows you to select your language (English or French) and enter your login details. These details can be found on your badge as indicated on the login page. In the past, the festival's web site design skills have left an awful lot to be desired, so don't be surprised if what you see once you've logged-in looks like a confusing mess.

Tickets for films in the Théâtre Lumière are typically released about 12 hours before the schedule screening time. Each film is normally shown twice on the same day so you will see a list containing multiple screenings, in order of start time, along with a 'cost' in points. Daytime screenings are cheaper in terms of points, with early evening screenings being the most expensive. To 'purchase' your ticket you must have sufficient points in your account to do so. The number of points you get at the start of the festival is determined by your accreditation type (and other factors which are opaque to all but the festival organisers).

Your points balance automatically increases each hour during the festival, but not nearly quick enough to necessarily see all the films you may wish to. As such, you will need to put a little thought into which red carpet screenings you really want to attend.

The list of upcoming screenings will also provide a basic indication of when tickets will be released. In the past there has been little rhyme nor reason to the way this appears to operate, so don't be surprised if you visit the site at the appointed time only to find that a screening's status goes from "Opening at..." to "No more invitations" without explanation. As mentioned, the system is poorly designed and chaotic - a significant blight on an otherwise impeccably organised event. Either way, it's only possible to obtain one ticket per badge for any given screening.

Assuming you've been successful if reserving your invitation online, you will need to visit *Billetterie Centrale* in Hall Méditerranée at the Palais to collect your invitation(s). Find it on your left immediately after you enter, but before you go down the stairs. The cut-off time for collection is 3.30pm for screenings that evening and 4.30pm for screenings taking place the following morning. If you don't collect your invitations by these times they will be returned to the general pool. To collect your tickets you will need the badge against which they were registered. It's possible to collect tickets for other festivalgoers, but you will need to bring their badge to do so.

On the day of the screening you should line-up outside the Palais around 30-60 minutes before the scheduled start time. You'll need both your badge and invitation for entry. Your invitation will indicate the area in which you'll be sitting – *Orchestre, Corbielle*, or *Balcon* – so make sure you join the correct line. The various entry points are well-signposted and an access map is normally included in your accreditation pack. You will need to sit in your respective area, but seats are not individually reserved and screenings are deliberately 'oversold' so being fashionably late is a privilege reserved only for the famous.

Ticket Returns
Demand for red carpet films is exceptionally high so the festival is keen to encourage you to either attend screenings you hold invitations for or return the tickets so they can be used by someone else. Unwanted tickets can be returned to Billetterie Centrale by 3pm on the day of the screening (for evening screenings) or 4pm the day before the screening for daytime screenings. All tickets are digitally associated with your badge and scanned on entry to the theatre. If you hold a ticket, but don't use it, the system will note this and as punishment for your heinous crime, restrictions will be placed on points available to you for future screenings. It's possible to give your ticket to someone else and so long as they actually use it, the ticket will show up as spent on your profile. But it's best to only give your tickets

to someone who you know will definitely attend, lest you get penalised for their no-show.

Last Minute Access

If you're absolutely burning to attend a screening, but didn't manage to secure an invitation, you can try your luck with *Accès de Dernière Minute* (Last Minute Access). About five minutes before the scheduled start time any remaining seats are given away to accredited festivalgoers on a first come, first served basis. The last minute access line can be found on to the right of the red carpet next to the *Entrée Personnaltés et Protocole* (Personalities and Protocol Entrance) of the Palais. As you can imagine, the line is normally fairly robust so securing your place early is recommended. And while last minute access can potentially get you into a screening, it sadly doesn't give you the chance to walk the red carpet. To join the line, make sure you are dressed appropriately and have your badge.

Dress Code

During the day, the dress code in Cannes is pretty relaxed. Neat casual will suffice for screenings as well as for meetings and general hanging out. But don't forget your badge.

For evening red carpet screenings, black tie is strictly observed. For the blokes, this means a tuxedo with bow tie, although national formal dress (e.g. a kilt) is also acceptable. It's also sometimes possible to get by with a black suit, but you will still need a bow tie. The humourless security goons can be very strict about this and will deny access to tieless attendees (or make you buy one on the door). It's normally best to bring your own tux, but if you don't own one or find yourself with a last minute need, tuxedo rental is available in Cannes from Air de Fête on Rue Gazagnaire (www.air-de-fete.fr).

Getting Papped

You can always tell when someone famous enters a screening – the red carpet suddenly erupts in a blinding array of paparazzi flashes. It would be nice to think that the photographers lined up along the red carpet might be interested in taking a photo of you, and the reality is they are more interested than you might assume. This is for two reasons. Firstly, shots of noticeable non-famous people can be used to fill last minute gaps in the press, but secondly photographers know that many festivalgoers are happy to buy a shot of themselves walking the red carpet. So dress to impress, get snapped, and if you don't appear in someone's magazine, you can always have the picture for your own album. Red carpet photos can be purchased from the *Photographes - Monteé des Marches* tent in the Village International. If you definitely want to use this service, it's a good idea to visit before your red carpet evening. The official photographers have their own mugshots on the wall in this tent, so you know who to strike a pose for when you're on the carpet.

As always, the rules for women have a lot more leeway. You don't need to wear a ball gown, but you must dress to impress for a very formal evening. Short skirts are not recommended and it's worth keeping heels on the edge of sensible as the red carpet and stairs can be treacherous. In the unlikely event you're stuck for something to wear, women's formal attire can also be hired from Air de Fête.

The dress requirements for sidebar screenings tend to vary according to the time of day, the nature of the event, and the desires of the venue management or hirers. It's always a good idea to dress up for evening screenings, regardless of what's playing, as it's virtually impossible to look overdressed in Cannes at night.

Subtitles
All films in the official programmes and sidebars will be screened in their original language (unlike in the rest of France where dubbing is the norm). Subtitles are added according to the festival's official policy, which means that films in French will have English subtitles; films in English will have French subtitles; and all other films will have both English and French subtitles.

Parties and Hanging Out

"But what about the parties?" If I had a dollar for every… well, you know how that one goes. Parties are the lifeblood of Cannes and therefore pretty high on most people's festival agendas. Unofficially, the party scene in Cannes can be divided into two types. The first is the early evening 'cocktail' receptions which normally take place at pavilions in the Village International and on terraces of the major hotels. These more low-key affairs start around sunset and normally run no later than about 9pm. The second type of party is the post-screening variety. These tend to be bigger and brasher dos in fancy locations or on yachts, complete with corporate sponsors, private guest lists, and heavy security. Many take place in the villas outside of Centre Ville with organisers throwing on free shuttle buses to ferry invited guests to and from the event.

The Festival itself does not run any official parties for general festival attendees, preferring instead to operate a small number of events with a select guest list. As a result, most parties in Cannes are private affairs; that is, they are organised (and paid for) by organisations which are completely separate to the festival. Unsurprisingly, guest lists are therefore jealously guarded and invitations reserved for friends, associates, and potential business partners. There are virtually no parties in Cannes which are open to all and sundry. Why? Well, if you look at it from the point of view of the organiser: your budget is limited, you have a bunch of people related to your business who you need to either impress or thank (or both), and it's expensive to put on a bash in Cannes. Why would you want open it up to people who are ultimately just going to be freeloaders?

To attend parties in Cannes, the best approach is to try and secure yourself as many invites as possible before you arrive. How do you find out what's going on? You work your contacts and keep your ear to the ground. The first step is to trawl your network and see who's going to be in Cannes and what events they might be hosting or attending. You can also contact other organisations like national film commissions to see if they have any suitable events for you to join. Once you're in Cannes itself, you need to keep your ear to the ground and discretely pump anyone you meet for information about parties which may be happening and more importantly, ways of getting invited. Sadly, there aren't any general lists of parties taking place in Cannes during the festival, although some people, such as UK indie filmmakers group Raindance (www.raindance.org) and the Cannes Party Facebook page (facebook. com/CannesParty), have tried with varying degrees of success. If you do find a party, but haven't managed to secure an invite, you can always try crashing.

Party-crashing is of course an art form unto itself and a bit like a career in filmmaking: there is no single route in, but if you are dedicated, talented, lucky, and smart, you'll probably find a way. The options are as limitless as your creativity. Blag your way in by pretending you're famous, delivering a very important package for an important-sounding executive, busting to go to the loo, suddenly remembering your little-used stage name after an illicit glance at the door list, insisting that the producer/chief executive/company honcho personally invited you, or undertaking a little bit of fancy footwork. Indeed, many a partygoer has been known to kick off their shoes, roll up their trousers or hitch up their dress, and literally wade into the beachfront soirée of their desire.

Regardless of your chosen route, you'll need to be pretty creative. The hired goons on the door have probably heard it all before. And speaking French definitely helps. To maximise your chances of success there are a couple of important things to keep in mind. Firstly, dress like you're meant to be there. As mentioned earlier, you can't be overdressed in Cannes at night and the less you look like a freeloader, the higher the chances of getting past the door security. Secondly, do not hunt in packs. The larger the number of people you are trying to blag in, the lower the chances of success. One to two people is best, three to four doable, five plus and you're in miracle-worker territory. Lastly, be patient and polite. At the beginning of an event, door staff will be under relentless pressure to check their lists and clear the throng of partygoers who are vying for first dibs on the arrival drinks and hors d'oeuvres. Wait patiently for them to deal with you, stay out of their way, and don't get arsy as this will simply result in the security goons moving you swiftly on your way.

Whether you're invited or have the perfect crashing plan, remember that unless you're famous, there's no such thing as 'fashionably late' in Cannes. Party space is limited and sponsored booze finite, so it's important to ensure you arrive on time. And no-one wants to host any empty party, so organisers often invite more people than a venue can hold. After capacity is reached you may find yourself barred from entry, even if you do hold an invite.

Lastly, *never* pay for a party invite in Cannes! At best, you'll be shelling out for access to a lame party full of posers and wanna-bes. And at worst, you'll be scammed into paying for an invite which is either fake or for a non-existent party. None of the parties you want to be at in Cannes have tickets which you have to pay for (with perhaps the exception of the AMFAR charity dinner).

Once You're In
Keep in mind that while this may look and feel like a party, in reality an element of work is ever present. Doing parties in Cannes always involves walking that fine line between having a good time and making the most of the plentiful networking opportunities that the festival affords. Parties offer a great opportunity to meet people in a relaxed setting, and indeed, people whom you otherwise would find it difficult to see. To get the maximum benefit of this, it's essential you spend your party time being friendly and outgoing. Don't just simply hang out in a big group with your mates. Be bold and introduce yourself to all and sundry whenever the opportunity presents itself.

It's also a good idea to make an effort to take most people you meet seriously. Inevitably, you will encounter some people who just seem to be wasting space on this planet, but you never really know how important they might be (either now or in the future). It's best to be polite, steer clear of conversation that might provoke strong reaction, such as religion, politics, or from personal experience, how crap the film you saw today was... lest you find yourself talking to the producer! And be careful with jokes as not everyone may have the same appreciation of your razor-sharp wit. Lastly, remember to take it easy on the booze. You'll want to stay astute and coherent in case you meet someone important.

Although the party scene in Cannes can be a load of fun, you shouldn't get too obsessed with trying to get into every single party, nor get depressed if your invite haul feels a tad light. There are plenty of other ways to network in Cannes and in many cases, the most valuable contacts tend not to be made at the biggest parties (where the ratio of blaggers to useful people can be skewed heavily towards the former). Often it's at the sunset cocktail receptions, and less glamorous places such as hotel lobbies, cafes, waiting in line, or at various pavilions in the Village International, where the best contacts are made.

Daytime Hanging Out

When not in meetings most festivalgoers can be found hanging out in cafes around town, at the beachfront restaurants, on the terraces of the big hotels, or in the pavilions in the Village International. The hotel terraces are one of the best places to be to meet people, but your wallet will need to be ready for the assault. The pavilions are also great places to hang and have the added advantage of being away from the main festival crowds and free from the obligation to nursing an expensive drink to keep your seat.

Most pavilions are operated by either festival sponsors or various regional/national film commissions. Their purpose is two-fold. Firstly, each pavilion is intended to be a place where the sponsor can promote their product, service, region, or country to other festivalgoers. For this reason, most pavilions are open to all accredited festivalgoers, at least during the day. The second purpose, and mainly applicable to the regional/national film commission pavilions, is to provide a base to support their nationals in their activities in Cannes. As such, national/regional pavilions can be used for meetings, offer basic business services (e.g. photocopying), and usually provide free internet access. In some cases, access to these services is restricted to people from the respective country, but the majority of the pavilions are open to all. Some key pavilions include:

The American Pavilion

For over 20 years the American Pavilion has provided the 'home away from home' experience that those of a Stateside origin tend to like when they travel overseas. Located in the heart of the Village International, it offers a bar and restaurant, free internet access (terminals and wifi), and hosts a range of industry panels and events throughout the festival. AmPav, as it's sometimes known, also runs a range of special programmes to bring high school and college students to Cannes.

Unlike all other pavilions in Cannes, you must be a member to visit AmPav. Membership is open to all (i.e. you don't need to be American) and comes in two tiers. Standard membership provides access to basic services and events/parties for the duration of the festival. A premium tier, known as "Red Carpet" membership, extends additional benefits such as bar tabs, priority event reservations, complimentary breakfast, and free guest passes. Pricing for both types of membership involves a sliding scale, with the cheapest option being the 'early bird' price offered where membership is purchase by mid-April. Standard membership starts at around $60 for the early bird rate, but will be around $100 if purchased in Cannes. Red Carpet membership will set you back about $650 early, or $850 in Cannes. Buy your membership online at www.ampav.com.

AmPav prices have steadily increased since they were first introduced in 2003 and membership is now quite expensive. Is it worth it? That depends. If you make extensive use of the events, or like to feel the reassurance of being surrounded by your fellow countrymen (if you're American), then maybe it is. However, if your main plan is to have somewhere to hang out, meet contacts, and/or get online, then you're probably better off saving the money and using one of the other pavilions where this comes for free.

The UK Film Centre

Run by the BFI, with support from national agencies such as Creative Scotland and Film Cymru, the UK Film Centre is the official presence of the British film industry in Cannes. The UKFC is the second largest pavilion in the Village International (after the American Pavilion) and has an open door policy so is a favoured hangout not just for Brits, but a range of other English-speakers. Facilities include a bar and snack service, free internet access (terminals and wifi), and a large programme of seminars on a range of British and international industry topics. Membership is not required – you simply need to present your badge on the door to be scanned (for statistical purposes) and you're in. The UKFC can however get very busy during the festival's opening weekend, particularly when a seminar involves high-profile panellists. More information is available at www.ukfilmcentre.org.uk.

The Irish Pavilion

A joint venture between the Irish Film Board and the Northern Ireland Film Commission, the Irish Pavilion is the focus for the business, information and social elements of the Irish presence in Cannes. Historically there have been less facilities on offer than at the American Pavilion or UK Film Centre, but the staff are normally friendly and it can be a good option if the other pavilions are crowded or hosting a private function.

Plage du Palmes

If you have market accreditation, or are with someone who does, you can make use of the facilities offered at an area known as the Plage du Palmes (Palm Beach). There are sofas, tables, and during the day there is a free basic bar service provided by festival sponsors. A lunch service (not free) also operates most days. You can find the Plage du Palmes at the far end of the Village International behind the Palais.

Other Pavilions

A host of other countries and organisations also pitch their tents in the Village International during the festival. Although the primary focus of the national pavilions tends to be about promoting their country as a centre for filmmaking, most also offer some degree of hospitality services such as Internet access, cafes, or simply just a quiet(er) place to sit. A few are more finicky about access than others, but it's always worth enquiring. Sometimes simply letting them know that you are meeting someone there is enough to keep the door staff happy.

Besides the pavilions, you also have an entire city at your disposal. The Centre Ville area is brimming with bars and cafes which will welcome your custom. And if you have the means, any of the big hotels will be more than happy to have you buying drinks on their terraces. For more moderate spenders, try Cristal Café on Rue Félix Fauré, the cafes around the Gray D'Albion (on Rue des Serbes), or take a walk along Rue du Commandant André where there are plenty of decent cafés.

Lastly, the Short Film Corner, located in the basement of the Palais, is also a good place to hang out if you're at a loss. Besides the viewing areas, the Short Film Corner also offers some café-style seating and best of all, has a daily happy hour with free wine and beer for all.

Hanging Out After Dark

If the early evening finds you without an invite to a sunset cocktail do, a good fall-back can be one of the many happy hours that take place in the various pavilions. Although not all do, many welcome accredited festivalgoers to the point where their capacity is reached or their sponsored booze has been exhausted. Different pavilions will have their happy hour on different evenings, but with a little research it's straightforward to find out what's on when.

As the evening progresses, there's normally a pause while people have dinner or attend a screening before the big parties start. Those without party invites tend to gravitate towards the big hotels - the terrace outside the Grand with its inflatable sofas being one of the most popular. You'll also see a lot of action taking place in the various beachfront clubs and restaurants along the Croisette. Most of these places are hosting private parties, but a few are open to the general public. In general, unless you're attending a party, these venues are best avoided. They are overly expensive and tend to be filled with non-festivalgoers who have more money than taste.

When it comes to late-night hangouts, the one Cannes institution you'll find hard to miss is the Petit Majestic. Early in the evening this bar, which has nothing to do with its hotel namesake, is fairly empty and serves dinner to those who want to brave it (most report the food to be average to poor). But from 10:30pm it starts to fill up and by midnight the crowds are so large they actually have to cordon off the street. While the Petit Majestic has all the charm of a student keg party, it's a great place to meet both friends and new contacts, and is normally a requisite stop for anyone heading home for the evening. Indeed, where the Petit Majestic is concerned, "just swinging by to see if anyone's there" are often famous last words preceding a big night and a cracking hangover. You can find the bar behind the Grand Hotel on the corner of Rue Tony Allard and Rue Victor Cousin. Take extreme care of your belongings at the Petit Majestic as the massive crowds of drunken people are a pickpocket's paradise.

Cannes of course also has its fair share of traditional nightclubs and similar fare, but these tend to be a little lame and are more likely filled with stargazing general public than industry people. So unless you're just planning to have a night out with your mates, regular nightclubs and the like are best avoided if you want to stick with the festival crowd. That said, downstairs at Auberge Provençal (Rue Saint Antoine) there's live jazz every Thursday, Friday, and Saturday, which can be great if you want a night out with your friends away from crowds and industry chitchat.

The Big Hotels

It's unlikely you'll get away with being in Cannes and not visiting one of the big hotels at least once during your stay. Cannes vets tend to prefer the bar at the Majestic and the Carlton terrace for their hobnobbing, although the Gray d'Albion is also a popular choice with the cashed-up indie set. With its inflatable sofas the late and lively alfresco atmosphere of the terrace at the Grand Hotel is also a regular favourite, but if you're meeting someone you're trying to impress, the elegant environment of the Martiez might be more suited. Lastly, if you're looking to rub shoulders with the A-list then you need to take yourself and a wad of cash out to the Cap d'Antibes and spend an evening in one of the various bars in the Hotel du Cap - Eden Roc. Regardless of which hotel you choose, you will need to be dressed appropriately and carrying your badge.

When spending time at one of the big hotels, make sure you're prepared for the drinks to be considerably more expensive than at other places in town. If you're travelling on an expense account, then it probably won't be too much of a concern, but if you're a cash-strapped indie it's best to avoid getting drawn into buying rounds. You'd be amazed at how many 'friends' seem to pop out of the woodwork when it's time for a trip to the bar, and before you know it you will have blown the budget of your next film on a single round.

The Biz

Red carpets, cinema auteurs, and flashes of paparazzo cameras are just one facet of the festival. Alongside, more film business is done in Cannes each year than in all but a handful of other places on the planet. This is because behind all the glitz and glamour lurks the world's largest film market. And for 12 days in May, virtually the entire international film industry is jammed into a few square blocks of this small Riviera city.

From humble beginnings in 1959, when a group of filmmakers hung a white sheet on the roof of the old winter casino to screen films for potential buyers, Cannes is responsible for inventing the festival-market relationship now emulated by a range of major international events such as Berlin, Toronto, Rotterdam, and increasingly, even Sundance. For those new to the film industry, 12 days in Cannes will teach you more about how the international business operates than most books or courses.

The official structure for business in Cannes is of course the Marché du Film, which welcomes over 10,000 cinema professionals from 83 countries each year. However, the concentration of film industry people in Cannes during the festival far exceeds these numbers as the figures don't take into account those who opt for festival accreditation or who come to Cannes to do business without formally registering through any official organisation. Estimates put the total number of industry attendees well north of 30,000 in any given year.

Aside from the press corps (which is a good 4,000 strong), the largest single contingent of industry people in town for the festival are those who work in sales and acquisitions, or in other sectors which directly support sales (i.e. publicity). Typically, industry people who are not involved in these areas tend to be filmmakers (predominantly producers, directors, and writers), but also equipment vendors, facilities providers, and of course agents. For these people the business side of the festival is mainly about meetings and networking, although some filmmakers may of course be involved in selling their films as well.

Business at Cannes

Cannes is the daddy of film business events and perhaps the single most important date on the international film industry calendar. On the whole, business for most attendees can be a pretty intense affair. Virtually everyone in town is peddling something, either formally (i.e. a film or film-related service) or informally (i.e. themselves). People's schedules tend to be very hectic and a high level of energy is required to keep on top of long days and late nights, which normally involve too much alcohol. It's quite common for people attending Cannes on business not see a single film in the official selection or sidebars during their stay. Some sales agents have even been heard to complain of seeing very little daylight over the entire 12 days - no mean feat given the physical environment the city offers.

In general, business activities in Cannes tend to fall into three main areas. So if you're heading to town with a business agenda it's important to understand how each of these areas work.

Sales & Acquisitions

The concept of an international film market was born when the first official Marché du Film was held in 1961. Back then, Cannes was used as the principle marketplace for American companies selling the foreign distribution and ancillary rights for their films. These days the market's focus has shifted to sales and acquisitions activities of all kinds – sales agents show up with a slate of projects under their arm and spent 12 days courting foreign and domestic distributors in an effort to flog their merchandise. While the festival is about toasting the cream of filmmaking, the Marché is about selling everything else. Glamour is pushed aside for profit, and art takes a distant second place to genre.

The Marché du Film is the single largest event of its type in the world. Other major markets include those attached to the Berlin and Toronto film festivals, and the American Film Market (AFM) in Los Angeles - the Marché du Film's closest competitor in terms of scale. Each day hundreds of films are screened in Cannes and millions of dollars change hands as films are bought and sold with all the vigour of a busy day on Wall Street. The main market action is centred in the Palais and Riviera buildings. The former is honeycombed by small offices used by visiting companies and media outlets as their base of operations, while the latter houses your standard tradeshow floor filled with companies peddling their wares.

Activity within the formalised market structure tends to focus mainly on small to mid-sized companies selling films made outside of North America or those with strong genre product such as action, horror, soft porn, and anything else that's selling well at the time. Larger players are normally less inclined to participate directly in the market, opting instead to conduct business from a suite in one of the big hotels or *résidences* (apartment buildings) along the Croisette.

Meetings & Networking

For those outside sales and acquisitions, Cannes is primarily about meeting with people who are likely to be able to help get the next project off the ground. But it's also about seeing movies, catching up with friends, and generally increasing one's contact network. During the festival the city is literally crawling with film industry people, from PAs to studio bosses, so it's a great opportunity to bolster the proverbial little black book.

Meetings in Cannes tend to be less formal than at home. Most take place over a meal, a coffee, or in a hotel suite which has been commandeered by a company for the duration of the festival. And nearly all meetings typically focus on discussion rather than action. Indeed meetings are often the primer or first step in a larger process, with the real business being done once everyone gets back home.

Networking also takes up a big chunk of most people's Cannes business agenda. This is really about making new contacts that might perhaps be useful in the future. Of course, for some networkers it's also about generating new business opportunities, particularly where agents or equipment/service vendors are concerned. Regardless, most of the networking in Cannes tends to get done after hours, while the daytime is reserved for more formal discussions.

Financing

Cannes is first and foremost a 'finished product' festival, so films which haven't been made yet are a little lower down people's priority lists than those that are complete. That said, with all the players in town plenty of discussion around the latter stages of development and project financing does take place. Programmes such as the Producers' Network exist to actively encourage co-productions, as do most of the national film commissions who are in town for the event. Private sector relationship building is also a key part of the festival, particularly for projects which are strongly packaged. But very few deals are actually signed in Cannes. It's common for discussions to start while everyone is in town, but the formalities are normally completed later on.

Preparing for Cannes

If you're planning on hitting Cannes for anything other than and an education and some interesting R&R it's essential to prepare your game plan well ahead of time. You need to have a clear idea about why you're attending and what you want to achieve. Without it you risk wasting your time in Cannes and possibly quite a bit of money in the process. But perhaps the biggest risk of heading to the festival *sans plan* is that of inadvertently messing people around. For a global industry the film business is very insular. People tend to hold grudges and if you mess someone about you might find it's much harder to make things happen in the future.

The first part of your Cannes preparation should therefore involve thinking about why you actually want to go to the festival in the first place. Are you going to see films, make contacts, sell your movie, pick up new clients, get an education, or even all of the above? Each of these reasons alone requires comprehensive planning and if you're considering all of them then extensive preparation is even more important.

Seeing Films

Although seeing films may not be the main focus of a business agenda per se, it's an important consideration if you're coming to town with any kind of business objective in mind. Once you're in Cannes and surrounded by all that is the world's most famous film festival you will almost definitely feel the temptation to catch a movie or two. So it's important to make sure that attending screenings is an activity built into your overall schedule, not just a last minute decision.

Once you've taken into account the queuing time, the possibility of the screening starting late, watching the film itself, and finally any post-show Q&A sessions, attending movies can take big chunks out of your day. During much of this time your mobile phone will be off (well, it should be) and being out of contact for so long can make doing business that much more difficult. In a nutshell, it's essential to make sure you've thought about how all of this impacts your business agenda. That way you can get to see some interesting films, but also get your work done.

If seeing films is an important part of Cannes for you, a good strategy is to try and attend screenings at the beginning or the end of the day. That way, seeing films will have the lowest impact on your business window and ensures you're free for that impromptu meeting which will undoubtedly pop-up.

Meeting People

Heading to Cannes is an excellent way to expand your contact network and also to see people from places which might normally require a plane ticket to get you to their front door. Meeting people usually happens in one of two ways: either you've made an appointment with someone prior to arriving in town (or perhaps while you're there), or you bump into someone along the way and, for whatever reason, you hit it off.

When it comes to pre-arranged meetings a big part of your prep should involve taking the time to set them up before you get to Cannes. Many people who are working during the festival can be extremely busy so pre-arranging meetings not only helps with your own planning, but having it in someone's diary ahead of time dramatically increases the chance of the meeting actually happening. In saying that, you should only pre-arrange a meeting with someone if you actually have a reason to meet. Discussing projects, pitching ideas, and talking finance are all good reasons to meet. Meetings to introduce yourself or to find out more about what someone does are bar-room or party conversations, not formal meetings.

The second way of meeting people is obviously a little more serendipitous – you have to be in the right place at the right time. The nature of the festival means you often can't help but meet people in Cannes. However, you can boost your chances of encountering more appropriate kinds of people by hanging out at the various pavilions in the Village International, the hotel terraces, or at well-known socialising venues like the Petit Majestic. Networking and meeting people is of course also a major part of attending parties, and you shouldn't discount the value of chatting to people when you're standing in line for anything from a coffee to a screening. While it's difficult to specifically prepare for these types of meetings, you can help your chances by building in some 'hang out' time into your Cannes schedule and picking venues where the concentration of the type of people you want to meet is likely to be reasonably high.

One of the beauties of Cannes is there's an 'accessibility' in people that often doesn't exist anywhere else. Maybe it's the change of scenery that makes everyone more open than they are at home, or that some of the normal barriers are dropped because everyone is a foreigner in a foreign land. Who knows? Regardless, you should use this Cannes accessibility to your advantage as much as possible. That said, it's also important not to come off looking and sounding like a chump. Make sure you prepare your story ahead of the festival, ideally in three versions: short, medium, and long. You should be able to effortlessly answer questions like "What do you do?", "What are you trying to do?", "What does your company do?", or "What have you done?". Not to mention pitching your active project(s). Depending on the situation and the audience you must be ready to roll out the short, medium, or long story at any time.

Selling Films

Of all the business activities undertaken at Cannes, selling films is by far the hardest and most intense. To achieve success in this area your preparation will need to meticulous, your execution flawless, and your enthusiasm boundless (with a good deal of luck thrown in on top). The first stage of your preparation for selling a film should be to seek professional representation. This means getting a sales agent on-board and if your budget can stretch it, a publicist as well. There are several reasons why having at least a sales agent for your film is absolutely essential.

Firstly, a reputable sales agent will know the marketplace and have the necessary contacts to get the right people to see your film. Without these contacts you're fighting an uphill battle to get distributors to attend a screening. Secondly, when it comes to talking turkey, having the negotiations done by a third-party who's familiar with the shape of distribution agreements, and is as keen as you are to sell the film (since their commission depends on it), will ensure you get the best possible deal. Finally, if you've approached a large number of sales agents and they've all decided to pass, then there's a good chance that your film just doesn't have commercial value. As harsh as that sounds, finding this out before blowing a load of your own money on a trip to Cannes is certainly better than coming home empty-handed with a lighter wallet.

So how do you go about finding a sales agent for your film? One word: research. These days the best place to start is a website called Cinando (www.cinando.com), which also has a companion app for iOS. The site was originally developed by the Marché du Film, but has since been spun off to allow it to work with other film markets as well. The core of its business remains managing participant data on behalf of the Marché.

In practical terms, Cinando is one giant searchable database of all companies and individuals participating in the Market, including names, contact details, and mugshots (so you know who to sidle up to at a party). In the past, this information was only available in the unwieldy official Cannes Market Guide and accessing it meant lugging around the world's heaviest book, plus spending hours thumbing through to find potential contacts. Having an online search facility now makes this task far less arduous. 12 months' access to Cinando is included free of charge with all market accreditations, but it can also be purchased for a stand-alone annual fee of around 90€. If you've got a film to finance or sell, it's well worth it.

The physical version of the market guide is still published each year and given free to market accreditees. But since it uses the same data as Cinando there isn't really much point to it anymore. The leading trade magazines also normally produce a 'market preview' edition ahead of the festival (and you can pick these up in Cannes too). The market previews contain listings for a large number of companies attending Cannes and the projects they have on their books.

Once you have access to Cinando or the market preview magazines, search for companies that seem to be selling films which are similar to your own. It's important to pick the right type of sales agent to approach as there's no point taking your quirky Gen-X comedy to someone who seems to specialise in period drama. Using the details in Cinando, compile your hit list and start approaching these companies to see if they're interested in talking about your film. You'll get plenty of rejections, but that's part of the game so you just have to keep plugging away. It's always best to start the process of locating suitable representation as far ahead of the festival as you possibly can. Your sales agent and publicist will then be able to work with you to formulate the most effective strategy for selling your film and also help you prepare fully before you arrive in Cannes.

Although it's far better to have your team in place ahead of the festival, it is possible (although considerably harder) to seek representation once you're in Cannes. If you're going to try this route, you'll still need to prepare your hit list and as many meetings as possible before you arrive. You should also put together a basic sales kit for your film which at minimum contains a logline, synopsis (short, medium, and long), key cast and crew list, and biographies of the key crew members highlighting recognisable credits where available.

It's always a good idea to have a copy of the film with you on DVD and on a memory stick, but it's unlikely any sales agent will have time to watch it while they are in Cannes. Trailers and clips can also be a useful tool to whet appetites, but ultimately the decision to represent a film will be based on seeing the completed film. Remember, you have one shot with most sales agents so do not let them see your film until you are 100% satisfied it's ready for prime time.

Development & Finance

As mentioned already, a large number of the people you would want to talk to about projects in development or requiring financing will be busy selling finished films in Cannes. That said, at the right stage of a project, the festival does offer a great opportunity to get your project on the radar of people that can help make it happen.

For your project to have the best potential for gaining traction in Cannes it should be at a late stage of development and be well-packaged (i.e. have a producer, director, and lead cast attached). And if the film is part-financed already, you'll find that considerably more doors will be opened to you. It goes without saying that projects should always be grounded in reality. Pitching a $30m film with a first-time director and no-stars is likely to get you nowhere fast. Likewise, *never* stretch the truth about who's involved in the project and don't mention names as being 'attached' unless you actually have an agreement with the person in question. With a couple of calls, it can be a simple matter for many people to find out whether you're on the level or just another member of the bullshit brigade.

If you're bringing a development project to Cannes, you should also spend a little time before the festival creating your sales kit. This will be similar to what you would create for a finished film in that it should contain the logline, synopsis, and cast/crew bios, but it should also include high-level budget information, the stage the project is at, and details of exactly what you are seeking. Don't bother bringing clips or trailers you've put together for a film that isn't made yet – these often do more harm than good. Previous work from the director is a much better option. Also, don't bring printed scripts to Cannes as no-one has time to read them, nor wants the excess baggage on the way back. Your script will be the first thing that's binned to save space in someone's return luggage. When someone wants to see your script they will normally ask you to send it via email.

At the Festival

Once you arrive in Cannes it's worth spending a little bit of time familiarising yourself with the locations of the key festival venues, and more importantly, how far apart they are. This helps you to be better prepared when you need to meet someone because you'll have some idea of how long it will take to get there and be on time. It's also worth remembering that as the day draws on the crowds outside the Palais get bigger (particularly on weekends). This can significantly slow you down if you're in a rush, so it's often quicker to scoot through the Palais (bag search delays notwithstanding) or go around the back where there are no crowds.

Meetings
Meetings are one of the most important activities you'll undertake in Cannes, so it's

important to allow plenty of time to get to the venue. It's always better to have time to kill than to be late and have to apologise. Before you get to your meeting make sure you're fully-prepared so that when you walk through the door you're calm and confident, and can blind them with your ability to get to the point in an interesting, but speedy manner. Know what you're going to say, but don't work from a script. You will be most effective where you come across naturally and with a personal touch.

Most formal meetings in Cannes will be fairly brief, so it's vital that you are focussed (particularly because it's possible the other person won't be). In general it's best to ensure your phone is switched to silent for the meeting, but if you're reasonably friendly with the person, decide at the beginning whether it's a 'phones on' or 'phones off' meeting. If you're meeting someone for the first time, don't be offended if they take calls during the meeting - *C'est Cannes!* as the French would say. However, your position in the grand pecking order of the film industry probably means you shouldn't take calls yourself.

After you've finished the meeting, spend a few minutes making notes about what was discussed. This might seem a little bit anal, but after 12 days of meetings you will be thankful for the memory jog. Follow up any successful meetings 1-2 weeks after the festival.

Networking

Cannes is a networking bonanza so you should make the most of it while you're in town. This means being forward, friendly, and striking up a conversation whenever the opportunity presents itself. As previously mentioned, it's a good idea never to be dismissive of someone's ultimate value to your career. Just because they're a wanna-be now, doesn't mean they won't be in a position of power a few years down the track. Play the long game because it's often the people you least expect who end up being the most important to your future.

If you do meet someone interesting make sure you swap business cards. You'll end up accumulating quite a wad of cards over the course of the festival, so a good trick is to jot down a note on the back about who the person was. This can be particularly helpful if you meet someone at a party or another event where the alcohol is flowing freely. That way, when you're staring through a hangover at someone's business card, at least you won't be left scratching your head over who they were or whether they were important.

The Market

Activity in the 'formal' market at Cannes - the Marché du Film - has its epicentre in the Riviera building and extends into the bowels of the Palais. Here you will find a standard tradeshow floor housing a whole bunch of different companies peddling their wares. Having a quick wander through will open your eyes to a whole world of cinema that at times defies comprehension (David Hasselhoff as a sensei in "Dancing Ninja", anyone?). Yet this stuff makes money, otherwise these companies wouldn't be here.

But it's important to remember that you don't need to fork out for a market booth sell a film in Cannes. Booths are mainly suitable for established companies with a slate of projects, and as you'll rapidly discover, these days it's mainly about non-English language films. Most companies from English language markets are normally found in a suite in one of the hotels or residences, or on yachts in the port. If you have a film to sell and don't have a sales agent, it's likely that most of your meetings will be in those places, or the Village International, rather than in the Riviera.

Screening a Film

Screening a film during a major festival is a dream for many independent filmmakers. Even though the concept was around long before, it was probably the various 'alternative events' that sprung up on the coattails of the Sundance Film Festival in the 1990s that popularised the idea.

Of all the world's film festivals, Cannes is probably the hardest event at which to screen an unknown film outside the formalised structures. There is so much attention focussed on the official selection and sidebars, and so much noise generated by the Market, that it's virtually impossible for films screened independently to get any attention whatsoever. And unless you've made it into official selection, Cannes isn't really the right festival to premiere your film to anyone other than potential buyers. Getting a space that even vaguely resembles a cinema is nigh on impossible and shouting loud enough to be heard amongst the noise of multi-million dollar marketing campaigns is sadly beyond the reach of most independent filmmakers.

If you still think you want to take a crack at screening a film independently during the festival, you probably have two realistic options. The first, and perhaps the easier of the two, is to sign up for the market and use the screening facilities available to those with accreditation. The market has a range of screening options on offer from small preview theatres through to full-size cinemas. The fees for hiring a screen will vary depending on the time of day and the size of the venue. Either way, you will need to reserve well in advance.

The second option is probably harder to achieve, but not out of the realms of possibility. Cannes has three main cinema complexes outside of the Palais: Les Arcades, Olympia, and

Star. Although these venues do show various films from the sidebars and market screenings, it is sometimes possible to make a deal directly with the proprietors for a screening slot (particularly at the Olympia). Again, you'll need to do this well in advance and know your budget before you start the negotiations.

Promoting Your Screening

If you've managed to secure a venue in Cannes the next major obstacle will be promoting your screening to the right people. If you're taking the DIY approach then it's likely your pockets are not going to be flush with advertising cash so whatever you do to promote the screening, it needs to deliver maximum bang for the buck. Prior to spending a cent on any form of marketing you should stop and take a moment to think about who exactly you want to come to your screening. The first rule of marketing is: know your audience. If you want to have any success in Cannes you need to figure out who you're going to be talking to.

If your main aim is to try to get your film acquired then you should be thinking of ways to market to acquisitions executives and the press, not to the general public. Marketing to buyers is a very different affair to marketing for a cinema-going audience. If acquisitions are the name of the game then putting a huge amount effort into getting a posse of cinema-lovers to show up for your screening is largely a waste of time. Even if the audience likes your film the chances of such a small number of people creating enough buzz to prick up the ears of buyers is rather remote to say the least. On the other hand, if your idea is to hold a screening that will go down in Cannes history then you're going to need to develop a good deal of interest ahead of time in order to get people to show up. You'll therefore want to focus your energies on building the anticipation amongst your audience and having them spread the word before your premiere.

Strategies for hyping your screening are as limitless as your creativity, but "unique" and "memorable" should be the two keywords that govern everything that you do. Remember that the second law of marketing applies to hyping films as well: it's all in the mix. In other words, there's no one sure-fire thing to do that will result in hundreds of people showing up, rather it's the combination of a bunch of activities which will hopefully achieve the desired results. Some suggestions include:

Hire Professionals
At a minimum a sales agent, but ideally also a publicist. Sales agents will take their fees from selling your film and publicists aren't as expensive as you might think... particularly if they like your film.

Talk to Journalists

Browse the trade magazines, local newspapers, and any other publications that cover the festival. Find the names of journalists who seem to have a style appropriate to your movie, then contact them via their magazines to see if they're interested. You will probably be ignored by many of them, but all you need is one or two on-board and you're in business.

Invite People Personally

Once you have your screening in place and understand your target audience, do your research and invite the necessary people personally.

Make it a Premiere

Don't show your film to anyone ahead of the first screening. Once you let the cat out the bag you will lose a major advantage.

Postcards

Make sure you always carry a bundle of postcards which have your film's screening time(s) and venue(s) printed on the back. That way, when you meet people in lines, at the Pavilions, or around town, and tell them about your film, you have something to give them to help them remember when and where they can see it.

These are just a few ideas. The finer points of festival marketing are beyond the scope of this book - there are complete volumes dedicated to the art of getting films noticed at festivals. For more on this subject check out, "Marketing & Selling Your Film Around the World: A Guide for Independent Filmmakers," by John Durie et al, or "The Ultimate Film Festival Survival Guide," by Chris Gore. Both books are available from the bookstore at CannesGuide.com.

Final Words of Wisdom

Before we leave you to strike out on your own Cannes adventure, here are some final snippets of advice which will go a long way to making your festival experience successful and that much more valuable.

Receipts

Make sure you get a receipt for everything you pay for. This is one of the only times you'll be able to claim a holiday on the French Riviera a legitimate business expense.

Film Commissions

Get friendly with your national and/or regional film commissions in Cannes. They are a source of party invites, free photocopying, and introductions to a whole range of people and events. Most of all, they are there to help you. And if you're from the US and therefore without a national film commission, no problem. Simply find a surrogate nation and cosy up with them. Most are welcoming in Cannes, particularly the Brits, Irish, and Scandinavians.

Free Lectures/Seminars

Many of the pavilions in the Village International run seminars and lectures during the festival. Often these are free and open to all accredited festivalgoers. Drop in to the various pavilions early in the festival to pick up a schedule and remember that space is limited so make sure you arrive early for anything you want to see.

Broaden Your Horizons

With over 30,000 film industry professionals in Cannes for the festival the potential for meeting new and interesting contacts is immense. You should resist the temptation to spend the whole time in Cannes hanging out with your cast and crew or people from your home country. There's no point in making the trek to Cannes simply to hang out with the people you could hang out with at home. Broaden your horizons and meet people who would otherwise be difficult or impossible to see.

Talk to EVERYONE

It's already been mentioned, but always remember that Cannes is a networking bonanza. Everyone is much more open to meeting new people at the festival than at home so make the most of it. Always be friendly and open, and take any opportunity you get to chat to people. You'll make new friends and colleagues... and maybe even meet someone who'll change your life.

Spotting Famous People

Cannes is literally crawling with celebs during the festival so if you're around town you will most likely see at least someone recognisable. If you get excited by such things, the best place for guaranteed celeb-spotting is of course the steps of the Palais prior to an evening screening. Get there early and stand behind the white barriers on the road looking straight up the steps. The sides might look enticing early on, but you'll be disappointed later when all you can see is the backs of a hundred cameramen and photographers. Otherwise, warm up the credit card and head out to the Hotel du Cap-Eden Roc for a drink.

Take Time Out

If you're planning to stay in Cannes for more than a few days, it's a really good idea to take some time out. The festival can be very intense, with long days and very late nights. If you're not careful it will burn you out quicker than you'd think. And besides, you're in the South of France... take a bit of time to see it.

"People who go to bed early lose out"

Words of wisdom from Stephan Elliott, director of "Priscilla: Queen of the Desert". He says he's done his "best work at night... well, early morning." You can sleep when you get home.

Keep It Real

It's a good idea to make sure you keep your expectations in check if you're trying to pitch your project or sell a film at Cannes. The reality is that only a small number of independent films get picked up by distributors at the festival and these tend to be films which have recognisable names involved (either in front of or behind the camera). Some films will go on to be picked up at other events later in the year – even if deals were talked about in Cannes – but sadly a good deal will simply fade into the annals of festival history, never to be heard of again. All of these scenarios are possibilities you should be prepared to deal with.

Cannes – A Festival Virgin's Guide... out.

The Lowdown

The Cannes Film Festival is a unique experience. A good analogy would be to think of the whole thing as being a little bit like an onion - peel back one layer and another emerges. And even after many years of attending, the festival still has the ability to throw up something new for almost everyone. To help you get a better sense of just how many layers there are, we present a series of interviews with Cannes veterans from across all walks of the industry. Each has visited the festival many times and in the interview, details their own experiences from being a Cannes virgin through to how the festival works for them today.

Dennis Davidson (PR) • Simon Franks (Distribution) • Patrick Frater (Press)

Harry Hicks (Finance) • Stephen Kelliher (Sales & Acquisitions)

Richard Millar (Producer) • Jonathan Olsberg (Producer) • Bill Stephens (Sales)

Jane Wright (Finance) • Ben Roberts (Film Commissioner)

Lise Corriveau (Film Commissioner) • Julie Archet (Film Commissioner)

Dennis Davidson
DDA (PR)

BC: When did you first visit Cannes and what were your impressions of the city and the festival?

DD: I started DDA in 1970 and in 1972, really to celebrate surviving for 18 months, my partner and I decided that we would go and look at this thing called the Cannes Film Festival. We were total virgins and had no idea what to expect. We booked a British Airways Sovereign Holiday and shared a twin-bedded room in the Sofitel Hotel, which was about as cheap as you can go. I'm sure you can't get packages like that anymore - it was very cheap. I was absolutely astonished at the level of activity in Cannes... and it was much lower key then than it is now. I was brought up in the English-language world and I suddenly found myself in the world of auteurs and people who respected film, respected film directors and filmmakers. It was a stunning place.

I think very soon after that first trip we realised that there was quite a lot of business to be done in Cannes. We were doing a really tiny bit of work for [British movie mogul] Lew Grade's company at the time, just brochures and flyers and so on. Between 1972 and 1975, we had taken over Lew Grade's account, starting off really with a couple of crumbs off the table, and then moved up to organising their Cannes activities. We set up the first office in 1975 and took an apartment at the Palais d'Orsay. That eventually became three apartments in the same building, but then they threw us out because we were too busy.

There was an old Palais where the Noga Hilton is now and after we were thrown out of the apartment, we weren't able to get anything in our first choice, the Carlton Hotel, which was close to the old Palais. They just wouldn't give us a room. So we moved to this then backwater, called the Majestic, where all the Europeans stayed. The US studios stayed at the Carlton, the major British players stayed at the Carlton or the Martinez, and the Europeans stayed at the Majestic. So we moved into the Majestic and set up some offices. We were perhaps handling Goldcrest by then and we launched Richard Attenborough's "Gandhi" down in Cannes before they started shooting the film. There was lots of activity, but we did it all at Majestic because we were not allowed into the Carlton. Then in the early 80s, they knocked the old Palais down and built a new one right opposite the Majestic. Suddenly I'm a hero because all my clients are now adjacent to the Palais.

BC: So these days, what sort of preparation do you do before you arrive in Cannes?
DD: We have two sides to the company. There's a logistic side which literally starts working on the following year's festival the day after Cannes finishes. We have a permanent representative in Cannes and they're locking in all the logistical stuff for the following year. They are paying the hotels, paying the cinemas, paying all the vendors, and at the same time, reconfirming for the following year. And that's a continuing process.

From a PR point of view, there are two or three stages. Cannes is multi-layered... far too many layers to even describe, but the principal one from an independent filmmaker's point of view is selling. That's the marketplace and it can either be the Marché du Film, or in the streets independently, or in the various strands of the festival and the Quinzaine [Directors' Fortnight]. For the market part, we know what's going on with our producer clients so we can pre-plan that two, three, four months out. The process really starts in January/February.

The strands of the festival obviously come into play much later because, although the Festival keeps you up-to-date as time goes by, often you don't know the final selection until the middle of April. Then it's a mad scramble because you've got to get the talent, you've got to get the hotels, and you've got to work with the protocol of the Festival or the Quinzaine, which have totally separate management. You've got to work with the French press attaché, you've got to work with the French film distributor, the sales agent, and that's usually a four-week scramble at the end. But our logistics people will have held back some rooms for key talent; they are prepared for that eventuality.

BC: How does a typical day in Cannes pan out for you these days?
DD: Well, we still have this sort of rather nasty regime... with eight o'clock staff meetings every morning. Although everybody is usually on call at quarter to eight, I actually get in at about seven to try and clear my head from the revelry the night before. So quarter to eight, it's general assembly and then eight o'clock we start - that is running through everything, arrivals, departures, screenings, trade press, junkets, staffing, tickets, fireworks, whatever it is that day. After that, it breaks into groups... account teams and the press office, which will start their meetings when we open the office at about 9.00 - 9.15.

From there, my day can be anything. Generally in the morning I spend a couple of hours troubleshooting or meeting with clients, just making sure that everything is working. If there is an important movie screening that night, then I'll be involved with the filmmaker, or not, depending on which filmmaker. The afternoon is pretty much the same... there are a lot of events and if we're doing an event then I normally would pass by. And there's always a crisis. There's always something that happens... somebody's bag has gone on the wrong plane, or someone doesn't have a dress to wear, or the tickets haven't arrived, or any of those things that could happen in the chaos of a major convention. So I often end up troubleshooting that as well.

BC: What about the evenings? There seems to be two camps in that respect, the party crowd and the wind-down crowd.

DD: I rarely go to the big parties. I will usually go to a few of the dinners, such as the AmFAR [American Foundation for AIDS Research] dinner because it's a nice, big glamorous occasion and my people do all the work. I go to the Vanity Fair dinner because again, most of my clients, most of the key people are going to be there. We did that "Lord of the Rings" huge event down in Cannes a couple of years ago I went to that, but in general I don't do parties... OK, one night, some time during Cannes, and hopefully towards the end, I will do a party, when the adrenalin is still there and I can actually keep my eyes open.

BC: How does a publicist work with a producer leading up to and during a festival?

DD: Again, in several ways. If we are involved with the producer from the start of production we will normally have a timeline and a strategy of what can be done based on the post-production schedule and whether that film is realistically able to get to a strand of the festival. Or if that isn't going to happen, no matter what the producer and director believe they've made, we'll be figuring out plan B. We're also looking at which sales company will be responsible for taking it to the market place. You will work with the producer and sales agent to try and find a way to move that particular film above the other 600 that are going to be available at Cannes... and that can be pretty much anything. The whole point is that there is no hard and fast rules; if there was a hard and fast rule, you wouldn't need companies like mine.

To give you some examples, we built a hill on the beach one year for "The Englishman Who Went Up a Hill But Came Down a Mountain" - the Hugh Grant film - and the stars climbed up on the top of this hill for a photo call. We had "My Little Pony" there another year so we converted the merry-go-round by the beach and put little ponies all over the thing for a photo call. So we manipulated it so that Elizabeth Taylor met Stallone at the top of the stairs for "Cliffhanger"... it was an AmFAR event, the first and only time there's been a charity event in the Palais. If you've got a piece of talent, you might try and do a red carpet at one of the back street cinemas... basically, you're trying to get someone important in to see a film and say, "Why hasn't this great gem been recognised?"

But the reality is, it's really difficult, particularly if you're going in to Cannes with the finished movie, with no distributors, no budget, no recognisable names! You've really got to think, "Can I find somebody to champion this?" And you've got to get people in to see this somehow. You see people doing it and they go up and down with flyers and faces painted, there's a million different things, motorcycles going up and down, but it really is very difficult to get attention in an environment like Cannes. But then, people do, you know, and it's a multi-layered thing.

I think when we work with producers, you first of all have to define who your audience is going to be. There's no reason to go for mass publicity when you know that there's only seven distributors that are going to take this film, you're not going to be able to sell it to Japan, and in the US you'll be lucky if it goes on cable. So you define who your audience is and you define who the consumer is. Is this a multiplex, is this straight art? Are we looking for a media sale in European cinemas, or are we looking for Warner multiplexes? I think it's a discipline. One of the main problems is filmmakers are too close to what they have created and they don't want to hear realism. Before they green-light a film they should hear realism.

BC: How far ahead would you start planning the campaign if you were going to do something for Cannes with a film and the producer?
DD: If we haven't been there from the start, probably about two months, but most producers don't think, "Cannes is happening in two months, we've got a finished movie, we'd better get a publicist onboard." Most of the time it is much later than that, if at all.

BC: Assuming that they haven't engaged a publicist earlier on, what sort of materials would you expect the producer to come with if they would like to work with you?
DD: Once the film is made, there are lots of things that are very difficult to recreate. Yes, you can get stills off the film digitally, you can shoot interviews afterwards, but they're never as good. In an ideal world, when you come to us you'll have some great, emblematic stills - digital images, slides and black & white - that you can really see being on the front cover of the Sunday Times colour supplement or at least on the inside page of Time Out. And they need to be professional. Most people do it in an amateurish way and you suddenly find you've only got something that looks very nice in a 10x8, very artistic, but it won't work in a newspaper or a magazine.

I think that people should shoot some B-roll during principal photography... they don't have to finish the B-roll, just that they shoot it and it's in the can, then if they do get distribution, they can hand it over for completion, which is the expensive part. I'm also amazed at how badly written and amateurish production notes can be. It's like "My Personal Odyssey." Who cares?! Is anyone going to be interested in reading this? If they're not interested in reading it, they sure as hell aren't going to go and see the film. So it's just basic materials I think, although unfortunately in this day and age, sexy young actors are also going do a lot better than a 60-year-old unknown character actor... but I guess the most important thing of all is to have a good film! If you've got a good film, then you'll find a way to get an audience.

BC: Cannes, particularly the market, is renowned for the enormous volumes or marketing and publicity. Are there any general strategies for getting heard above the noise, particularly for lower-budget/independent films?

DD: It depends on what you've got. There is the Critics' Week, Un Certain Regard, the Festival, and out of competition. You've also got the Marché du Film, you've got the Quinzaine, you've got the back street stuff, you've got the national film bodies doing their thing, you've got the Espace DVD, you've now got a video library - there are 600 or more titles in Cannes during the festival. So you need to invite people to your screening before Cannes, you need to identify the distributors. Most people in the position you're talking about are going to Cannes without distribution or have distribution in their home country and nothing else. There are only 200 buyers, that's all there are, so do your prep-work, write to them, or email them, and say, "At two o'clock on Friday afternoon on May whatever it is, there will be a screening of my film and it's going to be worth 15 minutes of your time. Come see it! I expect you're going to be there 90 minutes later." You've got to tell people what you've got. But there's no point in going to Warner Brothers with a little film shot on DV. Do your research and find the right person who will identify with what you've got.

BC: Do you have any particularly memorable experiences from the many festivals you been to?

DD: There's a lot of them over 30 years... I actually got married there [laughs]. We did a huge party for Carolco a number of years ago, which is sort of legendary now, where Stallone and Arnold Schwarzenegger just pretended to waltz. The photograph is still used. It was in the middle of a junket and it was just one of those incredible moments where you know that this is going to play forever.

We took Madonna to Cannes for her docu-thing, "In Bed with Madonna", and we played it in the Palais at midnight. It was a huge event. Madonna... she does what she does, she was at the top of Palais steps... the coat came off and the bustier was there, and you know... one of the most memorable Cannes photos ever was produced.

We took "To Die For" to Cannes a few years ago - it was the first time Nicole Kidman was there as a star in her own right, as opposed to being a spouse. It was a Gus van Sant film; it was just a magical moment.

I remember going to a party which had nothing to do with me - a nice change - for "The Blues Brothers". I popped in because it was some friends of mine literally thinking that I'd just drop in, do a quick beer and leave. I was still there four hours later because it was such a great gig.

We had the AmFAR dinner, which is the annual charity thing we organise. We got Victoria's Secret to be one of their key sponsors and Victoria's Secret did their fashion show which web-cast almost all over the world. I went down to a few rehearsals, and... I don't know how to describe it... just beautiful, beautiful half-naked women all over the place. I needed to get back to reality after that.

Jack Nicholson has been to Cannes many times and we took "The Postman Always Rings Twice" there, many many years ago. Jack used to go out from the Majestic Hotel and just walk through the market, walk through the streets, totally unmolested and undisturbed. One particular morning I was driving... I didn't stay at the Majestic in those days... I was driving in for my morning meeting and I knew he had a breakfast with 12 Italian journalists at eight o'clock. I was driving in, I was late that morning it was about twenty to eight, and he was just walking back to the hotel. I went upstairs and I thought, "Oh shit! How am I going to explain that Jack is not going to make the breakfast?" But I went downstairs and arrived in the room to find Jack already holding court with the journalists, looking like he'd just come off a good night's sleep.

I've been using that story about Jack's walks for years, telling people, "You know, you couldn't do that anymore, that just doesn't happen anymore." Well, we had "About Schmidt" in Cannes last year and most mornings, Jack would get up from the Majestic Hotel and go for a walk through the markets and the old town, exactly the same, no bodyguards, just by himself.

BC: Do you have a favourite place to eat in Cannes?
DD: I'm very lucky now that I'm back in the Majestic - I have a balcony, so one of my favourite places is to sit and eat a pizza on my own balcony and watch. You can see the Palais from there, and I know it's not far to my bed.

But there are lots of restaurants... I love Le Maschou; you eat there so well because it's really, really simple and pretty good value. I also like Le Festival, to which a lot of people turn their nose up and go, "Oh, The Festival?!" But I think their food and their wine list is pretty good and pretty fair. I also love the Hotel du Cap... the terrace at the Eden Roc. I have to go there for lunch, at least once every festival.

But there are really so many places to choose from. When we go, we just walk in the back streets and just try out luck. We used to love the Petit Carlton before it closed and there's nothing like that, because the Petit Majestic doesn't do it for me. I use Morrisons, the Irish pub a bit. I go in there, two or three or four times... I was about to say "a night," but during the festival of course!

I do think it's tough to do Cannes on a budget and I don't envy an individual without a 'home' in Cannes, you know, without a sale's agent or a PR company... some home. I think one of the problems you have in Cannes is you see all the Brits together, all the Australians together, and all the Scandinavians together. It's really silly... you could do that here in London or wherever. It's so much better to meet people who are not from your home country.

BC: Do you have any favourite socialising/networking venues?
DD: I think it's really quite tough because most parties are relatively exclusive. If you're a party-organiser spending £100 per head, or even £20 per head, you don't really want 100 great unwashed people you've never met in your life before flooding in. We have turned significant sums of money over the years from wealthy people who want to "facilitate" being invited to parties and dinners, or get tickets in to the Palais. We don't ever do it... we don't even do it for our clients and we certainly don't do it for people off the street.

A lot of people gravitate to parties and I don't know how, even when you're networking, you can make a judgment about whether you're talking to some loser who is fooling you, or whether they are legit. If you sit at table almost everywhere in Cannes you'll hear such incredible bullshit, which hopefully even the most virgin of virgins will recognise as such. However, sorting the wheat from the chaff I think is very difficult in a place like Cannes. I suspect that it would be more productive to be going to places at breakfast time and going to the Blue Bar and those kinds of places for coffee in the mornings, and also making a point of going to the various pavilions as opposed to just sticking with your national one. I suspect that networking after dark is just total crap.

BC: Do you have any specific advice for Cannes virgins, particularly producers looking to bring an unrepresented film to Cannes with a view to sell it?
DD: I think they need to seek representation. We're living in a real capitalist business and sales agents are desperate for new product. Therefore, if you are unable to get a sales agent on board, then there's something wrong with the product. You should be able to entice at least a local indigenous distributor to take your home territory. If you have a film which you've shown to half a dozen sales agents and they've all said "pass," then you probably have to re-evaluate the situation. And I'm not talking about major deals here... I'm not talking about them giving you loads of money, but maybe them paying the freight to take you

down there, maybe putting a proper press kit together, putting a sales team together, paying for a couple of screenings, you know... if they're not willing to invest 10, 20, 30,000 dollars, euros, whatever in at least taking the film down there, then there's something wrong. It's different if you turn and say, "I want a million euros in advance", but generally, most sales agents are looking for new hooks, even if they think they're only going to sell it on DVD, so there's something seriously wrong if you can't attach a sales rep.

So I think representation is essential, but I think it is sales representation - it's not an agent, it's not a PR company, it's someone who believes enough in your film that they are willing to invest a minimum amount of money in it, to buy a couple of ads and take you down there and do the stuff. You can go to their office and drive them crazy and somebody's paying for a couple of screenings. Without that, it's really, really tough.

Simon Franks
Redbus (Distribution)

BC: When did you first visit Cannes?

SF: I went to Cannes for the first time on business in 1996. At that point I was still working in the City [of London] and was just in the process of leaving to set up Redbus, so I went to Cannes as someone trying to learn about what goes on. I did know some people there, not from the film industry, but from my time in banking, so I used the Soho House boat [run by the London media club of the same name], I got an apartment in Cannes and spent probably three or four days there, just getting to grips with what it's all about.

On that trip I came to the view that there's two sides to Cannes and that I only had access to one of these sides. I think it's probably only in the last two or three years that I've seen the other side to Cannes.

BC: So what was your first impression of the city and the festival?

SF: Well, it's an incredible place and it's an incredible festival. The city is probably Southend-on-Sea with sunshine. The hotels aren't that great and they're overcrowded, but the shopping's lovely. I think that France has got a certain feel about it, better than Southend, but it's incredibly busy. I remember, I used to be amazed at how many American film students you could fit into one town, and I found that a bit of a pain because when you're there trying to do business, the whole razzmatazz just gets in the way. One of the problems is there's a market attached to the festival and people confuse them; they're totally distinct things, they just happen to be at the same time. We're there for the film market and the festival side of things just gets in the way. However, it is of course the festival that adds all the glamour and don't get me wrong, we do leverage off the festival, but it can also be a real pain. The crowds are there to see famous people and you can't get into a bar because there are thousands of people sitting around and all the tables are full. It can be really annoying.

I also remember being amazed just how many people were there. It was crazy. Oh, and loads of blaggers... people trying to get into parties. You see, I have this view that any party that other people are trying to blag their way into is a party that you don't want to go to, and any party where no one is blagging, that's the party you want to go to because no one knows about it. And no one knowing about it means the invite list is very small. The big parties are really for tourists. The MTV party for example... there's lots of famous people around you, but they're not going to talk to you. It's just thousands of people blagging it, trying to get drunk on free alcohol.

BC: How do you prepare ahead of Cannes?

SF: Preparation is quite important for us from an acquisition's point of view. In our company there are two primary acquisition groups. One is the development group, which takes onboard scripts and works with writers and books, and tries to develop those into movies. The other side is straight acquisitions - acquisitions of other people's films. We can sometimes have a crossover where we acquire something and we say, "Listen, we think you should develop it for a couple of months, then we can take it a bit further".

But Cannes is a market and for us, it is mainly about acquisitions of other people's films. As such we're on it year-round, tracking all the movies that are getting made. We can then have target lists of movies we want to see in Cannes and all sorts of data on every single movie screening. This will include who made it, when it was shot, who's in it, and industry gossip on it and any contact we've had to date. For movies that are of specific interest to us we will usually have had some contact with the production companies so we're not going in blind.

Often, if you're a big enough company, you get shown stuff early anyway. To be a big enough company, you need to be one of the top few distributors in a large territory like France, Germany, Japan or UK. So a big part of our preparation is about seeing films in advance. You're looking for that gem that no one has spotted, however in all honesty, movies that are made without distribution... they're just so unlikely to be any good.

Of course, the majority of what goes on in Cannes really is meetings with producers and sales agents who are pitching scripts, not completed movies. For this, we would have a look at the package and the script, and we would probably get the scripts three weeks before most markets. So we already know the scripts we're interested in and what we want to talk about with the various sales agents.

The reality is that for a company like Redbus, we're not trying to do that many movies, but the movies we do take on, we want to be doing $4m to $6m minimum box office in the UK. There are very few sales agents that handle movies which have got the calibre to do that sort of business. So really, there are probably only five meetings that count, and there are 25 other meetings with companies that are largely a waste of time. But you never know in this business, someone, even a very small sales agent with no track record, can just have that one great script. You never know. So we cover that as well.

BC: So do you mostly deal with sales agents in Cannes, or with producers as well?
SF: Our acquisitions group would probably only deal with sales agents in Cannes, but for me personally I deal with a few sales agents and a few producers, but those would be American studio kind of producer. I won't really see any independent producers - a first-time producer is very unlikely to get to see me. I don't mean to sound arrogant, but it would only be by mistake that I would see them because if I did, I wouldn't be able to run my business - I would be inundated all day. I can't even put my mobile number or my email address on my business card because I would get so much grief.

So I guess it would only be established, mainly American producers we'd talk to about co-financing on some project. In terms of other producers, it's unlikely that a first-time producer is going to have anything that would make me want to see them; unless it's a first-time producer who happens to be best friends with Tom Cruise, and then obviously I will want to see them. I'm not saying that Redbus won't see first-time producers as a company, it just wouldn't be me, it would be the acquisitions group, and it wouldn't be in Cannes because they're really busy there.

In most cases we won't see British-based companies or producers in Cannes. Obviously they're in the UK, so why see them in Cannes? It's ridiculous... it's like the guy next door, who doesn't try to see me the whole year, but when we're in Cannes, he drives me mad to see me. It's ridiculous, so I don't really tolerate that. We may see established foreign independent producers who we know and like their work. Cannes is a good place for that because they're in town, but this is really what I'm getting at when I say there are two sides of Cannes.

On one side, there's a certain circle of people you're seeing who you know and have probably been involved in many projects you have heard of, whereas the indie scene... these guys lugging around pitches, that's not really for us.

BC: What sort of things would the acquisition's groups expect to see from the producers that they are going to meet with in Cannes?
SF: Well, we won't read unsolicited scripts in Cannes, so I'm just trying to think how that would happen. The acquisition's group would probably say, "We can't meet during Cannes, however please contact us at the office and we'll talk." If the company is from out of town and they want to get to meet us in Cannes then their only chance is if, in a 30 second phone call or a short email, they can say something so exciting that someone thinks, "We really

want to meet this guy." That has happened a few times before. And by "exciting" I mean something like, for example, "I'm producing a movie and I've got Quentin Tarantino to direct it." Or someone even less big, but someone very interesting: "I've got Alejandro Amenábar" or someone like that. We did Amenábar's "Abre Los Ojos" ("Open Your Eyes"), which was the film that became "Vanilla Sky", before he was a huge director. We loved his first movie, "Tesis", and even though no-one had heard of him at that point, when we got an email saying that there's this project going on called "Abre Los Ojos", we obviously responded to it.

I think there's got to be something exciting, or who you've got attached, or who you know: "I'm friendly with Brad Pitt, or I'm friendly with Matt Damon or I'm friendly with Ben Affleck or I'm friendly with Heath Ledger." And then of course our ears pick up and go, "OK, we'll listen." But again I think our acquisitions group will have 50 meetings at Cannes, out of those there will be two that will be with non-established producers.

BC: Have you heard any memorable pitches in Cannes - memorable for either the right or the wrong reasons?
SF: Yes, I've had a few. The one I'm going to tell you about was a few years ago when we were entertaining a pretty famous popstar, who I believe will be a talented actor. We were doing other business with him at the time which wasn't related to his pitch, but he and I were having a glass of wine overlooking the sea - I think we were on a boat actually - and he started telling me this idea. He said, "Listen, I want to make a movie which is about me doing something noble, changing the world and all that." I said, "Great. Do you have anything in mind?" And he goes, "Well, yeah. I was flying to America and I came up with this idea, you know, it's about this schizophrenic popstar..." and this was totally deadpan "... it's about a schizophrenic popstar, who goes to Africa to save blind people and to work with them and help them do what they can't see with their eyes." So I'm sitting there just thinking, "What?!?" And he goes - and this is the best line - he goes, "Yeah, obviously it's a comedy." And I'm like, "What?!? A schizophrenic popstar goes to Africa to help blind people and it's a comedy? I mean, what are you talking about?!"

That's one of my most memorable pitches... I'm not going to tell you who it was, but it's someone, if you heard their name you'd probably laugh and go, "Wow!"

BC: Do you have any favourite anecdotes that you like to recount when the topic of Cannes comes up over the dinner table?
SF: If you're lucky enough to be on the buying side of Cannes, and especially buying for a key territory, people, particularly young American filmmakers, basically treat you like a king. I don't feel very comfortable with that whole scene because I think there are a lot of people who make fools of themselves. A lot of these guys think they can just make friends with a

film executive in a bar, and then the exec's going to give them $5 million to go and make their movie. You get that a lot.

I remember one time, which was just really funny. I was on a boat in Cannes in the main port. I don't know how this person knew who I was - it's not like I'm famous or in the papers every day - but I suppose that if you're making a film, you do the research.

Anyway, so this person had seen me on this boat and one of the hostesses came up to me and said, "Excuse me. There's a guy who wants to see you." I said, "Well, who? No-one knows I'm here. Could you go back, get a card, and find out who it is?" The hostess came back with this card saying something like 'Steve, Independent Filmmaker, Alabama' or something like that. So I say, "Listen, tell Steve, my very best regards, I'm happy to speak with him, but it's much better if he speaks with the acquisitions group. Here's their number, call them in London after the festival." She then comes back again saying, "Well, he really wants to see you," and I say, "Listen, he can't see me." So she goes away and I forget about it.

A couple of hours later, I'm getting off the boat and it just so happened that I had arrived in Cannes that morning and hadn't had a chance to get to our villa yet. I still had all of my luggage with me and I'm walking off the boat with my bags and this kid comes up to me, literally script in hand, and says, "Hi." I'm like, "Hello?" and he says, "I'm Steve, from Alabama," as if he's my best mate. I go, "OK, hold on... you're the guy... please tell me you haven't been waiting for two hours?" And he goes, "Yeah. I really really wanted to see you." So I said, "Listen, I'm sure you're a great guy and I'm sure your film is amazing, and I'm sure I'm making the biggest mistake of my life, but I'm really tired and I really want to go home. I just don't do this. You need to contact our people. I've given you the number." And he goes, "Look. I really think that this is going to change your life. Just give me five minutes." I said, "No. If I give it to you, I'd be giving five minutes to everybody down here".

As it turned out, my car and driver were down the very front of the port and the boat was at the far end of the port. Because it was our first day in town, we hadn't got the various passes sorted out yet the car couldn't get come down to meet me, so I had to walk down to the car with all my bags, a good five-minute walk. So Steve from Alabama says, "Well, how about I carry your bags for you?" And these are like some heavy bags! And I say, "No. Don't be silly. What do you want to carry my bags for?" He says, "No, no, no. Please, I just want to talk to you." I say, "No, I don't want you to. I'd feel very uncomfortable with you carrying my bags. I'll give you my number and please, let's just leave it at that." He says, "You don't understand. I'm telling you, you're going to love this idea. What do you have to lose? All I want to do is carry your bags, and in return for me carrying your bags, you'll let me talk to you whilst I'm carrying these bags." So I thought, "It's bloody hot, my bags are heavy... alright, 'Here are my bags.'" So he takes these big bags, and I've got this guy, script under arm, carrying my bags, pitching me! By the time we get to the car, the poor guy is dripping with sweat, panting. He's been speaking, he's a bit nervous, telling me his pitch. I literally just looked at him - it was such a terrible idea - and I turned around and said, "You know what..." And I never lie... I never have the heart, I never tell them it's not for us, but I found myself saying, "You know what? That was great. I'm not sure it is for us, but that was great. Please call us and maybe we can help you."

I think he did subsequently call and we did help him with something, but I always remember this guy, sweating his arse off, carrying my bags, just pitching me some ridiculous idea. And that is really what Cannes can be like.

BC: Do you have any particularly memorable encounters with very famous people?
SF: Not really, it's different for us as film producers. We work a lot of the time with 'famous people' and I don't think they would rush to work with us again if we went around spreading gossip. Now and then a few of what you would call 'famous people' stay at our house. One of the reasons we take a house on the Cap d'Antibes is that it's a little bit out of town, it's right on the sea, and talent often prefer to stay there than in town.

BC: Do you have any favourite places to eat in Cannes?
SF: I do, but I'm not sure I want to tell you them. My favourite restaurant in Cannes... I'm not going to tell you its name, but it's a small restaurant near the bus station... I'm not going to tell you what it's called simply because I struggle to get a table there as it is. But I would suggest that for people looking for a nice restaurant, go by the bus station, or up the steps in to Le Suquet.

BC: Do you have any specific advice for future Cannes virgins?
SF: For many independent filmmakers the key will be just getting completely lucky, bumping into the right person and them being prepared to do something to help. The chance of that happening is something like 1 in a 100,000, but literally, you have a chance of bumping into Barry Diller [former Chairman of Vivendi Universal Entertainment], him loving your idea and you're done. You have that chance in Cannes because he'll be there... so might Rupert Murdoch or the heads of most of the Studios. But although you have that chance, I wouldn't come to Cannes on the basis of that chance happening because it's extremely difficult to get near these people. And sadly, most people, even if they do get their chance, screw it up because they end up blabbing and straight away these Studio heads simply go, "Hold on. Sorry, call the office."

The thing to do, if you're going to go that route of literally camping outside the Hotel du Cap and trying your luck, is not pitch your project. Form a relationship yourself, form some kind of connection, where they think, "Wow, this is a smart person." And that means when you then contact them later down the track you can say, "Dear Barry, I met you at the bar at the Hotel du Cap, it was very nice to have a drink with you, I wondered if you could do me a favour?" They're much more likely do you a favour, if they did like you, because you didn't get in their face straight away.

If you're going through the more mainstream route, which is pavement pounding in Cannes, then the advice would be: prepare before you arrive. Don't come with scripts... we never take scripts home, they're too bulky, we throw them away. Send your scripts to whomever you want to read them ahead of Cannes with a covering letter explaining why you want them to read it, who you've got attached, who's going to direct, how much of the financing you've got, what you need to do the project, and so on. The more you've got in the package, the more chance you've got of it being read.

You should really go to Cannes to meet people you've already spoken to, and to meet people who've already read your script and want to talk to you about it. Don't go there cold saying, "Hi I'm Steve, I'm a producer, and here's my script." Don't do that, it's an absolute waste of time. Preparation is everything.

Another thing I would say is, don't waste your time blagging to get into parties. Most independent filmmakers, no matter how much they say they love movie-making, spend more time trying to blag into parties, than they do making their films. And it is just really not worth it.

This comes back to the other side of Cannes I mentioned earlier. The other side of Cannes is a scene which probably only 300 people participate in. It is the dinners, the parties, the AmFAR [American Foundation for AIDS Research] thing, where you get to watch Shirley Bassey and George Michael performing for a dinner party for 200-300 people, or the party Elton John throws each year at his house in Nice. It's the boats, the dinner parties, the Hotel du Cap, the villas... that's the other scene in which the more important meetings take place. People come back to our villa where you can look at the sea with a glass of wine, and it's a very nice environment through which to make business relationships. And that's the other side of Cannes, and it's a whole different world. It doesn't even take place in Cannes; it probably takes place on the Cap d'Antibes. If you get into the other side, then you've got a decent chance, but as I said before, don't come on the basis that that's going to happen.

Patrick Frater
Screen International (Press)

BC: When did you first visit Cannes and what were your first impressions of the city and the festival?

PF: It was 1991. I'd been a freelance journalist based in Paris for a few months and got myself involved in all sorts of little things, but was really looking for something a bit bigger. It was at this time that Screen International approached me and sort of said, "Would you be interested in working for us as our Paris correspondent?" I hadn't actually been interviewed by anyone at Screen, apart from over the phone, and it so turned out that my first day in the new job was to be the first day of Cannes, 1991.

So my first experience was of being thrown in completely at the deep end because Cannes is one of the four or five times a year when Screen goes daily in print, publishing ten market editions during the festival. The first day is particularly hard because the festival hasn't started, so there's absolutely no news to write. You've just got to bring something you think might interest readers on the first day of the festival, because nothing has happened that you could possibly report on.

I was very lucky on my first day. I picked up Nice Matin, which is the local paper down there, and found a story on their back page about a French film which had been invited to go into competition, but had been pulled on the eve of the festival. They were suggesting that this was only for political reasons because it was the first film to be produced by the Bouygues Group - this operation called CiBy2000. Bouygues was seen as the lowbrow end of the market because its core business was in construction and building materials and this guy with lots of money was seen as muscling into the film industry. Nice Matin was very much suggesting that this film had been kicked out for that kind of reason... that the Paris film establishment couldn't possibly bear to have this cement manufacturer on the steps at Cannes, even though he probably built the Palais. So I followed up that story and they ran it as the front-page lead on my first day, and from then on I was sailing with Screen.

BC: So what were your first impressions of the festival?

PF: It was colossal, huge, and massively confusing. I don't think that I understood until the end of that first festival what the different sections were about... the Quinzaine [Directors' Fortnight], the Critics' Week and so on. People kept asking me about films that I didn't know about. I thought I'd covered the competition and Un Certain Regard - the official sections - and they kept saying, "Well this film is here." and I thought, "But I know about all of the French films that are here?" And they kept coming up with more and more films that I didn't know were in the festival. That baffled me straight away, but also the scale of the thing and the colossal amounts of money that was swishing around Cannes being used just to impress people with really.

BC: What about the city itself... it's the French Riviera, it's supposed to be glamorous, how did you find it when you first got there?

PF: When I first got there I was blown away by the architecture along the Croisette, but I guess that pales quite quickly. It just becomes your working environment because, unlike other festivals where they dip in for two or three days, most people who go to Cannes are there for ten days. The whole of the independent film industry goes to Cannes to work and stay there pretty much for the duration. For those of us who've got a punishing daily schedule, the glamour side rapidly shifts into the background.

BC: These days, in your capacity as a journalist for Screen International, what do you normally do to prepare ahead of Cannes?

PF: There's no short answer to that - in a way, we spend virtually the whole year preparing for Cannes. Screen International's predecessors virtually claim to have invented the Cannes market. They're not saying that they put up the buildings and organised the screenings etc, but they realised a long time ago that that a market existed. People were buying and selling films, doing deals in the corridors of the old Palais, and they were doing the same kind of things in the other screening rooms and hotels around town - it was a market in all but name. Screen was the first trade publication to do dailies at Cannes, recognising that there was something to say and that people needed somewhere to get that information, rather than just through corridor-talk where some people had it and some people didn't.

So that's how Screen got started in Cannes and it has remained ever since then pretty much the high-point of our year. Everything starts or finishes with the beginning and end of Cannes. As soon as one year's Cannes is over, we all go on holiday for a bit, but after that we're already looking at which directors and which companies have got things in production or will be in production soon that will be ready for next year. It starts straight away. At the moment we're preparing the second edition of our "Cannes 101", which is a guide we did last year for the festival and who's got deal-making power. I'm currently looking at how I'm going to put together this year's list and which people are the 100 most important deal-makers internationally. I've found myself looking at it quite a bit more cynically this year because of just how many companies from last year's top 100 have gone bust or are diminished powers.

I'm also in touch with the festival organisers year-round. I see Thierry Fremaux and Christian Jeune [the two main selectors for the Official Selection] regularly, I talk to them, I talk to the press people at the festival, and more importantly, I talk to sales agents and producers all the time. The conversations people are having all year around are, "What is going to be ready for Cannes?" That's an obsession with a certain group of people, myself included. At the end of the AFM [American Film Market], I usually publish a list of films that I think have got a good chance of being in the festival - a kind of a teaser list for our readers and for film buyers. I collate masses of information and tips, from sales agents mostly, and run them by people who may or may not be in the know, particularly other festival directors as they tend to know what's been withheld from them. If it's the Berlin people for instance, and they say that a film is suddenly not available to their festival, it can be a good indicator that it might be going to Cannes.

I spoke to one sales agent at the end of one AFM and asked him what his tips for Cannes contenders were, and he said "I'm absolutely not helping you this time. We've got too many things that may or may not go, so I'm not going to help you. Just do your own homework." But he then added, "I can't wait to see your list."

BC: How does a typical day in Cannes during the festival pan out for you?
PF: My job tends to vary from year to year because I'm the International Editor and I don't really know what that means apart from that my responsibly is coverage for everything that is not American and not British. Some years I've found myself news editing, other years I've found myself covering particular territories where Screen hasn't got a correspondent, or other times I'm simply the floating person who's been around for a long time and can dip into any situation. So it has varied a lot. For the 2003 festival I was the French, German and Korean correspondent.

In general, my day pans out in a fairly regular fashion, but you never know what's going to come in between. We have a news meeting at nine o'clock every day and then we rush off to press conferences, meetings, breakfasts, and come back into the office with incredible regularity to try and hit various page deadlines. In Cannes, we publish up to ten pages of news each day, and each has a different deadline during the day, so you've got to just keep filing stuff. It's a bit of a treadmill if you think about it because you can't just wait until 11am or lunchtime to file the first story because there are three or four pages which need copy before then. Our office is in the ground floor of the Carlton. It's been there for a long time and nowadays people generally know where to find us - things like that make it all a little bit easier.

Then there's the meetings... I always have a series of meetings that I set up in advance, others which I arrange more spontaneously, and of course there are the things which you can't plan - like when someone announces a press conference because a deal they did during Cannes has finally come together - nobody knew that two days ago, so off I go. I do that throughout the day typically until about four or five o'clock, when we've closed the last pages. Sometimes I'll be involved in proofing pages, re-reading stories, or helping other correspondents with their copy, again that's what my job involves. Being International Editor I'm expected to be a bit of a know-all really.

The evening tends to start with the rounds of cocktails, parties, and so on, which for us are work. It sounds ridiculous, and it sounds obscene to people who are not down in Cannes I suspect, but whenever I news edit I tell our people, "By the time we close page one, I expect you to be empty of news, by the time you get into the office at nine o'clock the next morning for the news meeting, I expect you to have a whole slate of stories you can be offering me." So you've got to work the parties, talk to everyone there... producers, distributors, directors, publicists, and come up with angles and stories to put together throughout the next day. Consequently, the day may finish at one or two or three in the morning... I prefer not to think about that.

BC: As a journalist do you find yourself attracting the attention of filmmakers who are trying to promote their films, and if so, have you had any particularly memorable experiences where a filmmaker has done something really crazy to try and attract your attention?
PF: To get me personally interested in their film, not really. I actually find filmmakers are on the whole pretty modest about their ambitions and their talent and most of them don't make a fool of themselves at all. It's some of their producers and publicists that go over the top and get wacky. Filmmakers themselves tend to be pretty responsible and in some cases, overawed by the amount of attention that is given to films that are in the festival. They can't believe that there are 120 journalists queuing up to see their film and interview them, and it's got to be done in two days. The more crazy and eccentric things tend to be done for the films which are slightly more marginal, if they've actually been made at all. Often they're the films that are still looking for finance, so they tend to try and put on a big show suggesting that they're that are going to get made. Noise breeds more noise in Cannes.

Back in the good old days when there was lots of money sloshing around, when video was very healthy and the pre-sales market was buoyant, you could get films financed in Cannes that didn't even exist on paper even at the beginning of the festival. Someone would just say that Sylvester Stallone was attached to the film - Stallone had probably never even heard of the project, but if you created a buzz and noise around it and someone's offering to put money on the table, well... if there's $20 million on the table, Stallone will probably be there too. It used to happen like that a lot, but I've found in the last four or five years that there's much less of that 'excess for the sake of excess'. If there are people creating heat around a project it's because there is something there.

BC: It's nice to see heat where heat is due for a change.
PF: Yes. It's also a one of the signs of the difficulties in the industry that there's not as much spare cash floating around. Cash now for film finance comes more from public sources, at least in Europe, and the civil servants who are dishing that out are less impressed by 'flash' than some of the flamboyant producers who used to have all the money.

BC: Do you have a particularly memorable festival anecdote that you like to recount when the topic of Cannes comes up at the dinner table?
PF: I've got loads of anecdotes. One, which is a very journalistic experience, was during the second year that I went to Cannes in 1992. I was still in Paris and some of the other people had already gone down to Cannes. I called the editor when I heard the local news in Paris that Marlene Dietrich had died. Few people were aware of this to start with but as soon as they were, they realised they needed photographs. This was back in the days before the Internet really had taken off so it actually meant we needed physical photographs for the front page. Fortunately my wife had tipped me off on this story because her office in Paris was opposite Marlene Dietrich's flat. So she saw funeral things going on and rang me to tell me something had happened. I then called a photo agency friend of mine who gave me loads of photos before he'd handed them out to anybody else, because he hadn't had a call from anybody else yet. So I had 200-300 pictures of Marlene Dietrich to take down to Cannes the next morning on the plane. Our deadline for pictures was very early that day because it was the first issue, and they needed the pictures to be there absolutely immediately. So I took the helicopter [from Nice airport to Cannes]. It's the only time I've expensed a helicopter to Screen, and it's the only time I'm ever likely too. So that was one journalistic thing, but nobody bats an eyelid half the time at that kind of excess... they do at Screen, but other parts of the industry... "Take the helicopter? Great."

One of my other silly things was about five or six years ago, the year that Planet Hollywood opened in Cannes for the first time and took over the ground floor of the Splendid Hotel. For some reason they were handing out various different passes to people and I got a pass which gave me breakfast for every day I wanted it, so I wore that one, and another pass which gave me all-areas access anytime, and I thought, "This is great."

One of the days, I got invited to a party there... I've forgotten which film it was promoting, but in addition to all my Planet Hollywood passes, I also had the correct party ticket. Iggy Pop was playing - he's a favourite of mine - and what I hadn't realised until I got there was that this was such a select party - either that or the bouncers had been too heavy - because there was almost nobody there. So there's Iggy Pop on stage doing a fantastic set and there were about maybe 20 or 30 people in the audience, but they were celebrities. There was Demi Moore, one of the Sheen brothers, Mick Hucknell, Kate Moss, other supermodels... and me. I have no idea what I was doing in there with this lot - it felt like a private party that Iggy Pop was playing for. He was completely over the top, everyone was off their heads, he was doing a great set in private, and he was spitting into the audience of celebrities and they were loving it... it was absurd and over the top.

But to finish off this silly anecdote, I saw this rather lonely, spiky-haired figure turn up at the velvet rope, but he was debarred by the bouncers. They told him that they didn't need him in this party, he hadn't got an invitation, and that he probably should leave. It was Pedro Almodóvar and I recognised him. I don't know him, but I went up to the bouncers and said, "Are you really, really sure you should be doing this to this guy? He's probably the most successful foreign language director working today, and did you realise that he got the Légion d'Honneur [Legion of Honour] today from the French Government?" Nothing had worked until then, but telling him that he'd got the Légion d'Honneur that lunchtime... the bouncers opened up and in he came. I think it's the only time that pure reason has actually worked with bouncers in Cannes.

BC: Do you have any favourite places to eat when you are in Cannes?
PF: One is not really a restaurant. Near where we work at the Carlton, on one of the back roads - the Rue Rouaze - there's a Lebanese traiteur which has the best food in Cannes - I'm convinced of it. Their food is fresh, fantastically tasty and cheap, and they serve it with a kind of deliberately gruff insolence, but they recognise you year in, year out. You're made to feel welcome by them being ruder than ever to you. I kind of look forward to those lunchtimes where I don't have an organised lunch and just grab something from there and bring it back to the office. Their food is fantastic.

Real restaurants... my favourite is probably the Gaston Gastounette, which is near the old port. If you want a celebrity anecdote there... I organised a dinner for Michelle Yeoh last year - she's a friend of mine, one of the few celebrities I would call a friend - and she was on the jury last year. We'd met up at the Carlton on the terrace and I'd organised dinner for eight o'clock. With Michelle on jury duty, her time-keeping was not really of her own making. That evening, she only managed to turn up at the Carlton at eight o'clock, then had to get changed. We had drinks on the Terrace and we were running massively late. So I called the restaurant, not just once but twice to tell them that we were getting later and later. I'd warned them in advance that we had a VIP and the difference in service when you've got a VIP - "Come whenever you like" - was hilarious. But it was absolutely necessary because Michelle, who's quite athletic, decided she wanted to walk to the restaurant. So we walked from the Carlton all the way to the old town. She was on the jury, an absolutely recognisable celebrity and in high heels... it took forever to get there because, you can imagine, hundreds of people were asking for autographs all the way along the Croisette. So we got there about ten o'clock and the restaurant couldn't have been nicer.

BC: What about socialising/networking venues?

PF: Not really. They tend to vary from year to year actually, where the hotspot is. The one place I tend to gravitate to is the terrace at the Grand Hotel, but that's kind of very British. It used to be kind of French, and as I don't cover Britain it's not really that useful to me anymore.

BC: Do you have any advice for future Cannes virgins, particularly producers who are coming to Cannes with films?

PF: Prepare and be realistic about what you want to achieve. If you expect to get your film, which is at the moment barely developed, to be fully-financed by the end of Cannes, you'll be out of pocket and disappointed. If you know what you want, if you set yourself certain realistic goals, if you set up a few meetings beforehand, then that's going to help a lot.
Also, get a couple of good people on your side, whether it's another producer who's not in competition with you or a publicist. Indeed, some of the publicists are very friendly and amenable to people who are first-timers. You'd be surprised - they are generally very stressed people who've got masses of other things to do, but some can often find time to help people who could be clients five years down the road. And they have very good advice, always, because they've been inside every venue, they've been inside every party, they've worked with other producers, distributors, and they know how the festival itself can grind people down - because the festival organisation is pretty scary sometimes. So, make a couple of good friends before you get there and stick with them.

Other practical things... good shoes, you've heard that one a hundred times before. Stay there as long as you can, but that might mean being prepared to share rooms with people. Don't stay too far out of town, but don't necessarily try and stay on the Croisette either. Stay there as long as you can because relationships happen and can form very quickly. I often suggest to people that you can live a whole relationship with a person in a day in Cannes. You can meet them for the first time, be attracted, fall in love, fall out of love - I mean this in a professional sense of course. You can go through all that sort of thing, you can fall out, make up again, and go off into the sunset together in a day. That's probably a bit of a journalistic exaggeration, but within the twelve days that the festival is on you can achieve a lot.

Harry Hicks
Chiltern Plc (Finance)

BC: When did you first visit Cannes and what were your first impressions of the city and the festival?

HH: The first time I went to the film festival was only in 1999. I had done MIDEM [International Music Market] a couple of times before that, the first time in 1995, but the film festival was all very confusing. My first feeling was really, "Who does what?" Mainly I think because everything is so spread out. It's not like MIPCOM [International TV Market] or even MIDEM where everything happens in The Bunker [aka the Palais du Festivals]; everything is spread out so there's a very amorphous feel about it when you first go, certainly there was for me.

BC: These days, how to you prepare for a visit to Cannes for the film festival?

HH: Today I'm extremely focussed and I have my agenda for why I might be going worked out well ahead of the festival. For instance, the last time I went, one agenda was to make more contacts in respect of raising UK tax money, possible sources of finance, and the other one was to link up particularly with overseas sales agents and distributors in respect of those projects that we were doing through First Up Film. What I did beforehand was to make contact by fax or email with people I wanted to see and set up as many meetings as possible in advance. So my diary is very well planned before I go. I have to say, I also leave gaps in between each meeting because my experience is that meetings are always being rescheduled or running over. You have to leave those spaces to keep your schedule flexible, and also because it's all so spread out, you have to allow yourself time to get from one venue to another. You might have one meeting at the Carlton and your next meeting might be at the Palais, and your next meeting might be at the Martinez, or wherever, so it can be very very exhausting. I find leaving that space between appointments is essential.

BC: Accommodation is one of the biggest challenges for festival attendees these days. Some people get around this by staying out of town. What are your thoughts on places to stay?

HH: I prefer to stay in town these days. I have stayed outside of town in the past, but what I find is you get a taxi in first thing in the morning, then you're there all day and all night. It's just great to be in town and at some stage during the day be able to go back to where you're staying and freshen up.

BC: Once you're in Cannes, how does a typical day tend to pan out for you?

HH: It would usually be about three meetings in the morning, and some can start at 9am - it's not always necessarily a late start. Then there's almost always a lunch at one of the beach cafes, with people I want to see, or if people have invited me, and then maybe a couple of meetings in the afternoon. Then of course there's the round of cocktail parties, starting at 6pm and running through to 9pm or whenever. You could certainly go to three in an evening. Then dinner with contacts or clients. I have to say that by about midnight, and this is probably a bit disappointing, but I'm not one of these people that goes back to the Majestic and stays up until three o'clock in the morning - I just can't do that these days. Besides, I don't know what kind of real contacts are made at the Majestic in the early hours of the morning. It may be a place for swapping business cards but I'm not sure that the cost-benefit equation stacks up really.

BC: In your capacity as a financier, do you have people pitching projects to you at the festival, and do you have any memorable pitches that spring to mind?

HH: I tend to hear a lot of pitches at Cannes, particularly independent producers pitching projects or scripts to me. One pitch that was memorable was an animation project which looked very well thought out. The financing look convincing, it was well structured and I suppose that for me is why that did impress me. The artistic or creative value of the project wouldn't really be for me to judge.

BC: Have you heard any really awful pitches where you've just thought "these guys are wasting their time"?

HH: I've had quite a few, people that are touting around a script, which is just it... it's just a script. There's all levels of projects in Cannes, everybody's hustling from one end to the other. I've even had wanna-be actors hustling because they think I might be in some way important, and I've certainly had independent producers with scripts that had not really had a 'bat in hell's chance' of going anywhere.

BC: Cannes is known as a 'finished product' festival. Is it common for financing deals to be put together there?

HH: I would be surprised if they were finalised. I personally haven't seen a financing deal locked down in Cannes. My attitude towards Cannes would be that everything is a bit too frenetic for deals to be finalised in terms of financing, but it's a good place to start the discussion. Overall, looking at it from both sides, if I had projects that wanted financing, I wouldn't be having detailed discussions about it in Cannes. I might introduce the concept and idea, and then say "we'll continue the discussion afterwards."

BC: If you were to discuss projects in development with a producer in Cannes from a financing point of view, what would you be looking for them to show you?
HH: Obviously a screenplay, and at least a wish-list of major cast, so there is an indication that thought had being given to who might take the lead roles. Also, a director, or at least thought as to who the director might be, and indicative budget. I think that's what I prefer to see as a starting point.

BC: Do you have a favourite anecdote that you like to recount at the dinner table when the topic of Cannes comes up in the conversation?
HH: Yes, it has to be Cannes 2000. I was on the plane from London with a colleague, and we were coming down into Nice into thick fog, about an hour late or something like that. As we were coming in to land there was this almighty scaping sound - it was very scary actually. It turns out that at the last minute, the pilot realised we couldn't land because the fog was too thick and too close to the ground. We were temporarily diverted to Marseilles, and when we landed there were these two women who insisted on getting off, even though we'd been told that we would be returning to Nice as soon as the fog cleared.

Everybody on the plane was in uproar, there was nearly a riot and there was all sorts of chanting going on: "Nice, Nice, Nice." I'm amazed these women didn't get lynched. The pilot had to come out and it was absolutely amazing. All these otherwise civilised people, obviously most of them producers and the like going to the festival, got really anarchic.

I think in the end the women did get off, but it was decided to keep their luggage on the plane, because what was initially said was that if these two women get off, we're going to have to take all the luggage off the plane so we can get their bags. Of course that would have delayed us immensely. I think they got off, but it was announced that their luggage was staying on, and everyone went "Yay!!!" because that would have of course massively inconvenienced the two women. We finally got to Nice and caught a taxi from the airport to the hotel, out in La Bocca, where I was staying with a work colleague. When I got to the hotel, I was told that there was no room for me, even though I'd booked and stayed there before. This was the Friday night of the film festival. I'd arrived three hours late and I was told that there was no room for me. To cut a long story short, I had to share a small room with my colleague; not the ideal situation, but it was the only thing we could do.

BC: Do you have any favourite places to eat when you're in town?
HH: At lunch time it's usually one of the beach cafes, but I'm indiscriminate as to which one.

In the evening I particularly like going up the Rue St Antoine. There's a couple of good places on there. The places I can remember having enjoyed and having a good evening... there was Le Marais, but particularly Le Mesclun - I've had some really very good meals there. It's not the cheapest, but it's not massively expensive either.

BC: Do you have any networking/socialising venues?
HH: Well, if anywhere it would be the Carlton, but obviously when I'm on business accounts. I don't really like the Majestic. I find the Carlton more relaxed, quieter, and the Carlton Terrace is lovely. But if there was anything happening on a yacht... I think those are the best places. It's outside and it's just fun.

BC: Do you have any advice for future Cannes virgins, particularly first-time producers who are looking to come and sell their film or meet distributors/sales agents?
HH: The only thing I would say is, do some research first and have your meetings arranged before you get there. And quite honestly, there's not a lot of point meeting people from your own country in Cannes because they'll just say, "Well, we can meet back home." I think most people see Cannes as an opportunity to see people from abroad, so I would say focus on people from long haul destinations.

Stephen Kelliher
Beyond Films (Sales & Acquisitions)

BC: When did you first visit Cannes?

SK: The first time I went was eight years ago. I was working for another independent film sales company called Vine International Pictures, but I was literally the office junior and in a very lucky position to be going to Cannes at that age. I was 20 years old and it was my first time at a film festival so losing my 'Cannes virginity' was a big deal. I was there for the entire festival, running errands, making cups of tea, going to screenings, collecting business cards, and just really observing how the whole business works. Cannes and the other markets are the industry, or at least they are for a sales agent. That's where you do your business. So to see the biggest event in the film calendar for real was a very sharp learning curve and is largely responsible for making me see that this was the job I wanted to do. Previously, I thought production might be more suitable for me but experiencing Cannes first hand made me realise that I wanted to remain in international distribution.

BC: So what was your impression of the city? It's the French Riviera, it's supposed to be glamorous...?

SK: And I think it is on the surface. I mean you're walking down the Croisette and you've got all the designer shops and the imposingly lavish hotels, most of which employ security for the duration of the festival which makes them seem even more unapproachable. In saying that, from my perspective, it's never as glamorous as it appears. At the end of the day, Cannes itself is a small seaside town and, with exception of the Croisette itself, is mainly a maze of back streets which are populated by pensioners and their irritating dogs. But jokes aside... it can be intimidating, although I think most people are like a child in a sweet shop the first time around. It is frenetic and there's 101 things happening at once and it can be difficult to take it all in. I know I certainly had to stop and ask myself whether I was really part of this. If the answer is yes, you have to embrace it and wade in, I guess.

BC: Could you provide a bit of background on how a sales agent works with a producer at a festival like Cannes?

SK: The sales agent is primarily the bridge between the producer and the international market place. As a producer, your talents tend to be creative or financial, or both. But I would argue that many independent producers don't have the time or ability to ensure that their film is seen in around the world. So it's a sales agent's job is to have those contacts, to be able to take the film - it could be a completed film or it might be a script - to distributors and be able to target the right companies in the right territory. Hopefully they will close the deal so your film has the opportunity to be seen internationally. Of course, the sales agent also plays an integral role in the financing of films whether it be through pre-sales, putting up an advance against the international rights, or by bringing a gap financing bank to a project. In this respect, their role is also key to an independent producer.

In terms of how it works day to day in Cannes, I'd say that sales agents probably have the worst wrap of everybody. It's the longest market in the film calendar, lasting 12 days... and that's 12 days of solid work because weekends don't count when you are a sales agent. There are no lie-ins, your meetings start at nine o'clock in the morning, and they finish at seven in the evening. As a sales agent you are actually quite isolated from all the glamour that goes on around you, because you are sitting in an office day in day out, with meetings every half-hour for the duration of the festival. I think sales agents definitely have the toughest job in Cannes.

BC: So what do you do to prepare ahead of Cannes?
SK: It starts pretty much immediately after the American Film Market which ends at the beginning of March. We go straight into Cannes preparation at that point. We've probably already sent any films that are going to be completed in time for Cannes to the official selectors, whether it's for the main competition, Un Certain Regard, the Directors' Fortnight, or the Critics' Week. Hopefully they have seen the films by then and hopefully you're on top of them, trying to get back their feedback. Ideally, six weeks before the market we want to have our slate firmed up in terms of which projects we're going to have and which completed films will we be screening and what films are going to be in post-production. You need to get all that information out to as many people as you can, as soon as you can, because you want to get in early and avoid people coming back with: "Oh my schedules is full, but I'll drop by and see you sometime while I'm there." They never will. So it's best to get in early and make sure people know what you're up to. I've kind of summarised it all in a couple of brief sentences but it actually takes weeks to get to that point. You need to be in a position, when you get to Cannes, to be presenting your films at the highest possible level. Cannes can be the film equivalent of a cattle market, particularly if your film isn't in official selection. It's actually really tough to get those films noticed because people tend to focus on the films in official programme. In fact, I think it's important to ask yourself whether Cannes is the right

place to launch a finished film because even great films can very easily be overlooked there. In the build up to Cannes, you're working on creative publicity, with the producers and designers, coming up with visual images, trailers and that kind of thing. It's really a four-month effort to get to Cannes, and you always get there and realise you've forgotten something!

BC: So how does a typical day tend to pan out for you in Cannes?
SK: Well, as I said, meetings pretty much start at 9am... even earlier if you're unlucky enough to have a breakfast meeting in your schedule! One thing that's important to remember is that at the end of the day, you are there to do a job. You can be at whatever party until four or five in the morning, but you still have to be in the office at nine and be able to string a sentence together. Actually, the sales agent's life in Cannes can be quite unglamorous. You're meeting people from all around the world, delivering what is essentially the same pitch. And it can be hard, trying to keep it fresh, because you're not only pitching one film, you're maybe pitching six films to somebody in a half-hour period. It's extremely tiring mentally. And if you're having a successful market, or there's one title that is selling well, you'll still have to sit down at the end of each day to review the offers you've received, or the interest you have received, figure out what's the best deal, or who the best distributor is, and maybe chase people up who said they were going to see a film, or get back to you, but haven't. So you really need to spend an hour or more at the end of each day getting all that stuff clear in your head, as well as preparing a little bit for the next day. But then of course there are the infamous parties in the evening, some of which you need to go to for professional reasons and others which aren't perhaps so important from a work perspective; either way, it can be hard to find time to wind down and generally you arrive back home as something of a physical and mental wreck!

BC: How common is it for producers to pitch ideas or projects to sales agents in Cannes?
SK: The thing about Cannes is that anyone who has a project tends to be there. From a sales agent's point of view, I would say that it's not the best place for you to meet us because our primary function at a market is to sell. It is difficult to give time to someone who is thinking about shooting a film in six months time or in 12 months time, particularly if that person is based in the UK, but wants to see you in Cannes. You do try not to have an attitude about it, but it can be difficult.

Usually, the second week of the festival is the best time for us to see producers. At that point we tend to have a little more time to actually listen to what they are saying. We have recently appointed a dedicated acquisitions and development person who will come to the festival with us this year. Their job is solely to meet with producers and listen to the pitches so hopefully we will be a little more producer-friendly this year. I would say that the companies with an acquisitions person in Cannes are the ones to target. It's much easier to get to them than the sales people who need to be focused on selling.

BC: If you were going to meet a producer in Cannes, what sort of material would you expect them to be showing you?
SK: It all depends on what stage the project is at really. From our point of view, we can only become involved once a certain number of elements are in place, so it doesn't make sense for somebody to come and see us with a script and nothing else attached. We're not a financing house and we don't house a development department. So if somebody's coming to us with a project, they need to have the shooting script, they need to have a director attached, there needs to be a budget and a percentage of that budget in place, or at least working towards having a percentage of that budget in place. By it's very nature, a sales company can't be the first to commit to a project because they need to make an informed decision based on the script and the talent attached. You can't do that from a script alone. It's different if you're going to see people about development, or you're going to see production finance people, because they are less bound by the commerciality of the project, if you like, whereas for us, that is the be all and end all. We have to know that there's a market for it and that we can market it effectively. So I would say that as much of the package as possible should be in place. Once you've got that, I wouldn't necessarily say that you need to spend a lot of money creating expensive marketing materials because I think any sales agent worth their salt will be able to pick out the good projects from a verbal presentation, a script, and a typed list of the elements attached. I don't think it's necessary to spend lots of money on that kind of thing. That's not what it's about, it's about the script and the elements attached.

BC: Do you have a particular memorable anecdote from your time in Cannes over the years?
SK: The whole thing I think is an interesting experience. I don't think I can sit here and name one thing. The first year that you go is always going to be a lasting memory. You can't believe you're walking down the street... you're not bumping into film stars, but you're seeing them at events or you walk in to a hotel lobby and there's whoever with their entourage. There are memorable people I've seen though... I think Michael Jackson was one when he had his film Ghosts screening out of competition [in 1997]. But every year it's somebody new or something new. Cannes is definitely a life experience. I would almost say that everybody should experience it once because it is so crazy.

BC: Do you have any favourite places to eat when you're in Cannes?
SK: Everybody says that Cannes is expensive, but you can do it without eating expensively.

If you're going to go anywhere along the Croisette by the sea then you can expect to pay more for it. But you just take a walk in some of the less well-known places, and you can eat very reasonably. The Rue Sainte Antoine, which is in the old town, is packed with restaurants. There are a couple that are really expensive but the rest of them are priced pretty fairly. You're certainly not paying any more than you would pay in London, maybe a bit less sometimes.

For those on a very tight budget, there's always McDonald's or the fast food stall next door to the Town Hall which serves a very good horse burger - so I am reliably informed. I have never dared to try one myself though.

BC: Do you have any favourite socialising/networking places in Cannes?
SK: It is all networking really. Every night there are probably five or six cocktail parties that you could go to and those are the places where you meet people - it's one of the main reasons to go to them. For somebody who's trying to find opportunities to network, I would say get invited to as many cocktail parties as you can because that's where people talk and that's where people exchange information. There are also the international pavilions which run along the beach where there are the official film bodies for the various countries. Most of those have events and there are always interesting people to meet. I would highly recommend these as a networking exercise, just get invited to as much as you can, and speak to as many people as you can. Try not to drink as much as you can though - it's never a good look to be blind drunk when meeting a potential business partner!

BC: Any particular venues you like to hang out in or is it mainly the parties?
SK: I'm kind of over parties in Cannes at this stage. Every year I find I go to less and less because they're always such a bun-fight. It can take you an hour to get a drink at the bar, then you lose your friends and you never find them again. I would certainly never go to a party that I wasn't invited to; it's just not worth the hassle. I would much rather meet up with friends and just go for some quiet drinks around and about. Any of the bars along the Croisette or if you can get on any of the boats in the old port, that's quite nice too.

BC: Do you have any specific advice for future Cannes virgins?
SK: For first-time producers coming to Cannes to pitch their film, I think they have to be very careful about which companies they're going to target. There's a common misconception that you can just go to anyone and everyone. You should take your time and do a bit of research and see what kind of films particular companies specialise in. Ask yourself honestly whether your film is going to fit their criteria. I would also take the time to find out who the correct person to speak to is. You can look at the Cannes Market Guide and the bumper issues [of the trade magazines], and if there's someone in acquisitions or

development at the company you want to talk to, contact them for a meeting. It just saves a lot of unnecessary hassle in the long run.

I suppose the only other thing I would say is: don't be daunted by it. It is a huge event. You see people who've been doing it for years and it's all like second-nature to them, but just get stuck in and enjoy it. It is something to be enjoyed, it is hard work, but just don't be too frightened by it all.

Richard Miller
Available Light Advisory (Producer)

BC: When did you first visit Cannes and what were your first impressions of the city and festival?

RM: I first came to Cannes in the late 80s before I was in the film business, when I was still an investment banker. I had just taken three back-to-back red-eye flights from Hawaii to San Francisco, San Francisco to Boston, and Boston to Cannes, so I was completely burnt out. In my deranged state, Cannes seemed like this other-worldly place - seedy and strange but at the same time really beautiful and exciting.

I always say that it's really valuable that producers experience a festival before they need to deal with it professionally. So I was very lucky that I visited the festival when I had nothing at stake and could just enjoy it as a place to hang out and see films. Then later on, when I needed to work the event, I already had some understanding of how it operated. Since that first visit I've been to the festival about ten times, and in all my subsequent visits, I've probably seen half the number of films that I saw on that first visit.

BC: How did you find the city itself?

RM: Cannes is the encapsulation of the art/commerce nature of the film enterprise. Immediately everybody is overwhelmed with the massive billboards for these A and B-titles along the Croisette, but there are also a lot of dedicated cineastes and film fans queuing up to see obscure art films. Then you go behind the seafront and there's another world of French people with poodles going about the business of being glamorously French. And then you go up into the hills or out of town and there's even another world of people actually living normal suburban lives. That contrast is quite remarkable I think.

BC: What sort of preparation do you do these days before arriving in Cannes?

RM: Preparation is principally about setting up meetings. For me, both as a consultant now and when I was producing, Cannes is about meeting people that are more difficult to meet year round because they live in a different town or country. Or even meeting people that work just down the street from you, but somehow in Cannes they're there to take meetings and it's easier to get together with them. So it's all about setting up meetings - that's my preparation.

BC: So following on from that, your typical day in Cannes comprises of, surprise surprise, lots of meetings?

RM: Yes, lots of meetings, and in between the meetings, finding out where people are so that I can arrange other meetings. The great thing about Cannes is that there's a certain randomness to encountering people. You may have tried for weeks to set up a meeting through the normal channels and then at the first party you go to, you bump into somebody who says, "Oh, he's over there across the room", and takes you over and you've got your meeting. It's important just to be out and about so that you are exposed to this serendipity that is such a big part of Cannes.

BC: How was it that "Heavy" came to be selected for the Directors Fortnight?

RM: The film had played in Sundance and had been critically acclaimed, but had not been acquired at that point. I knew the number-two man at Directors Fortnight, Olivier Jahan, from previous Cannes festivals I had attended and also knew he was coming to New York to scout for films for the sidebar. I called him ahead of time, set up a screening, and he loved the film. He called us immediately and offered us a place. We were the first American film selected that year. It was that simple.

BC: What was involved in preparing to screen the film for the Directors Fortnight?

RM: At that point we did not have a distributor anywhere, but because we had an acceptance into an official section at Cannes we were potentially quite attractive to foreign sales agents. I arranged screenings in London for foreign sales agents and had a number of discussions and ended up selecting Fortissimo, out of Amsterdam. So I was able to go into the festival with a sales agent onboard. It's pretty important to do that because without a sales agent, if there is interest among distributors, it's going to be the producer doing the deals, and it's much more difficult for a producer than for a sales agent. A producer doesn't have all those relationships with distributors in the different territories, and also doesn't know all the deal terms and comparable prices.

Fortissimo then suggested a publicity person because publicity's also a big part of Cannes. There are two different types of publicity at the festival: the French publicity and the international publicity. They work side by side, but they're kind of different worlds. Fortunately we were able to put in place a publicist who was capable of dealing with both, and with a sales agent and a publicist onboard, we were ready to take orders.

BC: Did the film actually get picked up by a distributor in Cannes?

RM: We did a number of very good foreign deals; in the UK, in Japan, and in other major territories. So it was a very good Cannes for us. We actually didn't do a US deal, principally because the US distributors wouldn't come to the screenings because they'd seen the film in Sundance and consequently felt they didn't need to. In the end we didn't do a US deal until the Toronto festival where we showed a slightly trimmed film. Off the back of that we were able to get some new companies into the screening and did a pretty good deal there too.

BC: How was "Heavy" received by audiences in Cannes?

RM: It was received very well. It's a wonderful experience to screen a film in Cannes. They have the best screening facilities you'll ever see anywhere and technicians that really care about the quality of the screening. They had the director, Jim Mangold, and I come to this test at midnight the night before our first screening, just to make sure we were perfectly happy with the presentation.

Then on the day - to be in this massive hall and have people from around the world yelling and clapping - it's a remarkable experience. And the press conference afterwards, where they ask about cinematic influences, not distribution deals.

So it was a very good experience for us. We also had a bit of glamour with the screening because it was Liv Tyler's first festival experience... her second film, first festival... and that gave us a substantial amount of press attention.

BC: Do you have a favourite Cannes anecdote that sticks in your mind?

RM: It's tough to beat that experience of walking on stage arm-in-arm with my director and my star and having thousands of people stand up and applaud.

BC: Do you have any favourite places that you like to eat when you are in Cannes?

RM: I have two favourite places in Cannes, and I'm very tempted to keep them to myself, but I'll tell you anyway although I won't give all the details. Over by the bus station there is a wonderful little bar that has beers from all around the world. You go in there and generally there's nobody wearing a Cannes badge. You can sit and have a couple of beers and just get right away from the Cannes craziness. That's one of my favourite places. Another one is called La Brouette de Grand-Mère or 'Grandmother's Wheelbarrow' and it's on a side road off the Croisette. It has really good food, but the reason I like it is that you just go in and sit down and they bring you food and drink and you have absolutely no say in what you eat or what you drink. They just keep bringing it out. You have no decisions to make, you just go to your grandmother's and she takes care of you. Sometimes at Cannes you need that.

BC: Do you have any preferred socialising/networking venues?

RM: One always goes to the parties, but for bumping into people and meeting friends, there's nothing like what used to be the Petit Carlton and Petit Majestic, but is now just the Petit Majestic in behind the Grand Hotel. It's this little bar where the crowds just spill onto the street and everyone comes by. Most evenings will find me taking a quick walk through just to see if there's anybody I know there or need to meet.

BC: Do you have any advice for future Cannes virgins, particularly first-time producers looking to either sell a film or generate interest?

RM: Well the first thing is, if you can, try to go to Cannes for the first time when you don't need to do anything so you can just work out the lay of the land. The second thing is don't just hang around your national pavilion. I talk to a lot of Americans, for example, that seem to spend most of their time in the American Pavilion. It doesn't make much sense to fly all that way and just hang out with people from home. Certainly those pavilions are handy to use as a base, but part the Cannes experience is the chance to make contacts with the industry outside your own situation. Go to other people's pavilions and hang out. The third thing is, don't go naked. Make sure that, when it's important, you have the specialist expertise in terms of film representation, publicity, the experts... the people that know how to do it, if that's at all possible. And lastly, so much of Cannes is about serendipity that you want to be open to, but can't really control. You've just got to find time to relax and enjoy it as a place, and not just be so focussed on the task in hand - because it's a very pleasant place to spend a few days.

Jonathan Olsberg
Olsberg-SPI (Producer)

BC: When did you first visit Cannes and how did you find the city and the festival?

JO: Mine was a baptism of fire in 1982, but not as a producer - I went there as a sales agent. I had been an investment banker in New York until six months beforehand and I'd started a small film sales company with a partner. Low and behold, in our first few months we represented a film that got selected to be in Competition in Cannes - it was a surprise and we were totally unprepared for it. The film was called "Smithereens" and was made by a student at NYU called Susan Seidelman, who later went on to make "Desperately Seeking Susan". She made it for $50,000 on Super 16mm and when it was selected, we had to find all kinds of money... to blow it up to 35mm, for a marketing campaign, to hire press agents, and so on. And it wasn't as if we'd been in business for years. We didn't actually know what we were doing, but luckily we were recommended a very good French press agent to help us handle the whole thing and they taught us what to do. So in terms of selling, we had to prepare marketing materials and send them out ahead of time. We had to start to show the film before Cannes to a few selected buyers and we did a couple of quick deals that way. Unfortunately none of these stood up and we had to sue the buyers to get paid because they saw us as neophytes and they thought that they could say they'd buy the film and wait to see how it panned out - a bit devious really. Still, we won both cases and it was a good lesson!

BC: So what were your first impressions of the festival when you arrived there?

JO: Well for us, even though we weren't neophyte producers, we were neophyte sales agents, and the first impressions were that it was incredibly disorganised. For example, there was no central directory of where people were. There are the people who register, or are invited to the festival, and if they remember to send in the information, you could find out where they are, but that's only about 20% of all the people there. And it was so spread out with all these offices in the different hotels - it was just totally chaotic but also a little thrilling.

BC: And what about the city itself?

JO: I was already familiar with the city from going on holidays there when I was younger, so I knew the area in general. Of course Cannes when it's not a big festival or market is a delightful, relatively sleepy retirement town, but during the festival it gets mobbed by literally tens of thousands of people. It's wonderful if the weather's good and it's awful if it's raining because most people have to walk around from meeting to meeting. Walking around in Cannes in the rain is not much fun because you're always late and there are so many people getting in the way, whether they are there for the festival or just members of the public hoping to see a star. Something that is also terribly aggravating is that there are at least one or two public holidays that take place during the festival, so not only do you have the weekends where the place is mobbed, but if you have a holiday on the Thursday, it's a four-day weekend and a complete zoo. So it's an inconvenient and difficult place, but that is totally counter-balanced by the fact that if the weather's good you can have lunch on the beach with your toes in the sand and a nice bottle of wine.

BC: These days, what sort of preparation do you do ahead of Cannes?
JO: I think it depends on what I'm going to be doing there. I've been a producer in Cannes, I've sold movies, I've been a distributor buying movies, I've been a management consultant looking for other kinds of business, so I think it really depends on what hat you're wearing. If you're selling or buying films, there are certain things you have to do ahead of time.

For selling, obviously you've got to sow the seeds of your marketing campaign and make sure buyers are aware of your product. You might even start showing the film ahead of Cannes to certain people. If you're buying, you've got to be sniffing around for those sorts of opportunities to buy before the film gets to Cannes.

One essential piece of preparation is accommodation; you've got to get your hotel squared away months in advance, and you've usually got to dig deep in the pocket to do so. People going for the first time on a small budget often club together to rent an apartment somewhere close by, but nowadays if you're in a four- star hotel, by January you've got to slap down a hefty wad including various 'commissions' to people.

So accommodation has to be sorted out and then you've got to have a purpose or purposes for being there. You've got to have specific targets because otherwise you can be completely overwhelmed by some of the things that are going on. So ahead of time, you should set up your key meetings which you don't want to shift and then about two or three weeks beforehand, you email everybody who you know who might be going and let them know the dates you'll be there, how you will be contactable, and invite them to meet if there's a reason to do so.

It's generally a bad idea to completely fill your calendar with appointments before you go because you'll always be bumping into people there who you'll want to meet. You'll also be bumping into people who want to meet you, but you don't want to meet, so you've got to have enough appointments to say "Oh, sorry. I can't do it on a Thursday, how about breakfast at seven o'clock on Friday?" And inevitably they don't want to do it.

BC: How does a typical day in Cannes pan out for you these days?
JO: In my early days, when I was staying outside of Cannes, my day would start bleary eyed, getting up and getting into a rented car, heading in and finding a parking space. These days I stay at the Carlton so I usually have a breakfast meeting and then the day will usually consist of further meetings with people. I haven't seen a film in Cannes for about three or four years, which is a shame, but I just never get the chance to do it. So in a typical day, I could have as many as 10 meetings including dinner. Sometimes I might want to take it easy, in which case I make meetings for the afternoon and just chill in the morning. That way, I've got a chance to catch up on daily trades, which are a huge volume of stuff, make calls, and also deal with what's going on back in the office, which you can't just ignore. If the festival lasts for ten or eleven days, I'll usually try and block out day seven as a free day with no meetings and just get out of town. After a week of it, you're so exhausted that you just need a little time out to recharge the batteries.

BC: Obviously you've screened films in Cannes before in a position of selling. How did you go about organising that, and what was involved in getting a non-festival/market screening?
JO: If it's in the festival in an invited section then there's an established process you have to follow, but you also want to have market screenings. If you are just a producer without a sales agent you'll really have a tough time. You need to get some help, maybe from a publicist - they might be able to book the screenings for you. Or if you've got a sales agent, it's their job to do it but you've got to push them and be on top of it so you get the best dates, times, and cinemas. You also want to have it coincide with any publicity you're doing with your stars or your director because sometimes they're only available for a small slot. With your press agent, you've got to organise interviews, and if your film is in the official program, you've got to get it subtitled. I would say if you're there screening a film for the first time as an independent producer, get help from somebody otherwise it's going to be a major headache.

BC: Did you have any interesting experiences screening your own films or films you were involved with in Cannes?
JO: My first year we were there with "Smithereens" in Competition, this tiny film with nobody in it - nobody anyone had ever heard of anyway - but it had a lot of energy to it. This was in the old Palais which doesn't exist anymore but was a beautiful old Rococo-style building. For a neophyte, my first year in Cannes, my first year in the business, walking up the red carpet

with a film in competition was magic. You know, getting the limo pick us up so we could drive 100 yards and get out again further up - it was brilliant. But I have to say the biggest thrill of that first year was going to the closing night film. I'd never been to any film festival before, let alone Cannes, and the closing night film was "E.T". It was such an amazing experience that it sent shivers down my spine.

But it doesn't always go well. We had a situation when I was selling a film... a documentary called "Pumping Iron 2: The Women". This was the sequel to "Pumping Iron", the film that discovered Arnold Schwarzenegger, and this one was about female body builders. At that point we had quite a good reputation for working festivals and for promotional ideas, so we managed to get a lot of impetus behind the screening.

The film wasn't invited into any official category, so we booked a midnight screening in the old Palais, which [prior to its demolition] was used for the Directors' Fortnight. We brought over all seven stars of the film, who were six very gorgeous muscular women and one person who I still think was really a man. We organised a fashion show for the opening night where they modelled various items, and we did a radio promotion for the first screening with a local rock station. They did a sweepstake whereby local listeners called in and got tickets and their tickets gave them a chance in a lottery for two free trips to New York for the premiere of the film.

So it was just massively over-subscribed, the hype was incredible - this film was the film that everybody knew about. The screening was a mad house; the police had to come and bar the doors because there were so many people outside the building, but the upshot of it all was we couldn't sell the film. Because we massively over-hyped it above where it sat in the market, buyers' expectations were way too high. It was an ok, interesting film but we totally screwed it up. So I learnt that in Cannes especially, you've got to make sure that you pitch your movie right. People like to 'discover' pictures there and if you're dealing with independent films, it's normally going to be a discovery, so you've got to work it so that it is a buzz film, but without overdoing it.

BC: Do you have any favourite Cannes anecdotes that you like to tell over the dinner table?
JO: Our first year at Cannes, I was there with my business partner and a friend of hers who was helping us out. We had rented a one-room apartment with a balcony overlooking part of the Croisette, for use as our office and also to sleep in. So every morning at eight o'clock we had to wake up, literally fold our beds away and stick them behind the curtain, then bring out all the posters and display materials for our office. During a meeting one day I noticed

a whole pile of dirty underwear in the corner of our office (not mine I have to say) which the women had failed to remove. A little embarrassing, but Cannes is just a series of little skirmishes and battles that most of the time you get to win, but sometimes you don't.

BC: Have you ever had any memorable encounters with a big star in Cannes?
JO: I remember meeting Clint Eastwood one year at the Hotel du Cap. It's a very exclusive hotel - it's so exclusive that they only accept cash or travellers cheques. No credit cards, no personal cheques, but the big stars and big studio bosses stay out there. Punters like me can get in for lunch or dinner and I was invited by somebody who was staying there, and at a table close by was Clint Eastwood. It was actually great because at the Hotel du Cap, regardless of what you're wearing, you could be anybody. You could be a famous producer or financier or you could be a complete nothing, just someone who managed to squeeze in somewhere. But I managed to have a really good conversation with Eastwood who was very open and I explained what we'd been doing and he was very interested. So that was great.

BC: Do you have any favourite places to eat in Cannes?
JO: Unfortunately some of them have changed. You've probably heard about an old place called the Petit Carlton, which is now no longer, which is a shame. Now the late-night hang-out for the impoverished is the Petit Majestic, which is just behind the Grand Hotel. It actually caused me to no longer stay at the Grand Hotel - the noise was so great there at four o'clock in the morning I had to move.

I like to have lunch on the beach if the weather's good as they have these great restaurants that are set out directly on the beach. The food is relatively simple, but it's good enough and it's surprising how quickly a bottle of chilled rosé slips down. There's a beach restaurant called the Cannes Beach which I've just always been going to, which is great. In town, there's a restaurant called La Cave which is also good. Out of town, down the road in La Napoule is a beach restaurant called the Le Sweet which has great food and is a good place to escape to. To be honest, I think that the food in Cannes is overrated and very expensive. You can eat in London or New York or Berlin better than in Cannes, definitely.

BC: You touched a little on networking/socialising there when you mentioned the Petit Majestic. Do you have any other favourite venues in Cannes?
JO: I liked the old Carlton, which is where I used to stay. Even though it was very brash I preferred it to the Majestic. The other hotels... none particularly, but there's a place called Hotel Mondial which is a three-star hotel I used to stay in years ago which is nice, but for hanging out and networking it is the Carlton, it is the Majestic, but the terrace of the Grand Hotel is also a favourite of mine. The Grand Hotel is an old, not very impressive, but very

French hotel. It's set back from the Croisette behind a little green and has a nice big terrace. It's calm and the waiters there have been there forever and they're rather eccentric. So that's a nice place and quite a few independent film folk hang out there. The Palais itself, the conference centre, is a pretty gruesome building. They call it "The Bunker" and it's a concrete monstrosity. There are loads of offices inside, but I try and avoid it as much as I can.

BC: Do you have any advice for future Cannes virgins?

JO: If you've got a finished film, there's a certain procedure; if you're trying to set up a movie, then it's about making meetings and it's much better to make your connections ahead of time. The presentation... the email that arrives on your computer, one gets so many that you've got to make it different, make it exciting. Use your connections, use your lawyer, use people you know to get those meetings and then when you get to Cannes, make sure you figure out the lie of the land. It's a good idea to spend the first day just going everywhere and making sure you know where everything is. In fact, probably before you get there you'll want to get someone who's been there before who'll spend the time with you just to set it all out for you. There are also various pavilions that are set up just for this event on the Croisette - they're like big tents with little offices in them. And there's an American Pavilion, and a British Pavilion, and a Canadian Pavilion and these are really good places to hang out. They usually have a less-expensive little bar or a place where you can get a croissant, and lots of like-minded people will be there. It's easy to network and those are really quite good.

Another thing that's emerged in recent years is the protocol of mobile telephone usage - in a place like Cannes, a mobile is indispensable because you can never find anybody. So the thing to do is to rent a mobile locally otherwise the phone bill is going to be very expensive. If you do, make sure you know your number in advance and let people know your local number, or which number to contact you on if you're bringing your own mobile ahead of time. Then whenever you're having a meeting, agree in advance as to what the protocol is, whether or not you want to have your mobiles on or off during the meeting.

Bill Stephens
Nexus Consulting (Sales)

BC: When did you first visit Cannes and what were your impressions of the festival and the city?

BS: I went to Cannes the first time in 1982... that was my first visit of any sort and it was a bit of a shock! If you're interested in movies, it's something you've seen... you know what it is, but I think you disassociate the glitz from the business. The glitz is what they show you on the TV programmes... you know, the Barry Normans, the Jonathan Rosses [UK film critics] running around the Croisette with all the stars and the directors, the red carpet and the premieres etc. It was still very exciting... I think it must be for everybody the first time they go. It's a big thrill because you're finally there, it's a huge eye-opener, and you cannot imagine what you're in for but you soon find out!

BC: So how did you find the city itself?

BS: Expensive... it was scarily expensive. When I first went it was as part of an American company, and I think a lot of the Americans don't understand that there's anything behind the Croisette. Everything was Mougins [Le Moulin de] dinners, Croisette bars, the Carlton, the Majestic, you know, doing the sort of typically over the top expense account thing. I was horrified by the costs, it was just extraordinary. Even in those days... 1982... it was about £5 for a cup of coffee on the Carlton Terrace; it's probably closer to £10 now. It wasn't until after a few visits that I realised you could find very reasonable places to eat and drink.

So my first impression was, "This is hellishly expensive," but it was great to be there. You're a part of this huge buzz, and in those days it was bigger on the beach, the cameras... basically lots of paparazzi trying to get pictures of women in various stages of undress! Young girls would come from all over Europe, trying to be starlets or to hopefully be discovered. I'm not sure it's the same these days... maybe I just don't notice anymore; but it was all very exciting back then.

BC: It is quite common in independent film circles to hear the term "sales agent" used, but many people don't actually know what the job entails. Could you provide a bit of background on the role of a sales agent, particularly in relation to a festival like Cannes?

BS: A sales agent's job is essentially to represent films on behalf of independent producers or financiers because of their 'insider' knowledge of the players and the deals. Sales agents have a pretty poor reputation, in general. Producers are very disparaging about certain sales agents and you often have to "prove yourself" because everybody thinks you are on the make, you know... "sales agents don't earn their money, they simply sell something, take their commission and go home." I think when I die I will have emblazoned on my tombstone: "If the film sold well it was because it was a good film. If it sold badly, or not at all, it was because I was a lousy sales agent!" You can't win! There's a lot of work involved in marketing films effectively, a lot of 'before and after'. You represent the film on every level. You're taking it from the point of sealing a deal with the producer or financier... let's say producer because basically they represent the front-end... you're taking the film through it's entire build, meaning the marketing build. You're creating materials like show reels, posters, flyers, stills, publicity, press packs, whatever it is, you're taking the whole thing and building an image for that film.

You then take it out into the marketplace, tailoring every move to the type of project it is. And every film is different. You try and find the right buyers and that's about getting information to those people. What should be remembered, and producers often forget this, is that we're not marketing to the public, we're marketing to buyers. That's our target audience, so when we create posters, when we create flyers, when we create anything, it's done with those guys in mind. Not the guy in the cinema, that's a different game, that's done by the distributors.

So we build a profile, a campaign, for the film and get the details to our contacts in whatever method that one uses. It could be mail-outs, it could be emails, it could be letters, it could be CDs, it could be DVDs, it could be anything you want that gets their attention. You've then started marketing the film to those buyers, and we'll talk just in terms of Cannes... Cannes is two distinct and very separate things: it's a festival and it's a market. The festival is an entirely different game to what people are doing in the market. The whole affair is around 12 days long, but in reality, the market could and should be much shorter. It should be say, a week instead of almost two weeks as with the festival. Basically, you're screening the film to the buyer in whatever way that's best for the film. The festival clearly is the most effective way to do it because the film gets a massive profile, it gets wide coverage from the world's press which can be very helpful, but it can equally be very damaging. If you're in the market, it's a much harder game because it can be difficult to get noticed. Buyers are of course watching the market screenings but the impact is very different. So you try to get your film into either Competition, Un Certain Regard, Directors' Fortnight, Critics' Week... any one of those gets massive attention on a daily basis.

If your project does make an official section, you've got about three days in Cannes per film to make a hit for yourself, and three days to make the optimum sales. If they love it, it goes crazy; if they don't, nobody even looks at you, and a film can be destroyed like that. A producer will want to be in Cannes... they all want to be in Cannes! Great, if you've got the right product for it, but just to be in Cannes for Cannes' sake can be as destructive as it can be successful. I've had both ends of that scale. I've even been involved with successful films that were ultimately a box office failure... an example was "The Best Intentions", the Bille August film for which we won the Palme d'Or and the Best Actress award in 1992. The Palme d'Or... it was the worst thing that could have happened to us. We won, but the press didn't want us to win, so all the critics were saying, "If you want to see a boring Swedish film, this is the one to go and see." And as a result, the film didn't take a penny, anywhere in the world. So that was an example of a film that failed by succeeding. Had "The Player" or "Howard's End" [also in competition that year] won, and we just won the Best Actress award, we'd probably have been much more successful on release than we were. The support would have been more positive.

So sometimes you can go there, you get a film in, nobody pays attention - that's the worst thing that can happen, or you can get too much attention, as in this case, and the film just doesn't succeed. But essentially the sales agent's job is: "Here's my film, get attention for it, and sell the hell out of it." Then the other part of the role kicks in: doing the deals, the licensing, chasing the money, chasing the release dates, ensuring that the job is done properly, the proper title is used, the credit blocks are according to contract, that the right amount of money is spent on releasing the film, and then you have to collect the money if it makes it. So it's a whole strategy... it's a full-service agency deal. It isn't about, "Here's a movie, get the movie, take the commission, run home." You've got to work very hard to get your films noticed. From the moment you start building a marketing profile for the picture, to the moment it's released and you're out there collecting the money, there's a whole madness that goes with it. So, yes, sales agents earn their commission.

BC: These days, how far ahead, and what sort of preparation do you do for Cannes?
BS: Well, depending on which bit you're involved in, it probably begins back in November, or thereabouts, because the festival sections start looking at films around that time. You then have between November and, probably to be safe, the beginning of April, to get your films seen by whichever section you are after. It's a highly political thing because each of the different sections are not all close mates... everything has a pecking order and you have to adhere to that pecking order to do it right. It's highly political. That's the festival aspect of it

and that involves an expensive build up. The costs start when you are invited to participate and very often they don't accept you immediately. They'll say: "We can't tell you now... you'll have to wait, we'll let you know". This is a horrendous time because you don't want to start spending unnecessarily on work that you will never use. Then suddenly you get the call, six weeks before the start of Cannes and all hell breaks loose because not only do you have to subtitle prints of the film in French, you have to hire publicists, you have to get hotel rooms, you have to make sure that the director and artists are available and pay for them to get there, and so on. Cannes is a hugely expensive thing to be involved with, particularly the Competition. The festival itself doesn't pay for very much: three night's accommodation for the director and the two leading artists, that's it. No flights, no per diem, nothing. So anything that you do for the artists - and very few actors will fly anything less than first class - you have to pay for it out of the budget agreed with the producers. So you have to build a budget in keeping with the size of the film. Being a sales agent is a 'deep pockets' business because you've got to cash-flow all of these items... you'll recoup it from the sales made, but if you don't make the sales, you don't recoup the money!

If you're just in the Market section which is the screenings in the Riviera, or on the Rue d'Antibes, matters are very different because it's not dissimilar to the American Film Market or MIFED... you simply book a screening room, take an ad in a daily or a 'bumper', invite the buyers and people come or they don't. There's not the huge attendance expenses involved, there's not the whole build up involved, you probably don't need publicists, you don't have to have parties etc... but of course, you can if you want.

BC: How does a typical day pan out for you these days in Cannes?
BS: It's just meetings, meetings, meetings! It's a very long day and Cannes is a very long festival, it is extremely debilitating. You begin early... let's imagine you get up at 7am, you've probably got a breakfast, you're probably meeting someone at breakfast because there are only so many half hours in the day, or maybe you have staff meetings. So you have a breakfast at, let's say, 8am, you're in the office probably by quarter to nine. At nine o'clock the meetings start on the button. Depending on what sort of films you've got... if you've got films no-one wants it's probably not so difficult, but if you have a film that everybody's after or a slate of films that buyers are after, you are having a meeting every half an hour until around 1pm. Then with any luck, you get a break to go out for a while, but probably with a buyer or a producer. You get to leave the hotel or the stand, to eat either on the beach or you grab a sandwich somewhere, or you've got an official luncheon with someone. Back again, 2.30pm to do the whole thing again... half-hours. It can finish any time, but let's say around 6pm.

If you've got an official screening to attend, you've then got to run like crazy to get yourself dressed up because you've got to put on a tux every time you go to one of the main screenings.

If you're not going to the screenings, the chances are you've got an official drinks 'do'... somebody's always having a cocktail party! Then the chances are, you've got a dinner, either official or semi-formal, with somebody. Following that, if you're not attending a film party, there's that 'thing' everybody gets into, the networking that happens after screenings and after dinner, where people sit around at the various bars, such as the Petit Majestic. In the early days of going to Cannes you probably do it until three or four in the morning, go to bed, then you're back up at seven! Strictly for the young in my opinion! So the days are very long.

I think people have a vision of, "Oh, they're all sitting around drinking gin and tonics and thoroughly enjoying themselves and getting a nice tan." For a sales agent, that just doesn't happen. You're sitting in a hotel room or an office or a villa or whatever it is, just pitching to the buyers who come and see you. Usually you know the buyers - these are people you've dealt with for years - they come around, they want to know what you've got or have coming, when are you screening and so on. The idea is that they come in, see you, collect the news, leave, see the screenings, come back, and hopefully, do the deals. It's very busy at the beginning, hopefully you're even busier at the end, but that's only a result of whether the marketing and the film has worked or not.

So the day is a conglomeration of half-hour meetings, breakfasts, lunches, dinners, screenings, and then 'network drinking'. The Petit Majestic thing is seen as a bit of a, "It's the Brits getting pissed in Cannes," but it has its importance in terms of networking, particularly meeting new independent producers, because that's where they are. They're not in the Carlton - they can't afford it. You get to meet one person who introduces you to someone else etc... it's a great networking place.

So the day is long and there are 12 of them. I don't do as much of the evening thing anymore. I'm at the age where I can't handle it... I can't do that and still get up and do a whole day's work, so something has to give.

BC: Is it common for sales agents to listen to pitches from producers in Cannes, either for projects in development or completed films?
BS: I actually try and put producers off that, for a number of different reasons. Firstly, a lot of producers from Britain go and see British sales agents. Why? They're all here. It's better to meet with a sales agent in June or July when they're not as busy - you might as well see them when they're quiet and you've got their whole attention. I try and advise producers not to do this at festivals or markets. If you are talking to a large company where they've got dedicated acquisitions people, it's probably fine because the acquisitions people sit with the producers and talk about projects, and get pitched at, leaving the sales agents to doing their selling. But if it's a small company, it's quite likely that the people who do the acquisitions

are also the sellers. They haven't got the time. They're totally focussed on what they've got to sell: "These are my movies, this is what I've got to sell now, I haven't got time to talk to you and even if I have, I'm looking over your shoulder to see who's walking in the door."

It's far better to either arrange to see them before you come down, although the pre-market time can be equally busy in many cases. So it's best to think logically about when a sales agent will be the least busy. They're back from the AFM in March, so probably the whole of March they're free. They're probably also free for most of June and July. Once the 'selling' year starts, the whole marketing focus starts, most haven't got any time to give you at these events.

So actually, I think Cannes offices are the worst possible places for sales agents to hear pitches. The drinks things are different because at those events, sales agents tend to be a bit more relaxed and even though they are looking around the room trying to figure out who they need to speak to, they're away from the cliff face. If you want to see foreign companies, that's fine, but wanting to see people from your own country... that's crazy! So my advice would be: don't do it there, they're not really listening, not as much as they would be when you see them at home.

BC: Have you had any memorable pitches either at Cannes or outside of the festival; memorable for the right or the wrong reasons?
BS: I have heard some good ones, but mostly they are too apologetic. Not many people rehearse their pitch. They would do well to stand in front of a mirror and talk to themselves at home about their pitch because the apologetic approach is a bit daft given the importance of the presentation. It has to be sold to me, because I'm going to have to sell it to someone else. So it's important that you convince me... I'm feeding off the pitcher, so how can I get excited about it if they spend the whole time apologising for one element or another?

Because of the kind of background I've had... at Film Four etc, we had a commissioning structure and we didn't pick up many third party projects so pitches weren't high on my list of things to listen to. We were really only representing Film Four projects. People didn't pitch me because they knew we didn't really acquire. Similarly at Renaissance, we had acquisitions people, so I've never really devoted a huge amount of time to this. But my experience of the ones I've heard, and there've been many good ones, is that an awful lot of people are too apologetic and not enough rehearsing done.

Actually, a very important word for producers is: *homework*. Do your homework on almost every level; your pitch and who you're going to pitch to, because there's no use seeing every sales agent as some of them simply don't handle your kind of project. If you've got an art house project showing it to someone who handles vampire movies is completely absurd. You've just wasted an hour of your time, and theirs. You should go through the bumper editions [of the trade magazines] at any of the markets. They've got every sales agent in them, with all the projects they're handling. You can tell what sort of films they specialise in. You've got the people, what they selling, who to approach, phone numbers, all the rest of it. But very few people do this kind of homework. They would be far better off saying to themselves "OK, I'm going to Cannes, I do want to see these people. I'm British, so I don't want to see the Brits, so what I'll do is concentrate on the Americans. So I'll get 10 American companies, and I research those guys, and I know what they sell, so when I meet them I'm able to talk about their existing catalogue." Sales agents are naturally impressed if you recognise that they've done something you approve of. Do your homework on them, know what they sell, know what their successes have been, and don't talk too much about their failures! Then pitch your movie with confidence, and really learn the pitch, learn what it is you're talking about. Don't just go in with a bunch of, "This is going to be the best film ever made. This is a kind of cross between "Gone With The Wind" and "Spiderman"." They really don't want to hear that kind of stuff. They just want to hear about this film - they don't want it compared to anything. So, homework... a big word.

BC: Assuming you had formed a relationship with a producer and you were going to take their film to Cannes, what sort of materials would you have expected them to produce for you?

BS: Actually, none in terms of marketing. A lot of new producers think they need to produce posters and stuff. They don't because that's really the sales agent's job. As I said earlier, the sales agent is marketing to the buyer. It's a very particular kind of marketing and it's not creating a film poster in the same way as a distributor does. What you need is all the background information, you know, the credit block content, what are your arrangements with your artists, who's above whom, above titles, below titles, left of titles, who's on the front-end credits of the film itself. All the stuff which is background, the information that the sales agent needs to feed from to create their materials. It's extremely important. Many people forget things like music clearances... has this been dealt with? All of this background information should be provided to the sales agent in a form that is easily legible, in a file... "Here's my credit block, this is the music, these are the clearances, what you can do with this, what you can't," all of that is essential information.

Another thing that is terribly important for new producers, and I'm sure they've all probably had this beaten into them... is STILLS. Very few people think enough about stills. You can never have too many stills, or at least, too many of the right stills. And you need to hire a stills photographer for the production, not your brother-in-law with a camera! Other important things... unit publicity work, EPKs (electronic press kits)... fantastically important nowadays.

Artists can't travel as much as they used to so you need EPKs. It's all those things and it's not a big secret - you've only got to ask a seasoned producer, "Give me three things that I should have ready?" And they'll usually say, "Stills, unit publicity, and credits." So, it's information that the sales agent will use. They don't want you second-guessing them. They don't want you producing a poster, producing a trailer, producing a show reel, because all of those things are generally done wrong... in the nicest possible way! Agents know what their buyers need. So information is the key. Leave the rest to them.

BC: Do you have a memorable Cannes anecdote you like to recount?
BS: I can't think of anything wildly memorable... there have been some great moments, and I've had some enormous fun, but they tend to be part of an overall... like the "Trainspotting" party, a fabulous experience, endlessly tiring doing it, but when it happened and it was such a huge success... that was great.

BC: Have you had any interesting encounters with a big celebrity in Cannes?
BS: A couple of years ago I was on one of the boats... I don't know whether it was the Soho House boat or someone's boat... I was having drinks and I recognised this actor, who's name has completely escaped me now... an English actor. I'd seen him on some TV commercials, but mostly I knew him from the fact that we'd done a film at Film Four called "True Blue", which was about the [Oxford vs Cambridge] Boat Race and he was in the Oxford boat. I recognised the actor, and the main reason I recognised him was because a few months before, a Japanese guy had brought me a tape of a movie that this actor was in, and he said, "Would I look at this for representation of the film?" I watched the movie and there was this same actor, speaking fluent Japanese and I thought, "This English guy's amazing, he speaks fluent Japanese!" So I saw him standing there and I went over to him, introduced myself and said, "I saw this film of yours recently. A couple of months ago, this Japanese guy brought me..." And he went, "Oh yeah," and reeled off the title. And from right out from behind him steps... Salma Heyak (who I'm a huge fan of - this is a gorgeous woman!). She steps in, puts her arm in his and says, "You saw that movie?" And I went... I just blanked. I said, "Yeah..." thinking, "What the hell's she doing with him?" They were an item... this was pre Ed Norton. We talked about this movie for about 10 or 15 minutes and I'm gazing at, what to me was one of the most gorgeous women in the world, standing with a glass of champagne in my hand thinking, "Not in my wildest dreams did I think I'd be talking to her" because I couldn't have met her any other way. I wouldn't have walked up to her on the boat and gone, "Oh, Salma Hayek. Hi!" That completely gob-smacked me... I didn't think you could tip me over that way but she did! She was just as lovely as everything I'd imagined and I'm really thrilled about Frida and all that's happened to her since. That was a great moment.

BC: Do you have any favourite places to eat when you're in Cannes?

BS: Yeah, there are lots of wonderful places that I eat at for different kinds of reasons. You know, there's casual, there's formal... I love eating on the port or in the old town on the hill. I love going up there... there's the type of restaurants up there you'd be hard pushed to find anywhere else in the world. Also on the old port itself, the pizza place, La Pizza... that I like for totally informal eating. And next door to it is Gaston Gastounette, which is a terrific seafood restaurant; the best soupe de poisson! But mostly I'm bad at going back to places. I love moving on so I'm always looking for the next one... I don't really have places where I think, "I'm going to go back there." I like to find new ones and each year when I go, I find something different that I think, "Well, this is nice," and for that year it becomes the restaurant of choice. I found a Vietnamese restaurant a few years ago near the Martinez and it was just lovely. But generally I move on.

You certainly don't need to eat in expensive places in Cannes, and if you're not on expenses, you probably don't want to! If you go back towards the railway station, three streets behind the Rue d'Antibes, you can eat there very cheaply. I've done that as an independent a lot. You can have dinner for £10, with wine... you don't have to eat this side of the bright lights. I think a lot of people don't do enough experimenting and seeking that sort of place out, but you can eat cheaply if you want to.

BC: What about places to network/socialise, you touched on the Petit Carlton and Petit Majestic earlier?

BS: Well the Petit Carlton has gone now of course, but Petit Majestic... yes, it's taken over that mantle. It's just so crowded now; it's frighteningly busy these days. I suppose somebody will find somewhere else sooner or later. I think, depending on what you're looking for... the Majestic terrace is phenomenal, but you need a mortgage to buy a drink! It really depends who you're looking for because there are a lot of people there, but for networking in terms of what we do as independents, then I think the Petit Majestic is pretty much the place.

BC: Do you have any specific advice for future 'Cannes virgins', particularly producers who are coming to try and drum up interest in their completed or in-development project?

BS: Well, I do think get yourself a sales agent... I would say that wouldn't I, but I think you save yourself enormous amounts of time. I'll give you an example... I won't name names, but it involves a producer/actor/director last year at Cannes. He'd been to see me for advice but he'd never actually said, "I want to find a sales agent." He said, "We're doing this ourselves." He clearly had a bit of money behind him, from somewhere, because he'd helped to finance the film, acted in it, directed it, and helped produce it. He was down there with the writer and a producer. They spent a fortune on fly-posting, which by the way just doesn't hit the right people... you might think it does, but what it really does is hit all the other independent producers! There's no impact with that stuff. They must have spent £25,000 to go to Cannes, getting themselves there, living there, posters, flyers... and nothing happened. The film never got sold, it never went anywhere. You're wasting time, you're wasting your time AND you're ruining the prospects for the film. Get a sales agent, if you think it is good enough.

If it isn't good enough and no sales agents want it, you've got to do that stuff yourself haven't you? But if it can be avoided, avoid it. The job of the sales agent is to put up the marketing money, to market it right and to find the right buyer to buy it. Doing it guerrilla style... you might get lucky, it might work, but the chances are it won't. Not in that high-octane environment. There's lots of money there: I mean those posters you see on the Croisette cost $50,000 or more to place and I don't even notice them these days! They're there and a lot of seasoned attendees don't even notice them. To my mind it's just vanity advertising. I wouldn't dream of buying one of those things. I did it once when I first went to Cannes, I thought this was the thing to do, and then I realised, actually, there are many more effective ways of spending marketing dollars. The posters are just part of what the public sees, which isn't the point from the agent's perspective.

So I think my advice would be: think really hard about whether you want to spend this time/money. If you engage a sales agent, you won't be excluded; you just have to make yourself a part of it along with the sales agency team. You ensure they understand that you want to be included, you really do want to be involved, you want to come along and be involved in the decision-making process. But on the other hand, that doesn't mean that you can sit and watch the sales agent do their job because that's no help to anyone. Don't pester the sales agent... once you've got one, for God's sake, trust them! Going in to their offices every two minutes and asking, "Have we sold it?" doesn't actually endear you to the people in the office. If you are green, then it's hard not to do some of these things, but I would say, asking around a bit... again, homework. I would say, ask a few people about the sales agent's reputation. If you've looked in the bumpers and you've seen the films they represent, you might know one of the existing producers. Ask the producers if this particular sales agent is any good, because if the guy says, "Don't go near them, they're terrible," you don't want to waste your time... that's another one off the list.

So I think get the guys you want, the people you feel comfortable with, trust them to do the job and then let them do that job. You can be a part of it with them, you can always be involved. They'll keep you up to date... they'll only shut you out if you become a pain! I've had producers just come and sit in the office and often I've just had to say, "I'm very sorry... go have a coffee... leave. We're dealing with your movie... there's your poster, but I just can't have you sitting here watching us like a hawk! I didn't go and watch you on the set!" You have to trust pros. As a producer you hire a cameraman, an editor, you hire a soundman, they're all pros... so is the sales agent. Hire them, trust them, let them get on with it.

Jane Wright
BBC Films (Finance)

BC: When did you first go to Cannes and what were your impressions of the city and the festival?

JW: I first went to Cannes in 1987 when I worked for a US distribution company. I'd been to France before and I liked the city of Cannes... it was pretty and I was excited about being there again. I can't say I loved the festival. I found it huge, I found it daunting, and I had an experience there that's been repeated almost every year. For some reason it involves the Carlton Hotel: when I go in, the lobby is always full of huge posters and they all seem to have great splashes of garish red... red dresses flying up, red blood, guns, whatever, and I go into a two-day funk thinking: "What on Earth I am doing in this business?" Because my experience of the film industry, which is 20 years this year, has been mostly in art film, I tend to find the pure exploitation side of Cannes harder to take - it throws me off every single year. That's what I most remember about my first experience - being overwhelmed by the size of the industry and how many big players there are.

BC: These days, how do you prepare ahead of Cannes for the time you will be spending there?

JW: I think anyone, no matter what they're doing, needs to prepare a lot. In a sense, you are never prepared enough because our daily work lives are so busy. My own preparations have changed over the years. I first went to Cannes as part of an American distribution company, subsequently went to Cannes when I worked for the IFP [Independent Feature Project] as the Director of the Independent Feature Film Market... both had different purposes so therefore a different set of preparations. At BBC Films I'm part of an organisation that's a film financier, but we also have rights to sell, so I need to be prepared on both sides. I've also found myself at Cannes actually selling a slate of films when I was the Acting CEO at a London sales company, now called The Works.

So the preparation for each organisation and each function differs but basically, you have to know in each case what your product is and what you hope to achieve. You need to have read everything - you can't sell a project you haven't read, you can't sell a film you haven't seen. You really need to be in the know, and not just about the product you have, but how it relates to associated films, what's happened to that filmmaker in the past, and what's coming up. It's the extraneous information which is unending, but you have to gather what information and material you think is the most pertinent.

BC: So how does a typical day in Cannes during the festival tend to pan out for you?
JW: Generally I'm aware of having to get up very early. I usually start by looking through the day's activities and thinking about what I'm going to wear, particularly whether I am going to get a chance to go back to the hotel before an evening event. I'll also ensure that I have the correct materials I'll need for the day and know whom I'm meeting for breakfast. In my job at BBC Films, I go into the office and read the trades. Ideally I like to see the 8.30 movie at the Palais at least every other day. I find that because of meetings that have been set up, it's often very hard for me to get to festival films and it's so depressing if I get through Cannes without seeing a single film. So I think it's important for people like myself who don't have to see films for acquisition purposes, to try to see movies anyway. It helps us keep a sense of being in the film business.

As the morning progresses, my life becomes dictated by new circumstances... by my boss and by my colleagues, as much as by my pre-set objectives. So I have meetings, meetings, meetings, meetings, lunches, dinners, meetings, meetings, and then maybe a cocktail party and another event afterwards where you're again meant to meet more people or be seen.

BC: 8.30 screenings... that's 8.30 in the morning, right?
JW: [smiles] Yes, but all the good acquisitions people I know are having 7.30am meetings with their teams because that's the best time for them to get organised to see all the movies they need to cover. So 'early to rise, late to bed' is the rule of Cannes.

BC: In your current capacity at BBC Films, are you hearing people pitch concepts or films requiring funding?
JW: No, that's not what my job is so I rarely hear pitches. In fact, I tend to avoid them. Our development team are there and hear pitches all day long. My job involves pitching our projects to other financiers. I'm trying to meet with the key decision-makers at the major US distributors, sales agents and other funding bodies. Because I'm pitching BBC Films' projects, I'm discussing films of a pedigree that are already part funded which makes it much easier.

BC: Cannes is known largely as a finished product market. In your experience, both with BBC Films and prior to that, is it common for much in the way of development deals to be done during the festival?

JW: I think that there's a lot of it happening, but I would have to say that I think that most of the financing deals that are done are at an organisational level. I think it's very tough for independent producers who go there to try to finance their films from scratch.

The financing people are there - for example sales agents - but their primary focus is to sell. There are circumstances where they might listen to a pitch but they'll usually take the material back home for consideration. It's most likely that the deal isn't going to be tied up in Cannes. At an 'organisational level' you find that a lot of financing activity happens. A project will already be set up with one financier who then can bring others on board at Cannes.

BC: Again, in your experience with BBC Films or before that, if you were going to discuss projects in development, are there specific things that you are looking for the producer to show you?
JW: Something that sounds realistic and reasonably fully-formed even if only an idea. "I have a script, it's been written by so and so, we want to do it this year, here's why I think it's a fantastic property, I have interest from so and so." You don't have to have complete cast certainty but you do need to know who you want to cast in the main roles. What's important to avoid is pitching something that's not fully-formed, or displaying complete ignorance about the three films already out in the market place that are just like yours. Also avoid saying something which is plainly untrue. For instances, at BBC Films if we've got a particular actor already lined up in two of our movies, saying your film is going next month with this actor will not impress us. You need a compelling story and the elements you're attaching to it should be realistic.

BC: Do you have a memorable anecdote that you like to tell over the dinner table when the topic of Cannes emerges in the conversation?
JW: I think one of the nicest experiences for me was when my husband had his very first production, "Heavy", in the Directors' Fortnight, and that was lovely because we felt treated well. I had other work to do there but that experience on the filmmaking side of the business meant it was a fun year rather than hard work. That was great.

BC: Do you have any favourite places that you like to eat when you're in Cannes?
JW: Yes, Le Petite Lardon. I can't remember the street name, but I know exactly where it is. I just love it. It's a tiny little restaurant with a lovely atmosphere and I go there a lot. I have eaten at some of the finer restaurants outside of Cannes like Le Colum d'Or and Moulin des Mougins, but they are definitely not my regular haunts.

BC: Do you have any favourite socialising/networking venues in Cannes?

JW: I love the BBC Films party. That's very corporate I know, but I love our events - they're great because it does feel like family and you invite people you haven't seen for a long time. Of course the Petit Carlton is sadly missed [Ed - now resurrected!], and Le Petit Majestic is the number two. You also go to the bar at the Majestic hotel, and you go to the Carlton... but you know I have a problem with that! I'm kidding... the Carlton Terrace is absolutely fine, but it's really the parties and late night Petit Majestic that are my favourites.

BC: Lastly, do you have any specific advice for future Cannes virgins, particularly producers who are looking to sell their film in Cannes?

JW: Get a map before you go. Seriously, try to understand the layout and try to figure out where things are before you get there. Have a realistic set of expectations: worst case scenario, you go to see Cannes and only see how it operates; best case, your film gets financed. But you've got to be realistic about people's time constraints, and where you sit in the pecking order. People might see that as a little cynical and I don't mean it that way, but it's realistic. Everybody feels much the same way - you're just trying to do your own little thing which is going to be eventually a very small part of this big industry. And yes, of course we all hope we'll have hit films, whether we're with an organisation, or whether we're individuals, but if you're not approaching it with some degree of humility, then you can get psychologically crushed. That's why I believe building a realistic set of expectations for yourself is important.

A lot of people also get really upset if they're not invited to loads of parties or if they can't get tickets to the right parties. Once you've been there enough times, you can not go but tell people you did! They won't know because ultimately, it really doesn't make any difference. I think there's too much youthful anxiety over what kind of parties you can get into. Sometimes, going home and getting a decent night's sleep is actually far more worthwhile. Likewise, ending up at the Petit Majestic and just having fun can be a lot better than having tried to claw your way into some famous distributor party and not made it, where you're just going to end up feeling miserable.

Ben Roberts
BFI (Film Commissioner)

The BFI was founded in 1933 as a UK charity governed by a Royal Charter. The BFI combines cultural, creative and industrial roles, bringing together the BFI National Archive and BFI Reuben Library, film distribution, exhibition at BFI Southbank and BFI IMAX, publishing and festivals. The BFI also awards Lottery funding to film production, distribution, education, audience development and market intelligence and research.

BC: When did you first attend Cannes and what were your impressions of the festival?
BR: I don't remember the specific year, but it would have been about 15 or 16 years ago. I went as a junior buyer for an independent distributor called Metrodome. I remember my boss told me to enjoy it the first time as after that it would always be hard work. His advice was to go out and make the most of it, stay up all night, see as many films as possible, and just soak it up... which I did.

But I think Cannes is a huge experience. Until you get there, you don't realise it's actually lots of different things to different people. You've got a festival – a lot of which you watch from a distance – and then there's the market, which can feel quite down and dirty. Plus there's a lot of invisible activity happening in the apartments above and beyond the Croisette, which of course you don't even really see. So I think everyone finds their own version of Cannes. But what's most striking is that it feels as if every layer of the industry is there in some form or another – from studio executives down to someone going with their first film.

BC: And how did you find the city itself?
BR: It was very busy – impossible to travel in by car so forget any notion of mechanised transport getting you around. I actually stayed up the road in Juan-les-Pins my first year. We got accommodation late and figured it was cheaper there. The idea was we could use the train to get into Cannes in the morning and we'd just be able to get a cab back at night. But getting a cab late was virtually impossible.

As for Cannes itself, it's expensive. It's difficult to buy a sandwich on the go, difficult to grab a coffee without spending 10 to 15 euros, and difficult to find somewhere to plonk yourself down for any period of time. What I came to realise was, in Cannes you can end up with quite a lot of dead time between meetings, or if something cancels, or if you leave a screening early. So what do you do with yourself? I discovered it was quite good to find a wall that can become *your* wall – a place where you can sit and kill half an hour. Otherwise, you walk up and down the Rue d'Antibes a million times, spending a fortune in the process... better to find a wall.

But I think the city is also quite a fascinating place. It kind of unravels and reveals itself over time in terms of the expanse of where activity takes place. You realise it's not all about the Croisette. In fact, a lot of activity is associated with the Rue d'Antibes, the Village International, and beyond. It takes a couple of years to actually get your head around the whole place during the festival... things like what's easy to get to, where you're wasting your time, and where certain communities hang out.

BC: Where is the BFI normally based during Cannes?
BR: We're based at the UK Film Centre, which is in the Village International outside the Palais. But the BFI also has a kind of ambient presence elsewhere in that everybody is around to take meetings and watch films. The UK Film Centre also brings together the various public agencies from around the country and we host a programme of meetings, events, and talks. A certain proportion of our time is also spent catching up with films, filmmakers, sales companies, and distributors, as it's important for us to ensconce ourselves in the festival and keep abreast of all the activity.

Our priority with the UK Film Centre these days is to make it a business-focussed environment, whereas historically, I think it's had an element of just being a handy place to hang out. It will always be a base for people, but the programme is now prioritised for people to go there and do business, which probably slightly elevates the level of participant in the Centre. That said, there will always be programmes that relate to newer filmmakers as well.

BC: What services does the BFI offer in Cannes to UK filmmakers?
BR: Well, this is where we've had to think long and hard about our purpose in Cannes. If you're based in London most of the time – or elsewhere in the UK – why spend all that money going to Cannes to engage in UK-specific activity when it could be done any other time at home... when people are more sane, less tired, less drunk, and have more time to focus? What we want to avoid is making the UK Film Centre a space where, for example, we give out advice on the tax credit to UK filmmakers. We should be doing that year-round anyway, so I

would encourage UK filmmakers to come to us whenever they want that information, rather than in Cannes. There, it's just not a valuable use of anyone's time.

But what I would say is, on the ground in Cannes there are always going to be talks and programmes of events which will provide useful insights to UK filmmakers. There'll also be opportunities to connect with people such as international distributors, sales companies, and foreign co-producers – a certain amount of which we can help facilitate, or at least send UK producers off in the right direction. That said, from my experience as a sales agent, I'd discourage UK filmmakers from too much cold door-knocking with new projects. Your time is actually probably better spent learning about international opportunities, co-production, and getting a sense of the reality of the business, as opposed to coming with 20 copies of your script under your arm and hoping that will open some doors.

BC: And what about services for filmmakers from other countries?
BR: The BFI can provide a certain amount of connections through contacts and information. We also provide networking opportunities where people can meet and greet. We can explain to filmmakers from outside the UK how they can work in a financial production capacity with the UK. Obviously all the film agencies from the nations and regions are available to explain what they offer in terms of locations and skills – everyone is there with an export and inward-investment hat on to promote the UK's chief selling points. So you'd be able to get all of the information you needed about shooting in the UK, accessing crews, tax breaks, and other kinds of things which would be useful for international filmmakers. But again, nothing that you could not get from us at the BFI year-round through a phone call or an email. We always make ourselves available on that front.

BC: In your role with the BFI, what does a typical day involve for you in Cannes?
BR: It's quite a mix. It's very important that we're across new films that are screening in the festival and the market, that we're on top of new filmmakers, and what's successful and what's not working. So a certain amount of time is spent watching films, a certain amount of time spent manning the UK Film Centre, and a certain amount of time in the surgeries and events we run. In a 9-5 day, it is probably split evenly over those sorts of things. In the evening, it's pretty much like anybody else's Cannes. It's a stack-up of a couple of drinks events, a dinner, another film... it tends to be pretty varied.

BC: Do you have an interesting Cannes anecdote from any of your visits to the festival?
BR: Well, I can disavow myself of any credit for my first acquisition in Cannes, which was Andrew Dominik's "Chopper". It was my first Cannes and a very simple case of reading a map wrong. I was supposed to be having a meeting at a hotel, but the map I had showed

both cinemas and hotels. I got the keying wrong and went to a cinema instead of the hotel. By the time I realised, it was too late so I cancelled the meeting and stayed to watch the film, which was "Chopper". Nobody else was at the screening so we bought it and it was a big hit. Based on that, my bosses thought I was some sort of acquisitions genius and promoted me.

So I think there's a kind of haphazardness to Cannes which is often worth going with – a certain kind of pinball element you should embrace because you don't always know what you're going to see or who you're going to meet. A random connection might prove to be a useful one. Most of the time I think they probably won't, but it does happen. I did have dinner with The Rock [Dwayne Johnson] once in Cannes. He ate two cold jacket potatoes and that was it. I guess that's the secret to looking like The Rock.

I also had a terrible experience a few years back with Richard Kelly's second film, "Southland Tales". I knew Richard from "Donnie Darko", which we'd previously picked up. I'd moved to Universal and we took on "Southland Tales". It was a classic example of where Cannes can go horribly wrong. The film was in Competition against everyone's better judgement. The film actually wasn't ready, but they'd selected it anyway and everyone was wondering why they did. It was an unmitigated disaster. It killed the film. I think the lesson there is probably that Cannes isn't the best place for everything. You really have to think long and hard if Cannes is right. If you're not ready, go somewhere else, because if it goes wrong it can be quite a devastating experience and becomes incredibly disproportionate. It was terrible for us and terrible for Richard. In hindsight, Richard should have had some better advice like, "You know what? This isn't the right place for it. You've been selected, but what does your gut tell you?"

BC: That advice has come through from quite a few people I've spoken to. Filmmakers seem to get fixated on being at a festival like Cannes or Sundance, but end up hurting the film's chances by rushing and ultimately showing something that's not ready.
BR: Yes. You've got to think about how visible you're going to be. There's so much white noise at an event like Cannes so you have to be pretty confident that you can break through that. Obviously there are surprises every year, but I think you can be more strategic. When I was selling films in my last job we deliberately took two of our titles - Gareth Edwards' "Monsters" and Ben Wheatley's "Kill List" - to SXSW because we knew no other big films were going to be there. We thought there was a good chance "Monsters" could be the most exciting film at that festival. All we needed was to do an American sale to get the ball rolling and we knew all the buyers would be there because they had nothing else to go to. Whereas in Cannes, I think you have to accept that although you'll have a screening slot, God knows how many other films will also be screening at the same time. So somehow you have to cut

through the noise to get people come to your screening. You need to think very carefully and strategically about whether there are other more appropriate routes to take.

BC: Do you have any favourite places to eat in Cannes?
BR: There's a great pizza restaurant called L'Avion – it's got a biplane outside – which is on a side road near the Palais. I like to hide in the back of that. But if you want to see half of the British film industry on any given night... or actually the US indie sector as well, then La Pizza is the place everyone seems to hang out.

That reminds me of a hilarious story from a few years back... where I got slapped around the face by the woman at one of the restaurants on the Rue Saint-Antoine. I don't remember its name, but we'd booked a number of nights at this restaurant when I was working at Protagonist. For a variety of reasons, we had to cancel a couple of the bookings, but we did so ahead of time. One night when eight of us were there, it was just a catalogue of errors. We'd ordered some wine but had to send it back because it was corked. At the end of the night I gave them my credit card and the woman came back and said, "Who is Mr Roberts?" She then grabbed me by the chin, slapped me around the face twice and said, "That's for not cancelling your booking last night!" Which of course we had actually done... and we were about to spend 800€ on dinner! That was my favourite place, but I've never been back since.

BC: What about places to socialise and network?
BR: I have to say, I'm actually quite an 'early to bed' Cannes-goer these days. What I find amazing about Cannes is that it's the most important week in a lot of the film industry's year... it's the equivalent of an accounting firm doing a year-end tax return, but going out and getting hammered every night while they do. It seems remarkable to me that people are probably less 'on it', for want of a better word, at such as critical time. I've always gone to the festival with a specific job so I tend to go to bed by 10, which sounds ridiculous for Cannes. But I think the reason other people don't do that is because you never know who you're going to have a conversation with at two in the morning.

But the main hangouts for Brits are generally The Grand terrace and the Petit Majestic. There's also that road that runs from the Grand behind the Croisette [Rue Frères Pradignac] - that's a good place to hang out. For the last few years The Grand terrace has probably been *the* place to hang out, but it's expensive to drink there. Then again, there aren't many places where it's not. But overall I think people tend to get absorbed into Cannes as the evening goes on so it's probably quite hard to strategize who you may or may not see.

BC: Do you have any other general advice for filmmakers, either from the UK or elsewhere, who are coming to Cannes for the first-time?

BR: Well, going back to what I said earlier, I think the biggest question would be: should you go to Cannes? But if you've already made the decision to go, then I would say it's really a question of, what do you want to achieve from your visit? I think there's a lot of education to be gleaned from your first visit to Cannes. You can look at the Market and see where your project fits in, who's selling films and what types of films they are selling. You can also pick up the dailies [trade magazines] and see what types of films are being bought and how the press is responding. I think you can learn a lot just from getting a sense of that activity in the industry. Also, see as many films as you can and read their reviews... take the temperature of the market and the industry as a whole because it then informs you as to whether you're on the right track or not.

And as I said before, don't bother bringing scripts... or too much physical printed material for that matter. When I worked in sales a lot of people used to come and drop off materials for us. It certainly didn't go in the bin, but it all went into a crate that went back to London and we didn't really look at anything until after the festival. So I'd say, think long and hard about what you actually need to spend money printing and producing. It can be very expensive and you have to carry it around, but the reality is that, there on the ground, people have a job to do and often won't get a chance to look at much of it. There are probably other strategic moments to target people for sales representation or distribution. And you'll undoubtedly get a lot of grateful executives thanking you for not troubling them then and there.

But in a nutshell, I would just say, two questions... "Should I go?" and if so, "What am I trying to achieve there?"

Lise Corriveau
Telefilm Canada (Film Commissioner)

Telefilm Canada is a federal cultural agency dedicated primarily to the development and promotion of the Canadian film, television, new media and music industries. Telefilm Canada reports to the Department of Canadian Heritage. The Corporation provides financial assistance and strategic leverage to the industry in producing high-quality works – e.g. feature films, drama series, documentaries, children's programming, variety shows and new media products - that reflect Canadian society, including its linguistic duality and cultural diversity.

BC: When did you first visit Cannes and what were your impressions of the city and the festival?

LC: I first attended the Cannes Film Festival in 1997 and was overwhelmed by the sheer size of it. It is a very glamorous affair and can be quite intimidating for a first-timer. Cannes is a very lovely city but becomes totally invaded during the festival and it is very hard to circulate anywhere close to the Croisette.

BC: Where is the Telefilm Canada usually based in Cannes during the festival? Is this always the same place or does it vary form year to year?

LC: Telefilm Canada has been attending the Cannes Film Festival for over 20 years and various venues have been tried depending on the events taking place. The year 2002 proved to be a turning point for the Canadian presence. Telefilm Canada joined the International Village and along with provincial agencies, federal departments, the producers association and a few sponsors, we launched the Canada Pavilion. And since then we have expanded our presence as well as out activities at the Festival.

BC: What services does the Telefilm Canada offer Canadian filmmakers in Cannes?

LC: We coordinate the markets registrations for the Canadian companies participating in the Marché du Film. A series of networking events, such as breakfast meetings and other small gatherings are also organized within the Canada Pavilion in order to assist the Canadian producers to develop their international contacts. We also try to connect various producers looking for co-productions partners. We are also there to act as advisers and fixers to all the Canadian participants.

BC: In the past, has there been anything that Canadian filmmakers expected you to offer them in Cannes, but in reality you don't offer?

LC: Since Canada has been participating for so long, we have constantly reviewed our services and try to adjust from year to year.

BC: What does a typical day consist of for you in Cannes during the festival?

LC: Usually my days starts around 8.30am and ends around midnight. Since I coordinate the Canada Pavilion operations, you have to be ready to react to all sorts of demands from our own industry as well as foreign partners seeking information on the Canadian industry.

BC: What is/are your favourite place(s) to eat in Cannes?

LC: I have quite a few that I like, but I have one in particular that is off the beaten track, off the tourist circuit. I really like to go there to get away from the madness of what the festival is. It is more of a local spot and I would rather keep it to myself. It is my hideaway.

BC: What is/are your favourite Cannes socialising/networking venue(s)?

LC: The Canada Pavilion being a central point of all of our operations brings in many visitors and I am lucky to have the chance to meet very interesting and dynamic people. It is very stimulating. You really get a feel of what the industry is about.

BC: Do you have any advice for future Cannes virgins, particularly first time producers coming to the festival looking to sell their film?

LC: Before you arrive at the festival, you have to be prepared. You have to know why you are attending the festival and set some goals. Some leg-work prior to their arrival is also essential. You have to start planning your meetings at least a month ahead of the event. It is very hard to pin down people sometimes and it is best and easier if early contact has been undertaken.

I would also recommend that if you are looking for a partner, you best learn how to make a good pitch. Have good promo materials ready.

Julie Archet
Screen Australia (Film Commissioner)

Screen Australia is the key Federal Government direct funding body for the Australian screen production industry. Its functions are to support and promote the development of a highly creative, innovative and commercially sustainable Australian screen production industry.

BC: When did you first come to Cannes and what were your impressions of the festival and the city?

JA: My first Cannes was three years ago. I was already working for the Australian Film Commission at that time. I actually grew up in France, where Cannes is of course a big deal - everybody watches the news from Cannes on television. So for me it was a very interesting experience because if you grew up in France you feel that you're very familiar with the festival and all the glamour. But when you come to Cannes for work the first time it's a bit of a circus. For me, I was quite fortunate in that the first time I was coming to work for an organisation and I was very busy. So I probably didn't struggle like a lot of producers who come on their own and don't know what to do or don't have access to people. It can be a big deal if you come on our own.

BC: And how did you find the city itself?

JA: I'd actually been to Cannes before, outside of the festival, so I knew the place fairly well. I think it's a lovely town. Obviously it's a good festival, but I'm pretty sure the fact that it takes place in this charming setting, where you can eat well, has contributed to making it one of the biggest festivals in the world. When you talk to a lot of buyers and producers about Berlin, for example, which is an amazing festival, you tend to hear comments like, "It's great, but it's freezing, it's the middle of winter..." There's not the appeal that Cannes has got, where the climate's good, the town is nice, and there's lots of things to do around Cannes. I'm sure it contributes to the charm of it all.

BC: Where is Screen Australia normally based during Cannes?

JA: We're on the 8th floor at 52 Boulevard de la Croisette, which is between the Carlton and JW Marriott, and not far from The Grand, where all the sales agents are. I believe the

Australians have had the same penthouse apartment, which is transformed into an office, for over 20 years.

BC: What services does Screen Australia offer in Cannes to Australian filmmakers?
JA: We run an office which is open to all Australians. A lot of them end up being more of less based there to take meetings, use the wifi, or take advantage of the reception service. In the evenings, we turn around the space to allow us to run events such as working breakfasts with sales agents, distributors, financiers, festival directors, co-production markets and so on. It's also a place where Australians can network with the people that we line up.

BC: What about for people from other countries?
JA: Well, we just try to answer as many enquiries as we can. We produce a lot of booklets with the line-up of Australian films and a directory of producers attending Cannes. We also deal with a huge number of enquiries from foreign filmmakers looking to meet potential co-production partners. We also work with other screen organisations, such as Telefilm Canada, Scottish Screen, the UK Film Council, and Film France, to organise targeted co-production events where producers can meet these potential partners.

BC: In your role with Screen Australia, what does a typical day involve for you in Cannes?
JA: [Laughs] Start too early, finish too late. During the day I pretty much run the office, with the help of some local staff we employ. I also run all the events in the evening and have to squeeze in meetings in between. So it's quite busy. I don't get to see many films at all. If I see three or four over the festival, I'm really excited. My day normally starts around 8am and I finish my working activity around 11pm. So I spend way too many hours in the office, which makes it hard to see movies.

BC: What's your best Cannes anecdote from the times you've been here?
JA: I think it was the first year I was invited to the closing night party. I walked the red carpet – it wasn't my first red carpet and I normally walk up as fast as possible because it's not really my thing – and suddenly these flashes just started going off around me. I was thinking, "Well obviously this isn't for me" and I turned around and literally right behind me were Dennis Hopper and Benicio del Torro, who was coming to collect his prize for Che. That was quite cool. I don't really have any trashy anecdotes, or at least none I was involved in myself. I have to say it's all been very civilised.

BC: Do you have any favourite places to eat in Cannes?
JA: Yes, but if you put them in the book, I'm never going to be able to go there again [laughs]. I love a good steak, and I also love a good French steak because they know how to cook

them, or 'un-cook' them. I really like to go to La Cave, which is a bistro that doesn't pretend to do anything except meat and great wine. I think it's on Boulevard de la République, near Rue Marceau. My favourite pasta at La Cucina de Laura, on the corner of Rue Hoche and Rue du 24 Août, which is run by an Italian family and they do their own pasta. I also love another old school Italian which seems to be popular with the locals, Vesuvio, which is on the Croisette between the Miramar and the Martinez.

BC: What about places to socialise and network?

JA: Outside of the functions we run, it seems that you'll find a lot of Australians at The Grand. Actually, I've got a theory about that. Australians love a bit of the outdoors and as soon as they saw the garden they were like, "This is where it's at!" If you've got no plans and want to meet Aussies [or pretty much anyone else – Ed], they're all at The Grand on the terrace. I also love the Petit Majestic – there's nothing to it, but there's always people there any time of the day or night.

BC: Do you have any general advice for filmmakers, either from Australia or anywhere else, who are coming to Cannes for the first-time?

JA: I think Cannes is a wonderful place, but it can be absolutely terrifying so you have to come completely prepared. For Australians at least, it costs a lot of money to come to Cannes so you have to make sure you've got the right goals to justify why you're there, unless you've got money to burn. But for most filmmakers you really need to prepare way ahead and try to get in contact with people you're going to try and meet before you arrive. I also think it's helpful for filmmakers to try and think like a sales agent or distributor, and what their priorities might be in Cannes. A lot of producers don't realise that if a sales agent is coming to Cannes for the first week to sell, they've got that pressure, or if they are a buyer, they have to buy. They get everything else done afterwards, if they can. Also, it's worth remembering that partying is great, but being trashed every night and being hung over for your meeting the next morning isn't a good look.

If you're a first-timer, it can also be a great idea to have a mentor – someone who's been to the market before and can introduce you to people. Otherwise, it can be very scary and constant rejection can really sap your confidence. So in a nutshell, my advice would be that you need to be at the right stage of your project (i.e. have it ready to be financed), have made contact way before with people to introduce yourself, have the right marketing materials, and to be as professional as possible.

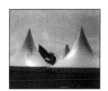  

The Appendices

Appendix I: Websites, Books, Apps

This book contains a large amount of information, but that doesn't mean you should stop here. There are many excellent resources out there that will also help with your visit to Cannes and provide useful or interesting information about the festival.

CannesGuide.com

The companion website for "Cannes - A Festival Virgin's Guide" contains a whole host of useful tools and additional information. Visit the site to get the latest festival news, meet other Cannes contacts, submit your own tips, and access a range of features to help you get the most out of your visit, including:

- Festival Information – updates and the latest buzz on the next festival;
- Accommodation Exchange – free message boards to find or offer festival lodging;
- Travel Desk – good deals on flights and hotels;
- Restaurant Guide – the lowdown on the best places to eat in Cannes for all budgets.
- Message Boards – to share information and meet new Cannes contacts.

Visit **www.cannesguide.com**. And don't forget to follow us on Twitter **@CannesGuide**

Official Festival Websites

Festival de Cannes
www.festival-cannes.org

International Critics' Week
www.semainedelacritique.com

Directors' Fortnight
www.quinzaine-realisateurs.com

L'ACID
www.lacid.org

Marché du Film
www.marchedufilm.com

Short Film Corner
www.cannescourtmetrage.com

Other Useful Websites

City of Cannes
The official web site for the City of Cannes.
www.cannes.fr

FilmFestivals.com
Covering many film festivals including Cannes, filmfestivals.com contains a huge amount of information and has dedicated coverage leading up to and during the event.
www.filmfestivals.com/festival/festival_de_cannes

Google Translate
If your French isn't fantastic, Google's free translation service can help with any websites or other French text you come across.
translate.google.com

The American Pavilion
The official web site for the American Pavilion at Cannes provides details of activities taking place and services available. Membership can be purchased via the site ahead of the festival.
www.ampav.com

UK Film Centre
Provides information and the event schedule for activities taking place in the UK Film Centre during the festival.
www.ukfilmcentre.org.uk

Cannes or Bust
Useful blog site for news and coverage of the film festival and other events in Cannes throughout the year.
www.cannes-or-bust.com

News & Media Coveage

indieWIRE's Cannes
indieWIRE reporters are on the scene in Cannes throughout the festival to provide the latest news, reviews, and interviews, with an indie bias.
www.indiewire.com

Variety
Provides extensive coverage of the festival through their web site, although to access the content in detail you need to be a subscriber.
www.variety.com

The Hollywood Reporter
Also provides extensive coverage of the festival in a dedicated area of their web site. Access to much of the content is for subscribers only, however of all the major trades, The Hollywood Reporter has the most free content available.
www.hollywoodreporter.com.

Screen Daily
Coverage of the festival from an international perspective. The online offering from Screen International is a subscription service, however the rates are reasonable and the reporting extensive.
www.screendaily.com

Recommended Apps

- Festival de Cannes (iOS, Android, Blackberry)
- Cinando (iOS)
- The Hollywood Reporter (iOS)
- Variety (iOS, Android, Blackberry)
- Screen International (iOS)
- Google Translate (iOS, Android)

These apps can be downloaded from the respective app stores for each platform.

Recommended Reading

The following books provide a great way to further explore the fascinating topic of the Cannes Film Festival and the culture and history surrounding it. All of these books and more are available from the bookstore at CannesGuide.com.

Avrich, Barry. "Selling the Sizzle: The Magic and Logic of Entertainment Marketing". Maxworks Publishing Group, 2002.

Dupin, Valerie, and Karen McAulay. "Eyewitness Travel Phrase Book: French". London: Dorling Kindersley, 2003.

Durie, John et al. "Marketing & Selling Your Film Around The World". Los Angeles: Silman-James Press, 2000.

Gore, Chris. "The Ultimate Film Festival Survival Guide (3rd Edition)". Los Angeles: Lone Eagle Publishing Company, 2004.

Langer, Adam. "The Film Festival Guide: For Filmmakers, Film Buffs, and Industry Professionals". Chicago: Chicago Review Press, 1998.

Stolberg, Shael. "International Film Festival Guide". Festival Products, 2000.

Turan, Kenneth. "Sundance to Sarajevo: Film Festivals and the World They Made". Los Angeles: University of California Press, 2003.

Walker, Stephen. "King of Cannes: Madness, Mayhem and the Movies". New York: Algonquin Books, 2000.

Williams, Nicola. "Lonely Planet France". Footscray: Lonely Planet Publications, 2011.

The following books are now out of print, but if you can get your hands on a copy they're also an interesting read. Try Amazon.com or second-hand specialists like abebooks.com and abrillis.com.

Bart, Peter. "Cannes: Fifty Years of Sun, Sex & Celluloid". New York: Hyperion, 1997.

Beauchamp, Cari, and Henri Béhar. "Hollywood on the Riviera". New York: William Morrow & Company, 1992.

Ebert, Roger. "Two Weeks in the Midday Sun". Kansas City: Andrews McMeel Publishing, 1987.

Appendix II: Cannes Listings

This appendix contains contact details for a range or organisations and services available from both the Festival and in the city of Cannes.

Bear in mind that calls to telephone numbers listed in this section are likely to be answered in French. If you're not confident in the language, you can always trying asking the question *parlez vous anglais?* (PAR-LAY VOOS ONG-GLAY) "Do you speak English?" In many cases operators are bilingual or can pass you to someone who is.

Official Festival Contacts

Festival de Cannes
3 Rue Amélie
75007 Paris
Tel. +33 (0)1 53 59 61 00
www.festival-cannes.org

General Enquires: festival@festival-cannes.fr
Festival Accreditation: accreditationpro@festival-cannes.fr
Press Accreditation: presse@festival-cannes.fr
Cinéfondation Enquires: cinefondation@festival-cannes.fr

Marché du Film
3 Rue Amélie
75007 Paris
Tel. +33 (0)1 53 59 61 30
www.marchedufilm.com

General Enquires: marketinfo@festival-cannes.fr
Market Accreditation: marketbadges@festival-cannes.fr
Producers Network: network@festival-cannes.fr
Short Film Corner: sfc@festival-cannes.fr

International Critics' Week
17 Rue des Jeûneurs
75002 Paris
Tel. +33 (0)1 45 08 14 54
www.semainedelacritique.com
contact@semainedelacritique.com

The Directors' Fortnight
14 Rue Alexandre Parodi
75010 Paris
Tel. +33 (0)1 44 89 99 99
www.quinzaine-realisateurs.com
infos@quinzaine-realisateurs.com

L'ACID
14 Rue Alexandre Parodi
75010 Paris
Tel. +33 (0)1 44 89 99 74
www.lacid.org

Tourist Offices

Cannes Tourist Office (Main)
Palais des Festivals et des Congrès
Esplanade Georges Pompidou
Tel. +33 4 92 99 84 22
www.cannes-destination.com

Cannes Tourist Office (Annex)
SNCF Station - Ground Floor
Tel. +33 4 93 99 19 77
(closed weekends)

Antibes Juan-les-Pins Tourist Office
11 Place de Gaulle, Antibes
Tel. 04 97 23 11 11
www.antibes-juanlespins.co.uk

Cannes La Bocca Tourist Office
1 Ave Pierre Semard, Cannes La Bocca
Tel. 04 93 47 04 12

Vallauris Golfe-Juan Tourist Office
84 Ave de la Liberté, Golfe-Juan
Tel. 04 93 63 73 12
www.vallauris-golfe-juan.fr

Mougins Tourist Office
15 Ave Mallet, Mougins
Tel. 04 93 75 87 67
www.mougins.fr/tourisme/

Press

The three main industry trade magazines, Screen International, Variety, and the Hollywood Reporter, all run local offices in Cannes during the festival. The locations of these offices tend to be the same each year, however the local phone numbers do change. To get the details for the next festival, either call the offices in LA or London, or pick up a copy of the respective magazine when you're in Cannes.

Screen International
33-39 Bowling Green Lane
London, EC1R 0DA
United Kingdom
Tel. +44 20 7505 8080
www.screendaily.com

In Cannes: Carlton Intercontinental Hotel, Boulevard de la Croisette

The Hollywood Reporter
5055 Wilshire Boulevard
Los Angeles, CA 90036-4396
USA
Tel. +1 323-525-2000
www.hollywoodreporter.com

In Cannes: JW Marriott, Boulevard de la Croisette.

Variety
5700 Wilshire Boulevard, Suite 120
Los Angeles, CA 90036
USA
Tel. +1 323-857-6600
www.variety.com

In Cannes: Grand Hotel Terrace, 45 Boulevard de la Croisette

indieWIRE
601 West 26th Street, Suite # 1150
New York, NY 10001
USA
Tel. +1 212-320-3710
www.indiewire.com

Other Major Film Markets

American Film Market
10850 Wilshire Boulevard, 9th Floor
Los Angeles, CA 90024-4311
USA
Tel. +1 310 446 1000
AFM@ifta-online.org
www.americanfilmmarket.com

European Film Market (Berlin Film Festival)
Potsdamer Straße 5
D-10785 Berlin
Germany
Tel. +49 30 259 20 666
market@berlinale.de
www.berlinale.de

International Film Festival Rotterdam (Cinemart)
Karel Doormanstraat 278b
3012 GP Rotterdam
The Netherlands
Tel. +31 10 890 90 90
cinemart@filmfestivalrotterdam.com
www.filmfestivalrotterdam.com

Toronto International Film Festival
2 Carlton Street, Suite 1600
Toronto, ON M5B 1J3
Canada
Tel. +1 416 967 7371
industry@torfilmfest.ca
www.tiffg.ca

Emergencies

Emergency Telephone Numbers
Medical - 15
Fire - 18
Police - 17

Cannes Police
1 Avenue de Grasse
Tel. 04 93 06 22 22

Suspect Packages
Tel. 04 92 99 25 28

Doctors, Hospitals, Pharmacies

First Aid
Provided by the *Sapeurs-Pompiers* (Fire Service). Located with the Riviera (north point) or call 04 92 99 25 28.

Allo Médecins de Garde (Doctor On Duty)
Tel. 08 10 85 05 05

SOS Médecins (Urgent Medical)
Tel. 08 25 00 50 04

SOS Dentaire (Urgent Dental)
Tel. 04 93 68 28 00

Cannes Hospital
15 Avenue des Brousailles
Tel. 04 93 69 70 00
Tel. 04 93 69 71 50 (Accident & Emergency)

Pharmacie Anglo-Française
95 Rue d'Antibes
Tel. 04 93 38 53 79

Pharmacie Lienhard
36 Rue d'Antibes
Tel. 04 93 39 01 29

All-night pharmacies are open on a rota system, known as in French as *pharmacies de garde* (pharmacies on duty). A list is maintained on the official Cannes city web site, www. cannes.fr, or you can call 04 93 06 22 22 to find your nearest open pharmacy.

Your Belongings

Lost & Found (Festival Venues)
Gare Maritime.

Lost & Found (City)
1 Avenue Saint Louis

Festival Cloakroom (No Bags)
Palais - Level 01, Aisle 01.

Festival Left Luggage
Gare Maritime.

Transport

Allô Taxi (24 hours)
Tel. 08 90 71 22 27
www.taxi-cannes.net

Bus Information (Bus Azur)
Tel. 08 25 82 55 99
www.busazur.com

Car Impound Yard (Fourrière Municipal)
Boulevard de la Croisette
Tel. 04 93 94 53 46

Train Station (Gare SNCF)
Place de la Gare
Tel. 08 92 35 35 35
www.sncf.fr

Nice-Cote d'Azur Airport
Tel. 04 93 21 30 12
www.nice.aeroport.fr

Cannes-Mandelieu Airport
Tel. 04 89 88 98 28
www.cannes.aeroport.fr

Phones & Computers

FNAC
83 Rue d'Antibes
Cannes branch of the giant electronics, books, video/DVD retailer.

Cellhire
Palais des Festivals – Level 01, Accreditation
Tel. +1 877 244 7242 (USA)
www.cellhire.com

SFR
23 Rue d'Antibes
www.sfr.fr

Orange
28 Rue d'Antibes
www.orange.fr

Bouygues
19 Rue des Serbes
www.bouyguestelecom.fr

Post & Copying

La Poste (Post Office)
22 Rue Bivouac Napoléon
Tel. 04 93 06 26 50
www.laposte.fr

TNT (Global Express Courier)
Palais des Festivals – Level 01

Marché du Film Business Centre
Palais des Festivals, Level 01

Buro-Copy
6 Rue Notre Dame
Tel. 04 93 39 19 49

Télécourses Bureautique
16 Rue Louis Blanc

Recommended Restaurants

Al Charq
Rue Rouaze

Astoux et Brun
Rue Félix Faure

Au Bureau
Rue Félix Fauré

Auberge Provençal
Rue Saint Antoine

Aux Bon Enfants
Rue Meynadier

Aux Rich-Lieu
Rue Meynadier

Bistro Casanova
Rue Casanova

La Brochette de Grand-Mère
Rue d'Oran

Caffe 50
Rue Frères Pradignac

Caffe Roma
Square Mérimée

Carré des Sens
Rue Saint Dizer

La Cave
Boulevard de la République

Chick 'n' Chips
Rue Jean Jaurès

Coco Loco
Rue Frères Pradignac

Cristal Café
Rue Félix Fauré

Délices Yang
Rue Emile Négrin

Restaurant Esméralda
Rue Tony Allard

La Galette de Marie
Rue Bivouac Napoléon

Gaston Gastounette
Quai Saint Pierre

Kiosque Gambetta Americane
Rue Chabaud

Le Ksar
Rue Georges Clemenceau

Le Jardin de Bamboo
16 Rue Macé

La Marée
Boulevard Jean Hibert.

Le Maschou
Rue Saint Antoine

McDonalds
Square Lord Brougham

Le Merchant Loup
Rue Saint Antoine

Le Mesclun
Rue Saint Antoine

Le Moulin de Mougins
1432 Avenue Notre-Dame de Vie, Mougins

La Palme d'Or (Martinez)
Boulevard de la Croisette

Le Park 45 (Grand Hotel)
Boulevard de la Croisette

Paul
Rue Meynadier

Petit Lardon
Rue Batéguier

La Piazza
9 Place Bernard Cornut Gentille

La Pizza
Quai Sainte Pierre

Snack Le Croq'in
Rue Félix Fauré

La Socca
Rue Meynadier

Sushi Time
Rue Notre-Dame

Restaurant Tovel Beth-Din
Rue Gérard Monod

La Villa Archange
Rue de l'Ouest, Le Cannet

Supermarkets

Carrefour Market
6 Rue Meynadier

Monop'
Place Gambetta

Monoprix
Rue Jean Jaurès

Casino
54 Boulevard Alsace

Intermarché Express
71 Boulevard de la République

Appendix III: French 101

It's quite possible that you, like many of us, remember dipping out of high-school French, or simply putting in the minimum effort required to pass, all with the justification of "when will I ever need to know French anyway?" Funny how things work out.

Luckily for all concerned, French is one of the easiest foreign languages to pick up since modern French and English share common roots. The English language we know today actually grew out of Old French following the Norman conquest of England at the famous Battle of Hastings in 1066. This makes it possible to get a basic understanding of French reasonably quickly.

Pronunciation

Perhaps the biggest difference between the two languages is pronunciation, a matter further complicated by the fact that some French words are spelt in exactly the same way as their English counterparts, yet pronounced very differently. To get started, let's look at how the vowels are pronounced:

a - like the first "a" in *marmalade*, or in *cart*, however less open;

e - like the second "a" in *marmalade*, or the "u" in *cut*;

i - like "ee" as in *bee*, however slightly shorter;

o - when in the middle of a word, like the "o" in *bottle*; and at the end, like "o" in *go*;

u - most commonly "u" as in *bush*, although it also has a sound that is hard to reproduce in English words, but has a sound similar to the German "ü";

French also contains accented vowels. For English speaks used to plain old Roman characters without accents, these can look a little scary. But in reality, these are largely a con, since most accents do not change the way the vowels are pronounced, with the following exceptions:

é - becomes "ay", like the "a" in *bay*.

è/ê - both sound like é, but lean more towards the "e" in *tennis*.

ô - like the "o" in boat.

In almost all other cases (à, î, ù, etc), the vowels are pronounced in the same way as they are without the accent. So why have the accented characters in the first place? The main reason is because the French are extremely protective of their language and reluctant to change it. Many of the accented characters survive from Old French in which these unpronounced accents were used show the contraction of a sound. These contractions simply came about through evolution of the language; for example, the word *hôpital* (hospital) in Old French used to be hospital and the "ô" simply represents the contraction of the "os" sound. Likewise, *hôtel* (hotel) was formally *hostel*.

In addition to the plain and accented vowels, some vowel combinations require different pronunciation:

ai - like the English combination "ay", as in *play*;

eau/au - like "oa" in *boat*;

er/et - pronounced like é;

eu/oeu - like "er" in *flower*, but not quite as long, unless followed by a "f" such as in *oeuf* (egg) or *boeuf* (beef), in which case it is more like the "urr" in *purr*.

in/ain - like "an" in *can*. Very important as when you ask for *vin* (wine) it's pronounced "van".

ou - somewhere between the "u" in *bush* and the "oo" in *boot*;

oi - difficult to reproduce in English, but it is pronounced like "wha", for example the combination of the "w" in *wagon* and the "a" in *attack*.

on - a bit like the "ong" in *long*, however more nasally and without the "g" on the end;

ui - like two sounds "oo-ee". No similar sound in English;

When it comes to consonants in French, most are pronounced roughly the same way as in English, however there are a few notable exceptions. Further, some are pronounced differently depending on their location within a word and indeed, which word follows in the sentence.

ç - pronounced like "ce" in *ice*.

ch - like "sh" in *English*.

d/n/p/r//t/x - are generally not pronounced when they are at the end of a word.

g - depends on the next character. If a/u/o it is pronounced like "g" in *garden*. If e/i like a French "j";

gn - pronounced "nya" like the "gn" in *filet mignon*;

j - pronounced like the "s" in *leisure*;

h - in all cases "h" is silent in French when located at the beginning of a word. For example, *homme* (man) is pronounced "omm".

ll - double "l" is almost always silent in French words. For example, the verb *travailler* (to work) is pronounced TRAV-A-YAY, ignoring the double "l";

r - a little softer than in English, closer to *air* than *arr* and with a slight roll;

s - when one "s" is in the middle of a word, it is pronounced like the "z" in *zoo*; when there are two "s" in a word, they are pronounced like the "s" in *snake*. Like English, French adds an "s" on the end of nouns to signify plural form, however this "s" is almost never pronounced, unless the following word starts with a vowel.

y - a double French "é", for example, the French word *pays* (country) is pronounced PAY-AI.

Gender

Unlike words in English, all French words have a gender; that is, they are either masculine or feminine. Definite articles (the...) are proceeded by *le* if masculine (pronounced LEH) and *la* if feminine. Indefinite articles (a/an...) are *un* (pronounced UH) if masculine or *une* if feminine. Unfortunately, there are no hard and fast rules for determining the gender of a specific word; the only way is to learn them by heart. But don't worry too much if you mess up your genders as most French people will know what you mean.

Numbers

Your numbers are important, particularly for shopping and anything to do with money. It's all pretty straight forward until you reach 70, which is literally "60 and 10" in French. 80 is "4 times 20" and 90 is "4 times 20 plus 10". No wonder there are no great French mathematicians!

Useful Words and Phrases

In the following section words are shown with the following convention:
English Word - *French Word* - Pronunciation

1 - *Un* - UH
2 - *Deux* - DE
3 - *Trois* - TWAR
4 - *Quatre* - KAT-RE
5 - *Cinq* - SANK
6 - *Six* - SEESS
7 - *Sept* - SET
8 - *Huit* - HWEET
9 - *Neuf* - NURF
10 - *Dix* - DEESS
11 - *Onze* - ONZ
12 - *Douze* - DOOZ
13 - *Treize* - TRAYZ
14 - *Quatorze* - KATOEZ
15 - *Quinze* - CANS
16 - *Seize* - SAYS
17 - *Dix-sept* - DEESS-SET
18 - *Dix-huit* - DEESS-HWEET
19 - *Dix-neuf* - DEESS-NURF
20 - *Vingt* - VAN
21 - *Vingt-et-un* - VAN-TAY-UH
22 - *Vingt-deux* - VAN-DE
23 - *Vingt-trois* - VAN-TWAR

30 - *Trente* - TRONT
40 - *Quarante* - KARONT

50 - *Cinquante* - SANKONT

60 - *Soixante* - SWASONT

70 - *Soixante-dix* - SWASONT-DEESS

71 - *Soixante-onze* - SWASONT-ONZ

72 - *Soixante-douze* - SWASONT-DOOZ

73 - *Soixante-treize* - SWASONT-TRAYZ

80 - *Quatre-vingt* - KAT-RE-VAN

90 - *Quatre-vingt-dix* - KAT-RE-VAN-DEESS

91 - *Quatre-vingt-onze* - KAT-RE-VAN-ONZ

100 - *Cent* - SONT

1,000 - *Mille* - MEEL

1,000,000 - *Un Million* - UH MEE-LEE-ON

Days & Times

Monday - *Lundi* - LOONDEE

Tuesday - *Mardi* - MAR-DEE

Wednesday - *Mercredi* - MERK-RE-DEE

Thursday - *Jeudi* - ZJHE-DEE

Friday - *Vendredi* - VOND-RA-DEE

Saturday - *Samedi* - SAHM-DEE

Sunday - *Dimanche* - DIM-MARSH

Today - *aujourd'hui* - OR-SURED-WEE

This Morning - *ce matin* - SEH-MAR-TAN

Tonight - *ce soir* - SEH-SWARR

Midday - *midi* - MEE-DEE

Midnight - *minui* - MIN-EW-EE

Yesterday - *hier* - YEHR

Tomorrow - *demain* - DER-MAN

Morning - *matin* - MAR-TAN

Afternoon - *après-midi* - APRAY-MID-DEE

Night - *nuit* - NEW-EE

Week - *semaine* - SAM-ENN

Month - *mois* - MWAR

Year - *an* - ON

Food & Eating

Breakfast - *petit déjeuner* - PET-EE DE-SURE-NAY

Lunch - *déjeuner* - DE-SURE-NAY

Dinner - *dîner* - DIN-AY

Meat & Poultry - *Viandes et Volailles*

Beef - *bœuf* - BERF

Lamb - *agneau* - AGNOH

Pork - *porc* - PORK

Chicken - *poulet* - POOL-LAY

Steak - *steak* - STEAK

Rib Steak - *entrecôte* - ONT-RA-COT

Veal - *veau* - VOH

Sausage - *saucisson* - SOR-SEES-ON

Seafood - *Fruits de Mer*

Fish - *poisson* - PWAR-SON

King prawns - *gambas* - GAM-BASS

Prawns/Shrimp - *crevettes roses* - CRAVETTE-ROAS

Lobster - *homard* - OMAR

Tuna - *thon* - TON

Salmon - *saumon* - SOR-MON

Trout - *truite* - TROO-EAT

Clams - *palourdes* - PAL-OORD

Squid - *calamar* - CALAMAR

Vegetables - *Légumes*

Asparagus - *asperges* - ASP-AIRG

Cabbage - *chou* - CHOO

Capsicum - *poivron* - PWAR-VRON

Cauliflower - *chou-fleur* - CHOO-FLER

Corn - *maïs* - MAYZ

Cucumber - *concombre* - CON-COM-BRE

Garlic - *ail* - AY-LL

Gherkin - *cornichon* - CORN-EE-SHON

Leek - *poireau* - PWAR-OH

Lettuce - *laitue* - LAIT-EW

Mushrooms - *champignons* - SHAMP-EEG-NYON

Onion - *oignon* - OARG-NYON

Peas - *petits pois* - PE-TEE PWAR

Potato - *pomme de terre* - POM DE TAIR

Pumpkin - *citrouille* - SIT-ROU-EE

Spinach - *épinards* - AY-PAN-YARD

Tomato - *tomate* - TOM-ART

Fruits & Nuts - *Fruits et Noix*

Almonds - *amandes* - AM-OND

Apple - *pomme* - POM

Cherries - *cerises* - SAIR-REES

Grapefruit - *pamplemousse* - POMP-EL-MOOSE

Grapes - *raisins* - RAY-SAN

Hazelnuts - *noisettes* - NWAR-SET

Oranges - *oranges* - OR-ONJE

Peach - *pêche* - PESH

Peanuts - *cacahoutètes* - KAKA-OUT-AY-TE

Pear - *poire* - PWAR

Plum - *prune* - PRUNE

Raspberries - *framboises* - FRAM-BWAR

Strawberries - *fraise* - FRAYS

Dairy - *Produits Laitiers*

Cheese - *fromage* - FROM-ARJE

Milk - *lait* - LAY

Cream - *crème* - KREM

Drinks - *Boissons*

Beer - *bière* - BEE-AIR

Orange Juice - *jus d'orange* - JOO-DOR-ONJE

Tomato Juice - *jus de tomate* - JOO-DE-TOMART

Red Wine - *vin rouge* - VAN ROOJE

White Wine - *vin blanc* - VAN BLONK

Water (Still) - *eau naturelle* - OH NAT-REL

Water (Sparkling) - *eau minérale* - OH MIN-ER-ARL

Bottle – *bouteille* – BOOT-AY

Glass – *verre* - VAIR

Other Useful Words & Phrases

Hello - *bonjour* - BON-ZJURE

Good Evening - *bonsoir* - BON-SWAR (after 6pm)

Goodbye - *au revoir* - OH-REV-WARR

Yes - *oui* - HWEE

No - *non* - NOHN

Right - *a droite* - A DWART

Left - *a gauche* - A GORSH

Straight Ahead - *a doit* - A DWAR

Sorry - *pardon* - PAR-DOHN

Please - s'*il vous plait* - SIV-VOO-PLAY

Thank you - *merci* - MER-SEE

Thank you very much - *merci beaucoup* - (MER-SEE BOO-KOO)

Excuse Me - *Excusez-moi* - EX-KUSAY-MWARR

I don't understand - *Je ne comprends pas* - (ZJUNE COMPRON PAR)

Where is...? - *Où est...?* - (OO-AY...)

Go straight ahead - *Continuez tout droit* -(CONTIN-YOO-AY TOO DWAH)

Turn right - *Tournez à droite* - (TOOR-NAY A DWAHT)

Turn left - *Tournez à gauche* - (TOOR-NAY A GOHSH)

I would like... - *Je voudrais* - ZJE VOO-DRAY...

How much is it? - *C'est combien?* - (SAY COM-BEE-EN)

The bill/check - *L'addition* - LA-DISHOHN

Can you take me to...?

Est-ce que vous pouvez me conduire à ...?

(ESKA-VOO POO-VAY MER KOD-EER A...)

Here is fine thank you.

Ici ça va, merci.

(EE-SEE SA VA MER-SEE)

Do you have any rooms available?

Est-ce que vous avez des chambres libres?

(ESKA-VOOS AVAY DE SHARMBRA LEEBR)

How much is it per night?

Quel est le prix par nuit?

(KEL-AY LA PREE PAR NOO-EE)

I would like a one-way ticket for...

Je voudrais un billet aller simple pour...

(ZJE VOO-DRAY UN BEE-AY ALAY SOMPLA POR...)

I would like a return ticket for...

Je vourdrai un billet aller retour pour...

(ZJE VOO-DRAY UN BEE-AY ALAY RE-TOUR POR...)

Could you let me know when we get to...?

Est-ce que vous pouvez me dire quand nous arriverons à...?

(ES-KE VOO POO-VAY MER DEER KA NOOS ARREEVERON A...)

Is this...?

Est-ce que est...?

ESK-AY...?

Appendix IV: Avoiding Scam Film Festivals

These days, it seems that every man and his dog wants to run a film festival, which is fantastic in many ways, not least because it provides a greater number of outlets for filmmakers to get their work in front of an audience. But sadly, the multitude of scammers and ethics-light opportunists who prowl the Internet also seem to have their dirty fingers in the film festival scene. Scam events represent a financial risk to unwary filmmakers everywhere.

Scam film festivals tend to come in two flavours – film festivals and screenplay competitions – but many often combine both. Most attempt to catch their victim's attention by using names which include prestigious-sounding cities (e.g. London, New York etc) or suggesting national or international pre-eminence (e.g. Canada Film Festival). Some have even been seen using names which are very similar to established and respected events (e.g. Alaska International Film Festival, which is a scam, compared to the legit Anchorage International Film Festival).

While these events are scams in the true sense of the word (i.e. dishonest schemes), it's unusual for them to be completely fraudulent (i.e. take the money and run). A scam by definition is not necessarily illegal, whereas fraud most definitely is. Typically, the underlying model behind the scam is to make money from submission fees for an event which nominally happens in some way, shape, or form, but almost certainly offers little to no value for filmmakers or writers who submit their work. More worryingly, many of these events use Withoutabox to collect their ill-gotten gains. This is unfortunate because the connection implicitly lends scam events an air of legitimacy. And sadly, Withoutabox seems to care little about scammers using its service; one can only assume because it too makes money from the submission fees collected.

Fortunately, scam film festivals and screenplay competitions are relatively easy to spot as they all share some tell-tale signs:

Long 'Call for Entries' Window.
Probably the easiest way to spot a scam is to look at the length of time the event's call for entries is open. Most legit festivals don't want the hassle of managing submissions year-round and therefore tend to open their calls no earlier than three months or so before the event. However for scam festivals it's about making money, so the longer the call is open, the more cash can be raked in. For example, scam events like the Cannes Independent Film Festival open their calls 12 months (!) before their next festival.

Generic or Prestigious Locations.

Most big cities have film festivals which have been established for years. Plenty of legitimate new festivals pop-up all the time, but new national festivals or those in prestigious locations should be viewed with a healthy scepticism.

Lack of Verifiable History.

Many scam events use language on their websites to suggest pedigree or history. Where a festival seems to suggest it's been running for a long period of time, it's easy to do a quick Google search to verify. Any legitimate event should have a Google footprint of some kind - a footprint beyond its own website and listing on Withoutabox. If a festival suggests it has a history, but you can't find any mention of previous editions online then it should be approached with caution.

Lack of Sponsors.

By itself not an indication of a scam, since many festivals are not lucky enough to attract sponsors, but if a festival is claiming national or international pre-eminence, then you'd think it could rustle up one or two. That said, some scam events have been known to list fake sponsors so where a festival does list companies you haven't heard of, spend a couple of minutes checking them out to ensure that they are legit and have no obvious connections to the scam event.

High Submission Fees.

Again, not an indication of a scam on its own, but obscure festivals which charge high submission fees should be viewed with scepticism. Most legitimate film festivals in Europe do not charge fees at all, particularly for shorts. Where they do, fees tend to be nominal. Fees in the US are normally higher, but again, even top festivals like Sundance don't charge $100 for a short film submission.

Administration Location.

Almost all festivals are run locally, so be very wary of events which have administrative or submissions offices in states or countries which are different to the festival's location. They're unlikely to be legit. You should also be on the lookout for local addresses which have been 'embellished' to suggest a local connection. For example, the Alaska International Film Festival, a scam event, listed an "office suite" address in Anchorage for submissions. Yet a quick look on Google Streetview showed this "suite" to actually be a PO box at a mail centre. On further investigation, evidence suggested the event was actually run out of either San Diego or somewhere in Kentucky.

Large Number of Awards.

Most legit festivals have a limited award-set. After all, the purpose of an award is to single out the best film in each category, rather than hand out as many awards as possible. Festivals which offer a lengthy award list, particularly where awards aren't well-differentiated, are likely to be scams.

Verifiable Winners List

If a festival publishes a list of winners from previous years, take a moment to check whether the films mentioned actually exist. A quick look at the IMDB is a good starting point, but you can also check for the Google footprint. Any film which is good enough to win an award (particularly something like 'Best Picture') should have at least some online presence beyond the festival's website. Scam events have been known to list fake films as 'winners' in an attempt to bolster the appearance of legitimacy to potential submitters. For example, the winners list for the 2012 Berlin Independent Film Festival and the 2011 European Independent Film Festival are identical, despite the fact that these events are supposedly completely separate of each other (in reality, they are two more scam events run by the same people who brought you the Cannes Independent Film Festival discussed earlier).

Opaque Judging Process.

Does the festival provide any information on the judging criteria it uses to determine winners or who the judges are? Festivals which are on the level will normally name their jury members or at least provide credible information on how the winner are selected. Festivals which only announce winners via email are definitely scams.

No Public Screenings.

Events which do not screen films publicly are not film festivals, period. Any event which calls itself a festival, but does not screen films to the public, is a scam.

Film festivals remain one of the best ways for filmmakers to get their work in front of a wider audience, but in the days of easy off-the-shelf websites (and lax verification from Withoutabox) extra caution is required to ensure you're maximising the benefits of the money you pay for film festival submissions.

Appendix V: Accommodation Services

Cannes - A Festival Virgin's Guide has teamed up with Venere, one of the leading pan-European hotel and villa booking services. Visit **CannesGuide.com** (www.cannesguide.com) to search hundreds of properties in and around Cannes. You can also make real-time online bookings.

And while you're at the site, don't forget to check out the Accommodation Exchange, a free message board where you can browse listings or post your own accommodation offered or wanted ad. **www.cannesguide.com/ax**

Apartment/Villa Booking Services

Azur Online
www.azur-online.com

Central Cannes
www.centralcannes.com

Destination Cannes
www.destination-cannes.net

Dovetail Foks
www.dovetailfoks.com

Everything Cannes
www.everythingcannes.com

Immosol
www.immosol.fr

Hotel Booking Services

Alpha Rooms
www.alpharooms.com

Booking.com
www.booking.com

Hotels.com
www.hotels.com

Late Rooms
www.laterooms.com

Trip Advisor
www.tripadvisor.com

It's worth noting that hotel reservation systems on most booking websites are not inter-connected. Instead, each booking service is typically given an allocation of rooms by the hotel which is separate from those given to other services. So if a particular hotel is showing as 'full' on one site, it may just be because that service's allocation is complete. You might find that other sites have rooms available in an otherwise 'full' hotel so it's always worth looking around.

Hotels in Cannes (1-Star)

Albert, Hotel
68 Avenue de Grasse
Tel. 04 93 39 24 04
www.hotel-albert1er-cannes.com

Baume, Hotel La
65 Avenue du Maréchal Juin
Tel. 04 93 94 36 77

Bourgonge, Hotel de
11 Rue du 24 Août
Tel. 04 93 38 36 73

Florella, Résidences le
55 Blvd de la République
Tel. 04 93 38 48 11
www.florella.fr

National, Hotel
8 Rue Maréchal Joffre
Tel. 04 93 39 91 92

Nord, Hotel Du
6 Rue Jean Jaurès
Tel. 04 93 38 48 79

Hotels in Cannes (2-Stars)

Alize, Hotel
29 Rue Bivouac Napoleon
Tel. 04 93 39 62 17
www.hotel-alize-cannes.fr

Alnea, Hotel
20 Rue J. de Riouffe
Tel. 04 93 68 77 77
www.hotel-alnea.com

Amiraute, Hotel
17 Rue Maréchal Foch
Tel. 04 93 39 10 53
www.amiraute.info

Appia, Hotel
6 Rue Marceau
Tel. 04 93 06 59 59
www.appia-hotel.com

Ascott, Hotel
27 Rue des Serbes
Tel. 04 93 99 18 24

Atlantis, Hotel
4 Rue du 24 Août
Tel. 04 93 39 18 72
www.hotel-atlantis-cannes.cote.azur.fr

Azurene Royal Hotel
28 Rue du Commandant André
Tel. 04 93 99 10 51
www.azurene-royal-hotel.com

Beverly Hotel
14 Rue Hoche
Tel. 04 93 39 10 66
www.benotel.com/france/cannes/beverly/

Chalet de l'Isère, Hotel Le
42 Avenue de Grasse
Tel. 04 93 38 50 80
www.hotelchaletisere.com

Chantilly, Hotel Le
34 Boulevard Alexandre III
Tel. 04 93 43 05 95

Charmettes, Hotel Les
47 Avenue de Grasse
Tel. 04 93 39 17 13

Cheval Blanc, Hotel Le
3 Rue Guy de Maupassant
Tel. 04 93 39 88 60

Cigogne, Hotel La
14 Boulevard de Strasbourg
Tel. 04 97 06 91 80

Climat de France, Hotel
232 Avenue F. Tonner
Tel. 04 93 90 22 22

Corona, Hotel
55 Rue d'Antibes
Tel. 04 93 39 69 85
www.hotel-corona-cannes.cote.azur.fr

Cybelle Bec Fin, Hotel
14 Rue de 24 Aout
Tel. 04 93 38 31 33
www.hotelcybelle.fr

L'Esterel, Hotel
15 rue du 24 Août
Tel. 04 93 38 82 82
www.hotellesterel.com

Florian, Le
8 Rue du Commandant André
Tel. 04 93 39 24 82

Ibis Cannes Centre
8 Rue Marceau
Tel. 04 92 98 96 96
www.accorhotels.com

Ibis Budget Cannes Centre Ville
3, rue Mozart
www.accorhotels.com

Jumelles, Hotel Les
24 Avenue Francis Tonner
Tel. 04 93 47 07 84
www.annuaire-hotels.com

Little Palace
18 Rue du 24 Août
Tel. 04 92 98 18 18
www.littlepalace-hotel.com

Lutetia
6 Rue Michel Ange
Tel. 04 93 39 35 74
www.hotel-lutetia-cannes.com

PLM, Hotel
3 Rue Hoche
Tel. 04 93 38 31 19
www.hotel-plm.com

Select, Hotel
16 Rue Hélène Vagliano
Tel. 04 93 99 51 00
hotel-select-cannes.com

Hotels in Cannes (3-Stars)

Alexandre II, Hotel
15 Boulevard Alexandre III
Tel. 04 97 06 37 37
www.hotel-alexandre3.com

Atlas, Hotel
5 Avenue Jean Jaurès
Tel. 04 93 39 01 17

Best Western Hotel Cannes Riviera
16 Boulevard d'Alsace
Tel. 04 97 06 20 40
www.hotel-cannes-riviera.federal-hotel.com

Best Western Hotel Univers
2 Rue Maréchal Foch
Tel. 04 93 06 30 00
www.longitudehotels.com

Canberra, Hotel le
120 Rue d'Antibes
Tel. 04 97 06 95 00
www.hotels-ocre-azur.com

Cannes Gallia, Hotel
36 Boulevard Montfleury
Tel. 04 97 06 28 28
www.cannes-gallia.com

Cezanne, Hotel
40 Boulevard d'Alsace
Tel. 04 93 38 50 70
www.hotel-cezanne.com

Chanteclair, Hotel
12 Rue Forville
Tel. 04 93 39 68 88
www.hotelchanteclair.fr

Citadines Cannes Carnot
10 Avenue Font de Veyre
Tel. 04 93 90 52 52
www.citadines.com

Comfort Hotel Atlas
5 Place de la Gare
Tel. 04 93 39 01 17

Embassy, Hotel
6 Rue de Bône
Tel. 04 97 06 99 00
www.hotel-embassy-cannes.com

Festival, Hotel
3 Rue Molière
Tel. 04 97 06 64 40
www.hotel-festival.com

Hotel de France
85 Rue d'Antibes
Tel. 04 93 06 54 54
www.hotel-de-france-cannes.com

Kyriad Centre, Hotel
24 Boulevard de Lorraine
Tel. 04 92 59 44 44
www.kyriad-cannes-centre.fr

Ligure, Hotel
5 Rue Jean Jaurès
Tel. 04 93 39 03 11
www.hotel-ligure.com

Mondial, Hotel
77 Rue d'Antibes
Tel. 04 93 68 70 00
www.hotellemondial.com

Orangers, Hotel des
1 Rue des Orangers
Tel. 04 93 39 99 92
www.hotel-des-orangers-cannes.com

Paris, Hotel de
34 Boulevard d'Alsace
Tel. 04 93 38 30 89
www.hoteldeparis.fr

Provence, Hotel de
9 Rue Molière
Tel. 04 93 38 44 35
www.hotel-de-provence.com

Regina, Hotel
31 Rue Pasteur
Tel. 04 93 94 05 43
www.hotel-regina-cannes.com

Renoir, Hotel
7 Rue Edith Cavell
Tel. 04 92 99 62 62
www.hotel-renoir.fr

Ruc Hotel
13-15 Boulevard de Strasbourg
Tel. 04 92 98 33 60
www.ruc-hotel.com

Suite Novotel Cannes Centre
46 Boulevard Carnot
www.novotel.com

Vendome (Villa Claudia)
37 Boulevard d'Alsace
Tel. 04 93 38 34 33
www.hotel-vendome-cannes.fr

Villa Tosca, Hotel La
11 Rue Hoche
Tel. 04 93 38 34 40
www.villa-tosca.com

Hotels in Cannes (4-Stars)

314 Hotel
5 Rue François Einesy
Tel. 04 92 99 72 00
www.314cannes.com

Park & Suites Presitge Cannes
12 Rue Latour Maubourg
Tel. 04 93 94 90 00
www.parkandsuites.com

Amarante Hotel
78 Boulevard Carnot
Tel. 04 93 39 22 23
www.amarantecannes.com

Beau Sejour
5 Rue des Fauvettes
Tel. 04 93 39 63 00
www.cannes-beausejour.com

Belle Plage, Hotel
2 Rue Brougham
Tel. 04 93 06 25 50
www.cannes-hotel-belle-plage.com

California's Hotel
8 Traverse Alexandre III
Tel. 04 93 94 12 21

Cannes Palace Hotel
14 Avenue de Madrid
Tel. 04 93 43 44 45
www.cannes-palace.com

Cavendish, Le
11 Boulevard Carnot
Tel. 04 97 06 26 00
www.cavendish-cannes.com

Cristal Hotel Best Western
13-15 Rond-point Duboys d'Angers
Tel. 04 92 59 29 29
www.bestwestern.com

Croisette Beach Hotel
13 Rue du Canada
Tel. 04 92 18 88 00
www.croisettebeach.com

Eden, Hotel
133 Rue d'Antibes
Tel. 04 93 68 78 00
www.eden-hotel-cannes.com

Excellior, Residence
93 Boulevard Carnot
Tel. 04 93 39 76 65
www.excelsuites-cannes.com

Grand Hotel, Le
45 Boulevard de la Croisette
Tel. 04 93 38 15 45
www.grand-hotel-cannes.com

Novotel Montfleury
25 Avenue Beauséjour
Tel. 04 93 68 86 86
www.novotel.com

Riviera Eden Palace
5-9 Boulevard de Lorraine
06400 Cannes
Tel. 04 92 59 16 12
www.eden-palace.com

Sofitel le Mediterranee
Tel. 04 92 99 73 00
Fax. 04 92 99 73 29
www.sofitel.com

Splendid, Hotel
4 Rue Félix Faure
Tel. 04 97 06 22 22
www.splendid-hotel-cannes.fr

Sun Riviera Hotel
138 Rue d'Antibes
Tel. 04 93 06 77 77
www.sun-riviera.com

Victoria, Hotel
Rond-Point Duboys d'Angers
Tel. 04 92 59 40 00
www.hotel-victoria-cannes.com

Hotels in Cannes (5-Stars)

Carlton Intercontinental
58 Boulevard de la Croisette
Tel. 04 93 06 40 06
www.intercontinental-carlton-cannes.com

Gray d'Albion, Hotel
38 Rue des Serbes
Tel. 04 92 99 79 79
www.lucienbarriere.com

JW Marriott
50 Boulevard de la Croisette
Tel. 04 92 99 70 00
www.marriott.com

Majestic Barrière
10 Boulevard de la Croisette
Tel. 04 92 98 77 00
www.lucienbarriere.com

Hotels in Cannes la Bocca

Amangani Resort Hotel
61/65 Avenue du Dr Picaud
Tel. 04 93 47 63 00
www.avanganihotelcannes.com

Bagatelle Pension
4 Chemin des Arums
Tel. 04 93 48 32 30

Brasserie du Marché, La
10 Avenue Monseigneur Jeancard
Tel. 04 93 48 13 00

Cannes Beach Residence
11 Rue Pierre Sémard
Tel. 04 92 19 30 00

Cannes Verrerie
6 Rue de la Verrerie
Tel. 04 93 90 72 00

Chateau de la Tour
10 Avenue Font de Veyre
Tel. 04 93 90 52 52

Du Midi
88 Avenue Michel Jourdan
Tel. 04 93 47 14 67

Ibis Cannes la Bocca
23 Avenue Francis Tonner
Tel. 04 93 47 18 46

Jumelles, Les
124 Avenue Francis Tonner
Tel. 04 93 47 07 84

Kyriad
204-212 Avenue Francis Tonner
Tel. 04 93 48 21 00

Neptune, Hotel
92 Avenue Francis Tonner
Tel. 04 93 47 04 47

Paris Provence
68 avenue Francis Tonner
Tel. 04 93 47 10 48

Villa Francia
33 Avenue Wester-Wemyss
Tel. 04 92 98 20 00

Hotels in Le Cannet

Sunset
Avenue du Campon
Tel. 04 93 45 35 35

Ibis
87 Boulevard Carnot
Tel. 04 93 45 79 76

Virginia
41 Boulevard Carnot
Tel. 04 93 45 43 87

De la Grande Bretagne Hotel
Boulevard Carnot
Tel. 04 93 45 66 00

Hotels in Vallauris

Palm Hôtel
17 Avenue la Palmeraie
Tel. 04 93 63 72 24

Siou Aou Miou
Quai St Sébastien
Tel. 04 93 64 39 89

Val d'Auréa
11 Boulevard Maurice Rouvier
Tel. 04 93 64 64 29

California
222 Avenue de la Liberté
Tel. 04 93 64 39 89

Chez Claude
162 Avenue de la Liberté
Tel. 04 93 63 71 30

Etap Hôtel
Rte de St Bernard - Font de la Cine
Tel. 04 93 65 48 08

Formule 1
3030 Route de St Bernard
Tel. 04 93 65 20 20

Hôtel du Stade
48 Avenue Georges Clémenceau
Tel. 04 93 64 91 27

Hotels in Golfe Juan

Auberge du Relais Impérial
21 Rue Louis Chabrier - Golfe Juan
Tel. 04 93 63 70 36

Hôtel de Crijansy
85 Avenue J.Adam - Golfe Juan
Tel. 04 93 63 84 44

Lauvert RN7
Impasse Beau Soleil - Golfe Juan
Tel. 04 93 63 46 06

Hotels in Antibes - Juan les Pins

Aigue Marine
1 Avenue du Pylone
Tel. 04 93 33 48 76

Auberge Provençale
61 Place Nationale
Tel. 04 93 34 13 24

Les Capucines
Boulevard President Wilson
Tel. 04 31 61 18 04

Hotel de la Gare
6 Rue du Printemps
Tel. 04 93 61 29 96

La Jabotte
13 Avenue Max Maurey
Tel. 04 93 61 45 89

Hotel Du Lys
81 Boulevard Poincaré
Tel. 04 93 61 53 77

Nouvel Hotel
1 Avenue du 24 Août
Tel. 04 93 34 44 07

La Parquerette
Route de la Badine
Tel. 04 93 61 59 60

Parisiana
16 Avenue de l'Esterel
Tel. 04 93 61 27 03

La Petite Reserve
20 Boulevard James Wyllie
Tel. 04 93 61 55 86

Les Tamaris
37 Rue Bricka
Tel. 04 93 61 20 03

Trianon
14 Avenue de l'Esterel
Tel. 04 93 61 18 11

Villa Christie
Rue de l'Oratoire
Tel. 04 93 61 01 98

Alexandra
Rue Pauline
Tel. 04 97 21 76 51

Hotel du Cap – Eden-Roc
Boulevard John F. Kennedy
Cap d'Antibes
Tel. 04 93 61 39 01
www.edenroc-hotel.fr

Appendix VI: Your Packing List

For many people, travel always brings with it that nagging feeling of, "I think I've forgotten something". To help, we've prepared a checklist of essential items for your festival adventure. So while you might be wearing the same pair of underwear for two weeks, at least you'll have all of the necessary kit to see you successfully through Cannes.

Mobile Phone
You'll need to be contactable at all times while in Cannes and having your own mobile phone is the only way to be sure of this. Don't rely on hotel messaging services or third-parties. Bring your own or rent one locally.

Hangover Kit
One night you'll be partying hard into the wee hours, the next morning you'll need to be bright-eyed and bushy-tailed for your pitch meeting. Whatever works for you, bring plenty of it.

Formal Gear
If you want to get into the evening screenings and many of the parties, you'll need to remember to bring your best black tie. It might be a hassle if you're staying in a tent, but it's better than hanging around outside while everyone else is having fun. And for the blokes... don't forget your bow-tie; lest you find yourself being forced to buy one at an extortionate price while you stand in line outside the Palais.

Beachwear
You're going to need a break at some stage so you may as well enjoy the beach when you get the chance. Locals tend to be a bit less inhibited by the clothing thing, but perhaps you would prefer to be a little more modest and go out in your favourite beach kit.

Sun Protection
May in Cannes is technically still spring, but the sun can be quite strong, particularly if your skin has yet to come out of hibernation after the northern hemisphere winter. If you're going to be spending a reasonable amount of time outside (e.g. running around between meetings or hanging in one of the pavilions) you'll need to apply sunscreen to prevent getting burnt. A good pair of sunnies is also a must as the morning glare off the water can feel like it's melting your retinas.

Umbrella

One day you will be soaking up the sun in beautiful 25°C (77°F) heat, the next you will be dodging a deluge which has decided to come right when you need to skip down the Croisette to an important meeting. Save yourself a soaking and bring a brollie.

Shoes

A successful trip to Cannes requires two pairs of shoes. The first should be the most comfortable pair you own - to provide some consolation to your feet for the amount of running around you'll be doing. The second pair should be your knock 'em dead shoes to match your evening attire; although ladies, it's advisable to keep your glam shoes as sensible as possible since it's conceivable that some fancy footwork may be required to pull off entry to a party.

Credit Cards

An essential tool for any traveller, credit cards allow you to manage your spending more effectively and in some cases, put off the payment pain until later. They also bring the added bonus of more favourable exchange rates on your purchases, since the currency conversion is done by your card issuer at home rather than locally. Savvy travellers always bring at least two credit cards just in case one doesn't work for some reason or happens to meet an untimely end.

Business Cards

You never know who'll you'll meet or when so you should carry business cards with you at all times. At minimum they should contain your vital statistics: name, telephone number, and email address. Don't get bogged down with fancy job titles – they mean nothing in the film industry. At best, no one cares, and at worst, people will just think you're a loser.

For those coming to Cannes with a film in tow, you'll also need to be packing the following materials:

Press Kit

A good press kit is essential for those who are looking to drum up interest in a film from either a distributor or the media. If you're working with a sales agent and/or publicist, they will have already made you go through this process, however if you're trying it on your own you'll have to create one yourself. A decent press kit includes a short synopsis of your film (one paragraph); a long synopsis of your film (3-4 paragraphs), bios of principle cast and crew, 1-2 pages of production notes describing how your film was made, and set of good stills (ideally in both digital and hard copy formats).

Your Script (Electronic)

People won't read scripts in Cannes so sacrificing a forest will only have one effect: making the printers and the excess baggage people rich. However, if you're trying to drum up interest in your project bring a digital copy in case you need to share (or God-forbid, print).

USB Stick

Containing electronic versions of all your support materials and script. You may need to print more while you are in Cannes, so it's always best to come armed with all the information you need.

Realistic Expectations

Perhaps the most important thing to bring with you.

About the Author

Benjamin Craig started his media career at the tender age of just 18 months when he was cast as the new child of the main family in "Certain Women", a popular 1970s Australian Broadcasting Corporation (ABC) soap opera. After leaving the show aged three, Craig spent the remainder of his childhood growing up in Perth, Western Australia. Always more comfortable behind the camera than in front of it, Craig spent much of his teens working backstage in theatre before starting a media production degree in 1990 at Curtin University of Technology. Graduating in 1994 with a Bachelor of Arts (Film & Television), Craig moved to London in 1996 to pursue his media career.

After becoming involved in the fledgling digital media industry in the mid-90s, Craig is now a veteran digital media producer who has spent more than 15 years working at a range of top London advertising agencies. During his career, Benjamin has run numerous large-scale projects for some of the biggest brands in the world – including Audi, Philips, Baileys, LG Electronics, Swatch, Nestlé, Microsoft, the BBC, and Vogue.

Despite a successful career in digital media, Benjamin has always retained a keen interest filmmaking and remained connected to the industry over the past decade through his role as founder and editor-in-chief of filmmaking.net, and as author of the leading film festival travel guide series, "A Festival Virgin's Guide" (with editions on Cannes and Sundance).

More recently, Craig decided to return to his filmmaking roots. In 2008 he produced and directed Cinemagine's multi award-winning 35mm short, "Waiting for Gorgo", and has recently completed the feature romantic comedy, "Sparks and Embers", the first of five feature films on Cinemagine's slate.

Benjamin Craig is currently chief executive of cross-media production company Cinemagine and resides in London.

Map of Cannes Centre-Ville (West)

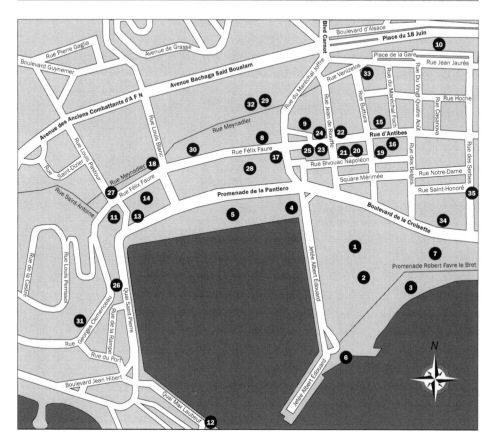

Festival Places	13. Nice Airport Bus Stop	Restaurants
1. Palais des Festivals	14. Hotel de Ville	26. Gaston Gastonette
2. Riviera	15. SFR (Phones)	27. Crystal Cafe
3. Village International	16. Orange (Phones)	28. McDonalds
4. Gare Maritime		29. Paul
5. Village International Pantiero	**Banks**	30. Au Bureau
6. Plage du Palmes	17. Crédit Mutuel	31. Le Ksar
7. Monteé des Marches	18. Crédit Agricole	
	19. HSBC	**Supermarkets**
Cinemas	20. Banque Populaire	32. Carrefour Market
8. Les Arcades	21. Société Général	33. Monoprix
9. Olympia	22. CIC	
	23. LCL	**Big Hotels**
City Places	24. BNP Paribas	34. The Majestic
10. Gare du Cannes (Train)	25. Caisse d'Epargne	27. Gray d'Albion
11. Gare Routiere (Bus)		
12. Ferry Port (Lérins Islands)		

Map of Cannes Centre-Ville (East)

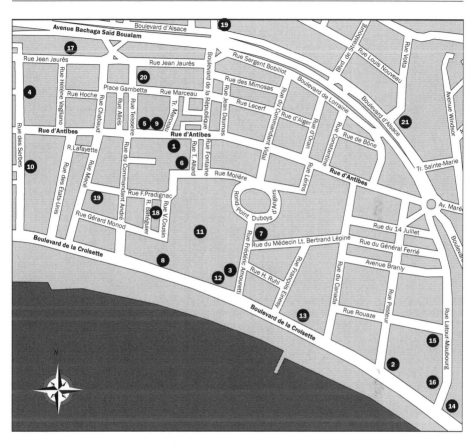

Cinemas
1. Star
2. Espace Miramar
3. Theatre Croisette

City Places
4. Bouygues (Phones)
5. FNAC (electronics)
6. Petit Majestic Bar

Banks
7. Barclays
8. EuropeArab Bank
9. Crédit Agricole

Big Hotels
10. Gray d'Albion
11. Grand Hotel
12. JW Marriott
13. Carlton Hotel
14. Martinez Hotel

Restaurants
15. Al Charq
16. La Chunga
17. Chick'n'Chips
18. La Petit Lardon
19. Coco Loco

Supermarkets
19. Intermarché Express
20. Monop'
21. Casino